MW00986570

From Anxiety Addict
To
Serenity Seeker

*Interpreting
and Working
the 12 Steps of
Phobics Anonymous*

ISBN 0-9627373-1-3   Copyright # VAU 195 522

ACKNOWLEDGEMENTS

Cover Photograph: William Brett Archer.

Graphics: Lorraine Danielsson.

Proofreading/Editing: M. E. Robertson, Rosemary Smith and Janice Wierzba

Printing: Carol M. Wierzba, Bang Printing, Brainerd, Minnesota.

The Twelve Steps of Alcoholics Anonymous: Printed and adapted with permission of A.A. World Service Inc. New York N. Y.

My Loving Thanks and Gratitude to:

Our Chapter leaders who found the strength, the time, and were willing to take the risk of initiating a Phobics Anonymous Chapter in their area and the many recovering phobics in our fellowship who had the courage to share their experience, faith, and hope with the readers of this book.

Marie (Mary) E. Robertson, our Phobics Anonymous Office Manager and my friend who answers the telephone, fills the requests for books and literature, takes care of all correspondence and provides perseverance, patience & pasta.

Joan Marie Archer, for her courage, support, spiritual sustenance, serenity and especially her friendship.

We have tried to give credit where credit was due, but some materials in this book were shared at our meeting by members from different areas, treatment centers and 12-Step groups, and we don't know the original source. If we have infringed upon any copyrighted materials we apologize. It was done innocently and if you write to us, we will gladly give credit in our next edition. Parts of this text have been reproduced from "The Twelve Steps of Phobics Anonymous" with permission from the publisher.

Before embarking on this or any program, please consult your physician. In no way is this book or the Phobics Anonymous 12 Step Program to serve as a substitute for medical treatment.

The Institute for Phobic Awareness
Phobics Anonymous World Service Headquarters
P.O. Box 1180
Palm Springs, Calif. 92263

TABLE OF CONTENTS

DEDICATION

This book is dedicated to Ann Landers, legendary, internationally-syndicated columnist and consummate humanitarian, with heartfelt thanks and gratitude for her commitment to helping those who suffer find the necessary expertise to alleviate their pain - be it emotional, physical or spiritual.

Proclamation
City of Palm Springs
CALIFORNIA

ANXIETY AND PHOBIC AWARENESS MONTH

WHEREAS, the Institute for Phobic Awareness, located in Palm Springs serves as the World Service Headquarters of Phobics Anonymous adapting the 12-step, format and principles (used so successfully by Alcoholics Anonymous) as a blue print for the recovery process of all anxiety and panic related disorders and,

WHEREAS, according to the National Institute of Mental Health and The Anxiety Disorders Association of America, anxiety and panic related disorders are the number one mental health problem in the world affecting between 5.1 and 12.5 percent of the populations, and are equal opportunity afflictions, crossing all barriers of race, religion and creed and,

WHEREAS, a large number of phobics for whom chronic worry, irrational fears, psychological stress, acute anxiety, and overwhelming panic invade all aspects of their lives, develop concurrent problems such as alcohol and drug abuse in a desperate effort to cope, often resulting in a major depressive disorder sometimes culminating in suicide.

NOW, THEREFORE, I, Sonny Bono, Mayor of The City of Palm Springs do hereby proclaim the month of March 1992

Anxiety and Phobic Awareness Month

in our beautiful city, and urge all citizens to join me in commending The Institute for Phobics Awareness and its Founder Marilyn Gellis for over a decade of service in the identification, education and rehabilitation of the affected persons.

DATED this 8th day of January, 1992

Sonny Bono

Mayor

AUTOBIOGRAPHY IN FIVE SHORT CHAPTERS

CHAPTER ONE:
I walk down the street.
There's a deep hole in the sidewalk.
I fall in; I am lost, helpless, but
it isn't my fault.
It takes forever to find my way out.

CHAPTER TWO:
I walk down the same street.
There's a deep hole in the sidewalk.
I pretend I don't see it;
I fall in again.
I can't believe I am in the same place,
but it isn't my fault.
It still takes a long time to get out.

CHAPTER THREE:
I walk down the same street.
There's a deep hole in the sidewalk.
I see it.
I still fall in.
I realize it is a habit;
My eyes are open;
I know where I am.
It IS my fault.
I get out immediately.

CHAPTER FOUR:
I walk down the same street.
There's a deep hole in the sidewalk.
I walk around it.

CHAPTER FIVE:
I walk down a different street.

INTRODUCTION

INTRODUCTION

From Anxiety Addict to Serenity Seeker, an interpretation of The 12 Steps of Phobics Anonymous, is the result of many years of dedication and hard work by our Founder, Marilyn Gellis, some of the Chapter Leaders and Charter Members of our Fellowship.

We began the process of developing a program and a book that would speak directly to those who still suffer from Anxiety and Panic related disorders after discovering that most programs addressed the physical, emotional and intellectual aspects of recovery but none focused on the spiritual.

Our first book, *The 12 Steps of Phobics Anonymous* was introduced at The Anxiety Disorders Association of America Conference held in Washington, D. C. in 1990— It is a 12 Step Program of self help for individuals who need tools to enable them to embark on their journey to recovery.

This book is a combined effort containing input from many sources, especially recovering phobics who are working the 12 Steps and who desire to share their experience, strength and hope, as they continue their recovery process.

We hope our efforts will help enable you to restructure your thinking, one step at a time, one day at a time, thus becoming free to make healthy decisions as actors not reactors. It is in no way meant as a substitute for medical treatment. Always eliminate the possibility of any physical problems. Before starting any program, consult your physician.

We also gratefully acknowledge and give thanks to Alcoholics Anonymous, Inc. for giving the world The Twelve Steps which has given birth to and nurtured our development.

People often attempt to live their lives backwards, by trying to have more things or more money, in order to have what they really want. The way it actually works is the reverse. You must first be who you really are, *then* do what you have to do in order to have what you need.

In 1923, a very important meeting was held at the Edgewater Beach Hotel in Chicago. Eight of the world's most successful men attended that meeting.

Those present were:

1. The President of the largest independent steel company.
2. The President of the largest utility company.
3. The President of the largest gas company.
4. The President of the New York Stock Exchange.
5. A member of the world's greatest monopoly.
6. The President of the Bank for International Settlement.

Certainly, if success is to be measured by the amount of money men make, this was a gathering of the world's most successful men.

However:

1. Charles Schwab, died bankrupt and lived on

borrowed money for five years before his death.
(Largest independent steel company.)

2. Samuel Insull, (President of Utility company),
   died a fugitive from justice and penniless in a
   foreign land.
3. Howard Hopson (Gas Company) became
   insane .
4. Richard Whitney (New York Stock Exchange)
   spent much of his life in Sing Sing
   Penitentiary.
5. Albert Fall (President's Cabinet) was pardoned from prison so that he could die at
   home.
6. Jesse Livermore (Investor - Wall Street) died a
   suicide.
7. Ivan Kruger (Greatest monopoly) died a
   suicide.
8. Leon Fraser (Bank for International
   Settlement) died a suicide.

They all knew how to make money, but not one of
them had really LEARNED HOW TO LIVE AND
ENJOY LIFE.

"Happiness is Found in Doing
Not Merely Possessing"

"The Difficulty in Life is The Choice"
Benjamin Franklin

A man had been wandering about in a forest for several days, unable to find the way out. Finally he saw a man approaching him in the distance. His heart was filled with joy. "Now I shall surely find out which is the right way out of this forest," he thought to himself. When they neared each other, he asked the man, "Brother, will you please tell me the way out of the forest? I have been wandering about here for several days and I am unable to find my way out."

Said the other to him, "Brother, I do not know the way out either, for I too have been wandering about here for many days. But this much I can tell you. Do not go the way I have gone, for I know that it is not the way. Now come, let us search for the way out together."

So it is with us. The one thing that each of us knows is that the way we have been going until now is not the way. Now come, let us join hands and look for the way together . We will embark on a journey from:

Darkness to Light
Sickness to Health
Fear to Faith
Self pity to Gratitude
Resentment to Acceptance
Dishonesty to Honesty
Desperation to Hope
Confusion to Peace of Mind
Self-contempt to Self-respect
Helplessness to Self Confidence
Loneliness to Friendship
Doubts to Understanding
Bondage to Freedom

This Precious Life

Life seems so futile, then again
it's precious all the way.

For there is still a glowing sun
however dark the day.

It seems in vain at times I know
but there's so much joy to gain.

No, I'll not ever agree
that life was all in vain.

It matters not how hard it is
how full of pain and strife.

Because there's so much good to do
in each and every life.

So many hearts that need our help
there's so much to be done.

It seems like life is near the end
before it has begun.

So strive to make moments count
All of them with endless trying,
and life will be a precious thing
that's void of usless crying.

THE
PHOBICS
ANONYMOUS
SYMBOL

THE PHOBICS ANONYMOUS SYMBOL

THE EIGHT-SIDED OCTAGON is recognized as the universal stop sign. We in Phobics Anonymous chose this symbol to serve as a constant reminder that we must STOP catastrophic, negative, fearful thought processes and behaviors. We must STOP blaming people, places and things for our problems and begin looking at our own reflection in the mirror.

THE BUTTERFLY at the top of the octagon symbolizes the freedom we experience upon working the 12 steps of Phobics Anonymous. It is the most human of all insects for the pain of its metamorphosis most closely resembles the pain experienced in human growth and the struggles which the Butterfly undergoes to emerge from its chrysalis is what gives the Butterfly the strength to live.

THE INITIALS "P. A." of Phobics Anonymous also serve as a devastating reminder of Panic Attacks which have given birth to the fellowship of Phobics Anonymous.

THE SOLID DOUBLE LINE around the octagon symbolizes the fact that we cannot do it alone. When we change the "me" to "we", we gain a sense of connection with the help of our Higher Power, to gain strength, become healthy, whole and free.

THE
TWELVE STEPS
OF
PHOBICS
ANONYMOUS

THE TWELVE STEPS OF
PHOBICS ANONYMOUS

1. We admitted that we were powerless over Fear, Phobias, Acute Anxiety, and Panic*, that our lives had become unmanageable.
2. Came to believe that a power greater than ourselves could restore us to wholeness.
3. Made a decision to turn our will and our lives over to the care of our Higher Power, <u>as we understood our Higher Power.</u>
4. Made a searching and fearless moral inventory of ourselves.
5. Admitted to our Higher Power, to ourselves, and to another human being the exact nature of our wrongs.
6. Were entirely ready to have our Higher Power remove all these defects of character.
7. Humbly asked our Higher Power to have our shortcomings removed.
8. Made a list of all persons we had harmed, and became willing to make amends to them all.
9. Made direct amends to such people wherever possible, except when to do so would injure them or others.
10. Continued to take a daily inventory and when we were wrong, promptly admitted it.
11. Sought through prayer and meditation to improve our conscious contact with a Higher Power of our choice praying only for the knowledge, the will, and the courage to carry that out.
12. Having had a spiritual awakening as the result of these steps, we tried to carry this message to others, and to practice these principles in all our affairs.

*The words "phobias", "acute anxiety" and "panic" have been added to the original version of the "12 Steps Of Phobics Anonymous" to make them more inclusive.

THE
PHOBICS
ANONYMOUS
PROMISES

THE PROMISES

- Recovery is an ongoing daily process that requires commitment and dedication that will lead to continuous progress and growth.
- We will be amazed before we are halfway through. We are going to experience a feeling of freedom and newly found happiness .
- We will not regret the past nor wish to shut the door on it but will use our painful experience as a stepping stone for growth.
- We will comprehend the word serenity, and we will experience calmness and freedom from fear.
- No matter how high on the anxiety scale our fear has peaked, we will see how our experience can benefit others, and in helping them, we will aid our own recovery.
- We will no longer fear or be anxious about how others respond to our feelings. Our need to be perfectionistic and people pleasers will diminish.
- We will no longer fear rejection nor being hurt by others.
- We will no longer respond in fear to other peoples' actions and attitudes.
- What we say and how we act will no longer be determined by our fear of others' feelings.
- We will no longer have difficulty expressing our feelings.
- Our serenity will no longer be determined by how others are feeling or behaving.

- That feeling of uselessness, rejection, abandonment, and self-pity will disappear.
- We will no longer be the nucleus of our own world but will gain an interest and understanding of our fellow phobics.
- Our self-will and compulsion for control will leave us.
- Our catastrophic and negative thinking and attitudes will change.
- Fear of people, places, things and situations will be replaced by faith.
- We will learn how to accept, cope with, and float through situations which previously panicked us.
- We will come to accept our Higher Power and realize our Higher Power is doing for us what we could not do for ourselves.
- We will gain the inner direction to stand and face our fears rather than retreat.
- Our shame, bondage, and self-made prison walls will crumble.

Are these extravagant promises? We think not. They are being fulfilled among us, sometimes quickly, sometimes slowly. They will always materialize if we work for them. A man would die of thirst if he failed to open his mouth to receive the water, even though there were gallons of fresh water surrounding him. So it is with the Twelve Steps—one must open up to receive them. Since even a thought, even a possibility, can shatter us and transform us. This is not the end. It's a new beginning.

The Game of Life

Help me to play the game Dear Lord
with all my might and main.
Grant me the courage born of right
and a heart to stand the strain.
Send me a sense of humor, Lord
to laugh when VICTORY's mine.
To accept if I should meet defeat
without a fret or whine.
Give me strength to follow rules
to fess up when I'm wrong.
When silence or some other thing
wins plaudits from the throng.
When foes are tough and fighting fierce
and I'm getting weak.
Dear God, don't ever let me show
a broad, bright yellow streak.
And teach me Lord, life's
game to play just one day at a time.
With thee as coach and trainer, Lord
real victory must be mine.

THE
ANXIETY
SCALE

THE ANXIETY SCALE

FUNCTIONAL
1. "Butterflies", A queasy feeling in stomach, trembling, jitteriness, tension, uneasy feeling.
2. Cold or clammy palms, hot flashes and warm all over, profuse sweating, or shivering and chills.
3. Very rapid, strong, racing, pounding or irregular heartbeat, tremors, muscle tension and aches, chronic fatigue, exhaustion.

DECREASED FUNCTIONAL ABILITY
4. Jelly legs, wobbly, weak in knees, unsteady feelings, shakiness, need to sit, lean or lie down.
5. Immediate desperate and urgent need to escape, avoid or hide, inability to concentrate, focus or make decisions.
6. Lump in throat, dry mouth, choking, muscle tension, difficulty with swallowing.
7. Hyperventilation, tightness in chest, shortness of breath, smothering sensation, racing thoughts.

LIMITED OR COMPLETELY NON-FUNCTIONAL
8. Feelings of impending doom or death, high pulse rate, difficulty breathing, palpitations, change in eating habits.
9. Dizziness, visual distortion, faintness, headache, nausea, numbness, tingling of hands, feet or other body parts, diarrhea, frequent urination, sleep disturbance.
10. COMPLETE PANIC, non-functional, disoriented, detached, feelings of unreality, paralyzed, fear of dying, going crazy, losing control, depression.*

*Frequently people experiencing their first spontaneous "panic attack" rush to emergency rooms convinced that they are having a heart attack.

Chapter 1:
FROM ANXIETY ADDICT TO SERENITY SEEKER

WHO IS A PHOBIC (ANXIETY ADDICT)?

We are a group of individuals who found that we are powerless over fear, phobias, anxiety and panic. We experience irrational fears often accompanied by acute anxiety and panic attacks. At times we experienced physical symptoms (refer to anxiety scale) to such an extent that they made our lives unmanageable.

Our fear of fear—of being trapped in our emotions, made us feel we were either going crazy, going to lose control, or die. The perimeter of our world became smaller and smaller as we avoided situations, people and places, such as markets, restaurants, theaters, social functions, driving, job related activities, etc.

We sought help from physicians, clergy, psychologists, psychiatrists, hypnotherapists, nutritionists, family and friends. Many of us self-medicated with alcohol, excess food and drugs. All of these provided temporary relief. They addressed the physical, emotional and intellectual part of man. Yet, there was a missing link. We found the recovery process was incomplete without addressing the spiritual aspect of man.

MARILYN'S STORY:
A RECOVERING AGORAPHOBIC

In 1976 I had my first panic attack. At that time, I had no idea of what a panic attack was and certainly no idea of what was happening to me.

I had been to the dentist earlier that day and he gave me a shot of novocaine before drilling my tooth. I then met some friends for dinner, where I had a glass of wine and off we went to the movies.

Nothing exceptional was happening in my life and, although there were many stresses in my profession, I thought I was coping quite well.

Then, out of the clear blue sky, about half-way into the film, my hands became cold and clammy, my heart started to race, I became dizzy and nauseous and ran to the ladies room, where I threw up. The suddenness and the severity of the attack was so devastating that I grabbed a cab from the theater (not even saying goodbye to my friends) and had him rush me to the nearest emergency room, sure that I was dying. After all emergency screening procedures proved normal, I was released and told to go home and rest.

As soon as I arrived home, I felt better and figured the novocaine must have reacted with the wine at dinner, and that was the cause of my distress.

I resumed my normal daily activities with no further incidence.

About six months later, once again out of the blue, I had a second attack. This time it was at Disneyland. A friend had some Valium with her so I took a half of a

5mg. tablet, went to the first aid station, laid down for an hour and felt better. I just wanted to go home.

The next day I felt fine so I easily rationalized my feelings. They were caused by too much excitement, never seeing the connection between the two isolated incidents.

Then, on a Sunday in 1977, I was feeling a little anxious and stressed, so I decided to take a hot bath to help me relax. I crawled into bed to watch "60 Minutes" and started to feel very uneasy, weak, and uncomfortable. My palms started to sweat, I couldn't breathe. I was having hot flashes, chest pains, and heart palpitations. I had this overwhelming feeling of impending doom and was sure that I was having a heart attack.

I was afraid to drive and felt I couldn't wait for a taxi, so I rushed across the street to my neighbor's house and asked her to drive me to the emergency room, where I was promptly admitted with a heart rate of 240 beats per minute. The doctors wanted to admit me to the hospital, but I refused. They kept me there for five hours, until my heartbeat returned to normal and sent me home after I promised to see my family physician the following morning. Once I returned home I felt better. I was frightened, but experienced none of the physical and psychological terror of a few hours before, so I went to bed and slept quite well.

The following day my doctor, finding nothing wrong with my EKG, diagnosed me as having tachycardia and preventively prescribed Lanoxin (a heart medication). He said I had a bad case of "nerves" and suggested I take a few days off from work and try to relax.

After that Sunday's scare, my panic attacks became more frequent. I started making the rounds of different doctors. I was sure that I was dying and nobody believed me, since they could find nothing physically wrong. I had all of the routine lab tests, another EKG, a treadmill test and blood chemistry work-ups. All results were in the normal ranges. Following my next panic attack, I seriously started doubting my doctor's diagnostic ability, so I made an appointment with the Chief Cardiologist at a neighboring hospital. Once again, he too, found nothing physically wrong.

During one panic attack, my symptoms included dizziness, tingling and numbness of my arms, and this time I was sure that I had a brain tumor, so I consulted with a neurologist. This time a whole different set of tests, studies and scans, with the same results, normal!

My panic attacks were becoming more frequent and my symptoms were not always the same. A month later, when I once again experienced difficulty in breathing and feelings of suffocation, I wound up in the emergency room again and there all procedures again proved normal.

I started listening in to all of my body symptoms and would catastrophize the slightest thing. When I had difficulty swallowing due to a tightness and lump in my throat, I arranged for a consultation with an Eye, Ear, Nose and Throat Specialist. Another false alarm. Still no diagnosis.

One day a friend showed me an article in a women's magazine which described some of my symptoms and attributed them to Hypoglycemia, so off I rushed to an

Endocrinologist for an eight hour glucose tolerance test. Same results: normal.

As a last resort, I went to a Gastroenterologist when another well-meaning friend suggested my chest pains might be gas. I had an upper G.I. series which also proved normal and with each "normal" finding, I became more and more terrified. I knew something was seriously wrong with me but no doctor could diagnose the problem.

All of my test results were returned to my original family practitioner who told me in no uncertain terms to "pull myself together" and I was nothing more than a hypochondriac and perhaps I should see a psychiatrist and stop wasting his time.

Due to the devastating effects of my unknown illness and the attacks, which were occurring much more frequently, my perimeter was getting smaller and smaller. I became virtually paralyzed with irrational fears. Like the ripples of a stone dropped into a placid pool of water, my circle of fear spread out to encompass all areas of my life. From a creative, personable, vibrant, articulate extrovert, I turned into a recluse with millions of excuses as to why I couldn't attend any social functions, go to the market, drive, eat in restaurants, go to the movies, etc. I only felt safe and secure at home. I continually checked my door to make sure the paramedics could get in when called, and lifted the receiver to maker sure the phone was working so I could call for help.

My main terror was the thought of mental illness, and now my own trusted physician was confirming my worst fears. Words like madness, insanity, crazy and lunacy raced through my mind, evoking images of padded cells and straight jackets. I didn't want to live, yet I was too chicken to kill myself, so I reluctantly made an appointment with a psychiatrist. He prescribed anti-depressants, but I rebelled against taking any medication. I had to be in complete control of my life and once I swallowed a pill, I had no control over the effect it would have on me, and I panicked at the thought of the possible side effects. Although I fought taking the medication, I did keep my weekly appointments with my psychiatrist.

It was the blackest summer of my life. Each day my fears and depression worsened. I couldn't sleep. The only time I left my house was to visit the doctor. I couldn't concentrate. I'd try to read something and wound up reading the same sentence over and over again. Even though I had the money, I couldn't pay my bills. Everything was too much of an effort. I had no energy and all I did was cry.

Some people lose weight when they are depressed, others self-medicate with drugs and alcohol. My "drugs" were chocolate, caffeine and nicotine. On the way back from the psychiatrist's office, (which was the only place I went that summer), I traditionally stopped at the market to stock up on ice cream, candy, cigarettes, coffee and dog food. (I had five dogs at the time and if not for them, I would have committed myself to a mental institution.) I gained forty pounds in two months. In addition to being an emotional basket case, I was a phys-ical wreck as well. I had bottomed out. The only light I could see at the end of the tunnel was an oncoming train.

And then it happened. Since I didn't want to see or

be seen by anyone during the day, and couldn't sleep at night, I watered my outside plants in the middle of the night. I don't remember the exact date, but I'll never forget the experience.

On the left side of my house, next to the driveway, I had planted a cactus that a friend had discarded. It was a night blooming Cercus, and quite ugly and thorny. I never paid much attention to it and left it there since it required a minimum of care and served as a good deterrent to burglars.

On this particular night when I went to water it, I saw on it the most magnificent flower I had ever seen. I couldn't believe my eyes. This cactus that had never bloomed in the ten years I had it, amidst its ugliness and thorns, produced a flower that was complete perfection. I get chills even as I write this, because that flower was a turning point in my life. When I saw such beauty could be produced and emerge from such ugliness, I realized from my deep despair something, too, might be able to flourish. I cried that night as I have never cried before and then a calmness followed.

The next morning, I called a trusted friend and asked him to come over and sit with me while I took the medication my psychiatrist had prescribed six months ago that lay untouched in the medicine cabinet. I then made an appointment with my Rabbi to discuss my "condition", ask for his advice, and tell him about the "miracle" which had occurred in my life.

I have never been devoutly religious, but this cactus blooming, to me, was a sign—a spiritual awakening. I was no longer alone—There was a Higher Power. I just had to acknowledge it and let it in.

Even though I still didn't know what was wrong with me, the medication was beginning to lift my depression and block some of my anxiety. I became semi-functional and was able to return to work, but I still existed in a state of anticipatory anxiety—not knowing when, where, or if the next attack would occur. I continued to avoid all other common places and activities.

Then another unexpected and unexplained development occurred. While watching television one night, I saw a program with an agoraphobic as its main character AND IT WAS ME! All my symptoms, all my fears, all my anxiety—was portrayed on the screen and I finally had a name for my "condition". I wasn't alone! I wasn't going crazy. What I had was agoraphobia! My self-diagnosis in itself was therapeutic and offered my first ray of hope for potential recovery.

Life at its best is not easy, but I found that as soon as I gave up trying to control my life, the pieces started to fit together like a well-made puzzle, and things started falling into place.

I suffered from the devastation of Agoraphobia (Acute anxiety and panic attacks) and vowed if I ever became functional again, I would dedicate my life to helping others with this problem. This gave birth to the Institute for Phobic Awareness.

Because of problems (health, legal, etc.) with my school district, I had to take a year off from work. This gave me the opportunity to research and read everything and anything I could get my hands on regarding Anxiety and Panic-related disorders. It also afforded me the time to fly to New York to meet with Dr. Manny Zane and Dr. Donald Klein, two of the most respected authorities in the field of phobias and panic disorders and to become more knowledgeable in current treatment modalities. Upon my return from Workman's Compensation leave, I was assigned to teach at a residential drug and alcohol recovery center in Desert Hot Springs. It was there that I became introduced to, and immersed myself in the Twelve Step program of A.A. that I saw used so success-fully in the recovery process of my students. This prompted me to start using the 12-step program for my own anxiety problems and I eventually founded Phobics Anonymous, which led to the authorship of this text, and my getting stronger and stronger as I use the 12-step tools to rebuild my life.

I know I have to rid myself of my "what if" negative pessimistic, catastrophic thinking. I also have my Bill of Rights.

BILL OF RIGHTS

1. I do not have to feel guilty just because someone else does not like what I do, say, think, or feel.

2. It is okay for me to feel angry and to express it in responsible ways.

3. I do not have to assume full responsibility for mak-ing decisions. Particularly where others share responsibility for making the decision.

4. I have the right to say "I don't understand" without feeling stupid or guilty.

5. I have the right to say "I don't know". I have the right to say "no" without feeling guilty. I do not have to apologize or give reasons when I say no.

6. I have the right to ask others to do things for me and I have the right to refuse requests which others make of me.

7. I have the right to tell others when I think they are manipulating, conning, or treating me unfairly.

8. I have the right to refuse additional responsibilities without feeling guilty.

9. I have the right to tell others when their behavior annoys me.

10. I do not have to compromise my personal integrity.

11. I have the right to make mistakes and to be responsible for them. I have the right to be wrong.

12. I do not have to be liked, admired, or respected by everyone for everything I do.

My "Shoulda" "Woulda" "Coulda" thinking
only leads to **FRUSTRATION**

F ear of people, places and things
R etreating to my "safe place"
U nconditional surrender to my fears
S eeking excuses
T raitor to myself
R esignation and resentments
A nxiety and agitation
T error, instead of tranquility
I nadequacy and low self esteem
O ppression and obsessive thoughts
N egative feelings

I also know that I must live in the present, one day at a time and in order to prevent a set back I must avoid:

1.   Exhaustion - I can't allow myself to become overly tired or in poor health caused by work addictions, compulsive over-eating, or taking on responsibilities that really belong to someone else. Good health and enough rest are important. When I feel well, I am more apt to think well.

2.   Dishonesty - This begins with a pattern of unnecessary little lies and deceits with fellow workers, friends, and family. Then come important lies to myself. Rationalizing, making excuses for not doing what I do not want to do, or for doing what I know I should not do.

3.   Impatience - Things are not happening fast enough. Or, others are not doing what they should or what I want them to do.

4.   Argumentativeness - Arguing small and ridiculous points of view may be a sign that I am not dealing with my real issue. Arguing over and over again indicates a need to be right, and an effort to control. I must be alert for "If I could just make you understand".

5.   Depression - Unreasonable or unaccountable despair may occur in cycles and should be dealt with and talked about. Depression may be an indication that I have been stuffing feelings. Talking is one tool of recovery.

6.   Frustration - At people or because things in general don't seem to be going "right". Everything is not going to be the way I want it or think it should be.

7.   Self-Pity - "Why do these things happen to me?" "Nobody appreciates all that I am doing (for them)". "Things would be better if only..." I always have choices. Self-pity indicates blaming outside circumstances.

8.   Cockiness - I've got it made, I can handle it. It will never again happen to me. This is dangerous thinking. I must continually remember most relapses occur when I let up on my own recovery program.

9.   Expecting too much from others - "I've changed; why hasn't everyone else?" It's an extra plus if they do, but I cannot expect others to change their life style just because I have. The only changes I can make are with myself.

10.   Letting up on the discipline - Of prayer, meditation, daily inventory, because of complacency or boredom. I cannot afford to be bored with my program. The cost of a setback is always too great.

11.   Wanting too much - Perhaps in a hurry to make up for lost time. I do not set goals and I expect too much. "Happiness is not having what you want, but wanting what you have."

12.   Forgetting gratitude - Looking negatively at my life, concentrating on problems that still are not totally corrected. It's good to remember where I started, and how much better life is now.

13.   Protecting - Remember I am responsible for myself, and others are responsible for themselves.

14.   Powerlessness and Unmanageability - Admitting and accepting are the cornerstones of recovery. I apply this to my life on a daily basis. I go to meetings, learn to work the steps and TALK ABOUT WHAT'S REALLY GOING ON WITH ME.

I find the best way to deal with my problem is with <u>Acceptance</u>. It is the answer to all my problems today. When I am disturbed, it is because I find some person, place, thing or situation, some fact of my life unacceptable to me and I can find no serenity until I accept that person, place, thing or situation as being exactly the way it is supposed to be at this moment. Nothing, absolutely nothing, happens in God's world by mistake. Unless I accept life completely on life's terms, I cannot be happy. I need to concentrate not so much on what needs to be changed in the world as on what needs to be changed in me and in my attitudes.

I believe it is my duty to myself to develop a well rounded life using the abilities which I possess within myself.

1. I shall do something today about my health, my figure, my appearance, my voice and my speech.

2. I shall learn something today because I believe in personal growth.

3. I shall employ the light touch today and bring joy and laughter to at least one person.

4. I shall use gracious ways today in my contact with others.

5. I shall develop my senses a little today in the appreciation of beauty.

6. I shall have faith today in the great creative force and realize that I am an important part of a great play.

7. I shall live serenely and free of fear today.

12 WAYS TO ACCEPT

1. ACCEPT, that I am a phobic, and need help and that help can be found by attending Phobics Anonymous meetings, reading literature, taking medication if necessary and by practicing the 12-Step program at all times.
2. ACCEPT, that I am powerless over anyone, but that I have the power to change myself.
3. ACCEPT, that I am not responsible for anyone's actions, but I am responsible to myself.
4. ACCEPT, God or a Higher Power back into my life, to LET GO AND LET GOD. To learn to have patience by not taking things back too quickly and trying to manage or play God myself.
5. ACCEPT, that I am a good person and it is OK to be good to myself. Don't be afraid to be happy and enjoy what is beautiful. Always remember, I'M OK, GOD DOESN'T MAKE JUNK.
6. ACCEPT, tolerance with others and especially myself, having faith that can grow in our P.A. program and become a whole person again.
7. ACCEPT, things I do not like, realizing that all things do not have to be good to be acceptable. By having to let someone we love suffer for their own mistakes, or actions, by detaching with love.
8. ACCEPT, that I do not have to be right all the time and that it is OK to be wrong or make a mistake, our mistakes can be a learning experience.

9.   ACCEPT, that it is OK to say I'm wrong and ask forgiveness when I hurt or wrong someone.
10. ACCEPT, that I must be open-minded enough to listen thoughtfully to the opinions of others.
11. ACCEPT, that each day is a new beginning. It is within my power to make that day as good and happy as I want it to be.
12. ACCEPT, that I have no control over the PAST. That TOMORROW is beyond my immediate control for it is yet unborn. This leaves only TODAY. Let me therefore live but ONE DAY AT A TIME.
     If I can just follow the motto:
     Live for today - Dream for Tomorrow
     Learn from Yesterday.

I know I will stay on the right track, and last but not least, I know that I must learn to trust myself to know what's best for me, to have complete trust in my ability to determine my own needs. My role is to fully express myself. Today I embrace every opportunity to be who I am. I am not ashamed of my needs.

I am a unique and special individual and my needs are a positive extension of my personhood. There are those who feel they know what is best for me and there are others who tell me what my needs are; I thank them, but I listen to my inner voice. I determine my choices and needs and the directions I'll take in recovery. Today I am willing to take time to listen to myself. Today I make a conscious decision to trust my inner voice and fulfill my needs and must remember even the great Cathedrals are built just one brick at a time.
Easy Does It!

FRED'S STORY "THE FRIGHTENED CHILD"

My story does not start with experiencing out of the blue panic attacks. It started with the day I was born, I believe I was born a frightened child. Biologically, chemically predestined to live a life of fear, anxiety and addiction. My family background and my childhood laid the foundation for my eventual social phobia and agoraphobic condition. I am a very shy, quiet, and emotional person; a loner who sometimes very much needed my privacy. My family was very quiet and reserved. I cannot even remember my parents having any close friends or entertaining people in our home. My father died when I was sixteen and both my mother and sisters are very much like me, anxious and shy, except they show no signs of extreme phobias.

My mother says I barely started to talk until the age of three. As a young child I only had one close friend and he molested me at the age of six. I was being preconditioned not to trust people, let them get close to me or know me. At age seven we moved and again I only developed one or two close relationships.

I was always the smallest child in my class. The last to be picked for sport teams and called names like "shorty" or "shrimp". I experienced a lot of negative conditioning about my size and abilities. As the years went on, I didn't want to go to school. It became a very fearful experience. It was just too painful. Home was the only place I felt safe and secure. If I was not prepared for a test or if I had to take a physical fitness test I would fake illness and lie to my mother. I constantly laid awake sick to my stomach fearing that I would fail the test or come in last in the sports contest.

My parents recognized my shyness and tried to get me involved in programs to open me up. I joined the church choir, but could not sing and was asked to leave the group. I enrolled in drama and suffered such terrible stage fright that the teacher only gave me non-speaking parts. In the seventh grade I had to take Spanish, which required practicing speaking the language out loud. I performed very poorly and was always embarrassed. I could barely get the words out and knew all the other students noticed my problem. My heart would beat fast, my hands would sweat and my mind would become dizzy. This is when my anxiety became a daily habit. Every morning I woke up with a stomach ache and a general frightened anxious feeling. I just wanted to stay home. At school the palms of my hands would sweat all day and I would have a sick feeling in my stomach until school was out and I could go home. Even though I knew the answer, I was always afraid the teacher would call on me to answer a question. If I had to present an oral report, I would think and worry about if for days, not being able to sleep at night. When I finally had to give the report I would become very quiet and shaky. In high school I never attended school events, dances, football games, etc., because I felt so out of place. I didn't think I belonged and that other kids didn't want me around. I did have three or four friends but they always wanted to go places and participate. My area of security was home.

One activity I did participate in was the sport of tennis. It was an individual sport that did not require me to play with a large group of people. I became very good and spent almost every day playing. My father paid for private lessons with one of the best teachers in the area, but every time I had a lesson, I'd be terrified, my palms would sweat, my body shook and my mind would start racing. My father would always drive me and I would feel such shame and guilt at the way I played, because I knew if I could only relax I could be an excellent player. I wanted to please my father so much, but had no idea why I was always so scared and anxious. Finally the coach told my father my play just was not good enough to take up his time. At school, during team matches or at tournaments, whenever I had to play in front of people, the same anxious condition would appear. During this time I had some good tennis friends that I played with on a daily basis. I was secure with them and felt none of my severe anxiety. Then one day, when I was about twenty, I suffered my first full blown panic attack on the tennis court. My best friend and I were just going to workout for a couple of hours. His father was sitting off to the side watching us. As soon as I stepped up to the base line to hit the ball, a terror came over me that I had never experienced. I started shaking and hyperventilating. I thought I was going to faint. I couldn't hit one ball over the net. The more I tried the worse it got. My friend knew me well, so he asked his dad to leave. After that I had to quit and left feeling confused and shameful. Soon the only way I could play was if I had a couple of beers to relax me before I played. I quit playing tennis entirely at age twenty-seven, the pain was too great and all the fun had been taken out of the sport.

During my last year of high school, I met my first and last real girl friend. We dated for two years. She always asked why my palms were sweating and why we never went to any school dances or social events. I didn't have an explanation for her. I was just scared to go out. Finally she broke up with me, and dated other guys. I can understand why. Throughout high school I wanted to be just one of the guys, but never felt comfortable or had any self confidence in myself. At eighteen I took my first drink and found that it helped remove my shyness, fear, and anxieties. I went to parties, dated a lot of girls, and had many more friends. I felt more self confident about myself. I still had a lot of anxieties about public speaking but found if I had four or five drinks before, I could get through the speech even though I was feeling terrible.

My self-medicating alcohol treatment lasted about two years and then the panic attacks started again, this time more numerous and intense. I attended college for five years, but never graduated. I enrolled in speech class five or six times, always thinking this time I could do it. Each time I lasted about five minutes, when the teacher wanted to go around the classroom and have us give our names and history of ourselves my attacks would be triggered instantly. The only thing I wanted was to get out of the room as fast as I could.

Every time I experienced a panic attack I hoped and prayed that I would grow out of it; that they would eventually disappear and I would feel calmness and have control of my life. I always wished I could have received help as a child or young adult, but nobody knew what I was going through or had a name for it, including myself.

My next major panic attack occurred while working for the Bank Americard Credit Center. I was twenty-three and one of the top employees in my department. My supervisor asked me to take over the department while he went to dinner. He also said a tour group of men and women would be coming in our department and he wanted me to speak to them and show them around. Oh my God, I thought. My stomach sank. He left and five minutes later they arrived. I instantly panicked, I froze. Even though I know the department inside and out, I could not think of a thing to say. As I approached them I started sweating and becoming sick to my stomach. I had nowhere to hide, so I decided to do the best job I could. I started talking, trying to go slow and think through it, but with every word I just got worse. I started hyperventilating and choking on my words. I was dizzy and confused in my thinking. As I looked into the eyes of these people, I could see the pain and hurt they felt for me. Some felt embarrassed and walked away. I felt so much guilt, shame and embarrassment that I went directly to the men's room and didn't come out for a half an hour. When I did return I felt as if all my co-workers were looking at me, but not saying anything. They all looked at me as if they knew something was terribly wrong.

I quit that job three times in seven years, because I was always being offered a promotion to supervisor. That would mean having to lead group meetings and attend middle management meetings but I always came back after a couple of months vacation and got my job back. All my supervisors knew was that I was their best employee, but after quitting three times they finally realized I had a problem and did not want to be promoted.

In 1979, I quit the bank and did not work for five years. My world became smaller and smaller. I could not write in front of people, I could not go out to get a haircut, eat in a restaurant, or go anywhere without a drink to steady my nerves, and calm the fear of having a panic attack.

I moved to Palm Desert to take care of my grandmother. This was my way of avoiding a job. She went through five operations and the stress of running her affairs, hiring nurses, doctors and lawyers was running me straight into the ground. I drank to fight the fear of attacks in any situation I had to handle. My grandmother passed away in 1982 and I moved to Redlands and found an apartment. I lived off the inheritance from my grandmother and I fraudulently stole from my sister's trust fund. At that point I felt no shame at what I was doing or how I was living. I was trying to survive, never leaving my apartment except for food and an occasional trip to visit my mother. I felt I was going crazy and had to move again.

This time it was back to the San Gabriel Valley where my family lived and I had one or two friends. I moved in with one of them and only left the house for food and now drugs. My family finally realized I might have more than just an alcohol and drug problem. They begged me to see a psychiatrist. I made an appointment and then took seven mgs. of Valium to gain the courage to go. He understood my problem but said I had to get off the drugs before he could help me. My addiction was so great that I couldn't do it. I finally had to total my mother's car before I was hospitalized for help.

In 1984, I was admitted to the Betty Ford Center. Those six weeks were the hardest thing I ever experienced in my life. While waiting to get in, I detoxified at the home of one of my grandmother's friends. I was drug free for two weeks when I entered.

The first night I had a panic attack while lying on my bed. I started shaking, hyperventilating, crying and I could not stop. I could not stand it and asked the night nurse for something to help me. She looked at me and accused me of being on drugs. Finally a night supervisor took me out to the pool and jacuzzi and I was able to relax. The next day I was told we were going to have a group therapy meeting. I immediately became sick to my stomach. I entered the room and there were twenty chairs in a circle. I sat down. My heart was racing and all the other symptoms started appearing. As we went around the circle my anxiety got worse and worse with anticipation. I was hyperventilating and looking for a door I could run out of. When it was my turn to talk I could barely get two words out.

It took two weeks before I could talk in a group. I would have a panic attack each time, twice a day and always at the nightly A.A. meeting. After two weeks, the panic attacks in groups subsided and I opened up, but they never stopped during the A.A. meetings. The entire time I was there I was in constant anxiety and fear. After six weeks, I felt a lot better and had no desire to ever drink again. I felt more relaxed around people, more self confident and hopeful.

I was sent to a recovery house in Omaha, Nebraska. I stayed two days, until I was told that I had to memorize all Twelve Steps of A.A. forward and backward and be prepared to recite them orally in front of all my peers, who were all free to call on any step for me to recite, for as long as they wished, until they were satisfied that I knew them. When I heard this, terror raced through my mind. Here I was, two months clean of drugs and another massive panic attack. I knew that there was no way I could put myself through this and ran back to California. I moved in with my sister and started looking for a job. I felt great and even went to some speaker A.A. meetings.

The first two jobs I applied for caused a panic attack as soon as I walked in the door. My hands shook so badly I could not fill out the application forms so I walked straight out the door.

I found a job in the classified ads. It involved working outdoors, inspecting new cars. Very nervously I went in for the interview, but found the environment very calm. I got the job and they even invited the branch manager up to see if I wanted to work in Long Beach at a higher level. I was scared to death, all I wanted was to work outside and not have to deal with people so I turned down the offer to work in Long Beach. The job turned into a positive situation. I felt comfortable with my workers, but after a few months the panic attacks started again. If I was in the office and the phone rang, I would start getting panicky; if it was our manager or anyone with any authoritative position, I started hyperventilating and shaking, barely able to speak; if I saw a group of men in suits walking in the work yard I would always walk the other way, afraid that they were coming to see me and ask questions. This devastating floating fear, that now was coming back really confused me, because I was still drug free and continuing to do a great job at work.

Another year went by and my agoraphobia continued getting worse. I went to work and also worked out physically, weight training and running and then straight home. My world was starting to get smaller again. I avoided having to write my name, go out to eat and do anything social. I was convinced there was something else wrong with me. I decided to see the same psychiatrist that I met with three years ago, but this time since I'd been drug free for over two years, he was ready to help. He started me on a drug called Xanax. Anxiety left me and I felt more comfortable working with people. I attended group therapy and was given several promotions at work. I now had my own business accounts and was making more money. I had my own apartment, but there was still something missing in my life. A terrible void.

Even though the panic attacks had stopped, I still dreaded attending social functions and speaking before a group. I still lived in an isolated world. I didn't make any new friends. All the old ones drifted away, because I did not use drugs any more. The only friend I had left was my best friend for over twenty years. He never understood why I was always so scared of the world and people and was always pushing me. The more he pushed the more I ran. I finally wrote him a letter two years ago, telling him how I felt controlled and smothered by him. I have not seen or talked to him since.

It's 1990 and I have not seen my psychiatrist in two years, but am getting my Xanax from my personal M.D. I have started drinking again and the stress of my job has become unbearable. One day I just gave up, quit my job and checked myself into the nearest hospital. They detoxified me in three days and I felt like hell. I couldn't sleep or eat. I was in one large panic attack the entire time I was there. They wouldn't give me anything to help me function. I asked to see a psychiatrist and they sent one over. I told him my whole story, the best I could, and he immediately said I showed all the signs of being a social phobic, along with being agoraphobic. He said he would be glad to help me when I got out of the hospital. I said couldn't wait that long, that I was going crazy. Two days later I walked out of the hospital.

I still had Xanax at my apartment. I returned there, cleaned everything out and went to Big Bear, where our family owned a vacation house. I went to the market to stock up on food, went back to the house and dumped all the Xanax down the drain. I stayed in that house, going through the worst withdrawals I had ever imagined. Two weeks later, I was able to leave the house to walk around. I had lost twenty pounds and was very weak. But I managed to leave the mountain and see the psychiatrist I had met at the hospital. I was shaking all over and breathing very heavily. The floating anxiety was present twenty-four hours a day. He started me on

Xanax again in small doses. I started to feel better. He wanted me out of Big Bear because I was isolating and told me to move back down to the valley. I moved in with my mom, who is very supporting but very co-dependent to me.

My doctor urged me to go back to work and get out of my mother's house. My old company gave me my job back. I made amends to my manager and told him my whole story. He understood and even admitted that his wife suffered from the same problem. He asked if I wanted to move to Port Hueneme for a fresh start and handle our account there. I said Great! I wanted out of the L.A. area and a new chance to be on my own. The past year and a half was not easy. Work was still stress-ful. I was still isolating and not working on any program for my recovery.

The first week of January 1992, I saw an article in the paper offering a 12 Step Phobics Anonymous spiritual program. I knew instantly this is what I wanted. I attended their second meeting and felt right at home. The meeting felt so much more comfortable than A.A. meetings. I felt no pressure and was able to share my deepest fears and feelings. I am an alcoholic and need to work on my sobriety just as much as my agoraphobia. I'm dual diagnosed which makes it twice as tough, but I'm not going to quit. I just have to go slow, take it one day at a time and keep coming back.

I thank Marilyn for this program, and Karen, our leader, who brought this program to Ventura County. Through their help and the help of my Higher Power and the friends I now have in Phobics Anonymous, I pray I will grow as a person and be able to help others along the way.

The road we all must travel toward serenity is forever, every day for the rest of our lives, but after thirty-seven years of hell, it's well worth the walk. I just wish I could have been helped as a child and pray that all children and young adults that have these irrational fears and anxieties can get help early, so they don't have to waste years of their lives, as I did, misunderstood and lonely.

SANSKRIT PROVERB

Look to this day,
For it is life.
The very life of life
In its brief courses lies all
The realities and varieties of existence.
The bliss of growth,
The glory of power.
For yesterday is but a dream,
And tomorrow is only a vision.
But today, well lived,
Makes every yesterday
A dream of happiness
And every tomorrow
A vision of hope
Look well, therefore, to this day.

KAREN'S STORY

When I was 21 years old I had my first panic attack. I had been married at 18 and had a baby at 19. We lived in our own home. We were happy.

I was standing in the kitchen, I felt terror come over me like I had never known. My eyes went dark. I felt that I could not breathe, my heart started pounding, then felt as if it would stop. I experienced nausea, my legs gave way and I was on the floor.

What was happening to me? Was I going to die? The fear I felt that day has never left me.

When the condition subsided I did not know what to do. What had happened?

I rationalized it away - it won't happen again, etc.

But deep down the fear was always there.

I went on about my life in a normal way. Then in the supermarket, I felt the terror begin, the darkening of the eyes, the nausea, couldn't breathe. I had to get out of there.

I left my groceries and ran with my baby to the car, getting there before my legs gave way.

I knew that I had to get help. I went to a doctor. He would know.

That began my search for a cure. I had a thorough examination. I was in perfect health. It was all in my head. This is what I feared, mental illness.

I was sent to a psychologist. I told him my story. Remember, this was 25 years ago. He said I came from a screwed-up family (dysfunctional family), that I was deeply insecure, had very low self-esteem and had suppressed anger.

I saw him once a week. It was nice having someone to talk to, but I still had the attacks. He put me in group therapy, which was good fun, but I still had the attacks. He told me to get lots of exercise, so I went to a gym and was terrified. I was getting worse, not better, but he didn't believe me.

I didn't know what was worse about the attacks—the actual symptoms, or never knowing when or where it would happen.

I went to another doctor—more tests, same results: you're fine.

I became more desperate. I was afraid to leave my house. The terror of having your body attack you from inside out. Not having control. Not knowing why.

People asked me to go to church, to go to the movies, to go shopping—I did want to go, I knew I couldn't. It's very hard to tell people, "Well, I have fits", like they would understand. It was happening to me and I didn't understand. The doctors didn't know. The shrinks didn't know.

I had become familiar with alcohol in my teens and liked the effect. I started to drink. It didn't cure me, but it made me a much happier agoraphobic.

I had given up on doctors, shrinks, exercise, nutrition and even God. I tried not to think of anything.

The funny thing was that I always knew, intuitively, the attacks were physical, not mental. I knew I was nutty, but not much nuttier than anyone else.

From 21 to 31 years old, I kept a good house, took care of my children, looked good (or so I thought), was a loving mate to my husband, and kept the secret and hid.

When I was 31, my husband said "You are an unfit mother. I'm getting a divorce, I'm taking the kids, and I don't love you anymore."

This was a shock. My family was everything to me—except the drinking and the attacks. That's what my life had become.

My drinking had turned to alcoholism. I had become allergic to my "medicine". It no longer worked—actually, it never had.

I went to A.A. I never had another drink. I got my family back. Happy Ending.

Big Surprise: three weeks into sobriety my panic attacks returned.

I went to another doctor and said "You must help me"—more tests (normal, of course). He put me on Valium and it worked.

I could go to A.A. and follow my 12-Step program, go to church, and be with my husband. Freedom, well sort of, I always sat by a door. I never trusted the pills fully. I never knew.

The 8 years I was on Valium were productive. I went to A.A., Church of Religious Science, lots of volunteer work, busy with my family.

Deep down, though, I knew it was all a lie—and I was a liar. If I was following the 12 Steps of A.A., wouldn't I be cured? If I really believed the principles of my religion, that thoughts are things and if you believe them and have faith you would be cured, healed, and I knew I wasn't.

The aloneness I felt—the guilt I felt—well, you know

—and I could tell no one. I'd tried that.

The doctor I'd been going to informed me Valium was a bad drug, highly addictive (putting it mildly). Drugs were now going out of fashion.

I withdrew from Valium. My hair fell out, I couldn't sleep—convulsions, nausea, diarrhea—and of course I could tell no one.

A few weeks off Valium, happy surprise, the panic attacks came back worse than before. My world became very small. I became housebound.

Then a new hope, more docs, more shrinks.

They had miraculous new treatments for my condition and I was willing to try them all.

I went through desensitization—it didn't work. In fact, I scared a few people to death.

Hypnosis; it didn't work—acupressure; it didn't work—biofeedback; it didn't work—visualization; it didn't work—positive affirmations; they didn't work—assertiveness training, more shrinks, cognitive therapy, more exercise, more vitamins; nothing worked. I was getting tired and discouraged, not to mention broke.

I felt these doctors thought I was not a good patient. They couldn't help me and it was my fault. I felt guilty.

A new wonder drug, Xanax, for panic disorders. Would I try it? Boy, would I!

The drug took away my panic attacks. It didn't give me the slight high Valium had. I still had highs and lows like everyone else, but I felt normal.

By this time we had moved to Paso Robles to a ranch 25 miles from town, a mile from the nearest neighbor. Very beautiful.

Good A.A., good friends. The only trouble: my husband had to work in L.A. for long stretches of time.

I was on my own for the first time in my life. The kids had grown and had lives of their own.

So more Xanax as my isolation and stress escalated. Instead of getting out more, getting more exercise, I isolated.

I went to more and more doctors to get the pills. The insurance company caught up with me. Good old honest me—I was leaving a paper trail all over the place.

I was seeing a counselor at this time to help me through my mid-life crisis, isolation, troubled marriage, mainly so I could get my pills. I knew what being without them was like.

One day the insurance company called all the doctors: stop the pills. My shrink calls and says "you dishonest crook". Of course, deep down, I knew I was the most dishonest crook in the world. The shame, the guilt, the lies, not enough prayer, not enough faith, not enough...

I felt the total criminal.

My husband must be right, go off those damn pills, as he threw them in my face, screaming at me.

My shrink says go off the pills, you bad person— that's all that's wrong with me.

The doctors all cut me off, except one who was to withdraw me gradually.

I did not sleep for 41 days or nights, could not eat, could barely see, had convulsions, nausea, diarrhea, could not walk. When I talked, I stuttered. I had to crawl. I was bed-ridden for 3 months. I was down to 98 pounds.

Finally, I took my last pill. Yeah, I was cured. Everybody loved me again. I wasn't an addict.

I would never have to see another doctor or lie or be humiliated or to feel guilty all the time. Denial time.

But underneath I knew.

Two weeks after my last pill the monster came back, but not as before. Worse—seizures. As my body had aged, I guess so had my brain.

All the old symptoms came back, but stronger, life-threatening—the real thing, and I was alone.

I thought of drinking, but knew that wouldn't work. I would let nothing threaten my sobriety, not even death.

I'd tried docs, shrinks, and God. This was total demoralization. I had given my all, I was defeated. I was a failure. I wasn't good enough, and I was ashamed. Mental illness. I was scared. I didn't want to die.

My daughter came up from Cal Poly. She looked at me and started screaming, "You're dying!"

I said, "Yes, I know, I'm sorry."

She said to hell with addiction. They don't treat diabetics, heart patients, and other patients this way. They don't worry about medicating them. They just want them to live, chemically dependent if necessary. I tried to explain when it has to do with the brain, they don't know.

She did not know what to do, so she left me.

I realized then there was no hope. Between seizures - about 5 minutes apart—I got my gun out. I just wanted the pain to end. I said a prayer, "God, if there is a God, please help me."

I then remembered a number in one of my self-help books. How to Cure Agoraphobia—a hotline to a place in Maryland.

I phoned the number. It was answered by a woman named Ivey.

She listened to my story. I was honest about everything and it felt good.

I told her all the things I had done honestly and dishonestly to get well. I told her how ashamed I was—all the lies, how hard I'd tried, and that I was finished. I was tired. I was very ill and I just wanted it to be over.

Ivey listened. She said she believed me. <u>Someone had heard me.</u>

She said my story was quite common, that I could be all right. She said there were people who could help me.

I had felt so guilty about the pills but she assured me anybody would have done what I did and more to survive.

She said it really said something about me, that I had been sober for 14 years in spite of everything.

Ivey gave me the number of a psychiatrist in Santa Barbara who knows about Chemical Imbalances and panic attacks.

She gave me the name of the woman in Palm Springs —Marilyn, who had founded Phobics Anonymous. She gave me her phone number and told me to call her.

She talked to me a long time and kept reassuring me that I wasn't bad, just sick, and that I could get well. She gave me hope. I am very grateful for Ivey and people like her.

I called Marilyn. She listened. She said she had been

through the same thing. She told me what to do. She said I would be all right. She knew me, she knew the pain. Here was someone who had felt everything I had felt. I was no longer alone. I put the gun down. Thank God.

Marilyn Federal Expressed every piece of information and knowledge she had to me immediately. This busy, busy woman took time for a stranger.

I will forever be grateful to her. She also told me to get a book called "The Anxiety Disease", by David V. Sheehan. She told me to take the book and all the information she sent to my doctor.

When I read the book, I thought I had read every book on how to cure panic attacks. It made sense, this guy knew! I wasn't crazy. I had a physical problem that could be controlled with medication.

Somehow, I got to the psychiatrist in Santa Barbara. He did all kinds of tests. He found out I had Temporal Lobe Syndrome. He said I would need anti-anxiety medication possibly.

He said with proper care, nutrition, exercise, out of isolation, and a 12-Step program for support, I would function and have a normal life. He said there was nothing to be ashamed of.

From him, I learned that anxiety disorders can be caused by many things. Genetic predisposition seems to play a part.

He told me that anxiety disorders can be caused by trauma to the brain.

He also told me head injuries (ignored) could be a cause.

He told me that very little is known about the brain. In some cases anxiety disorders can be caused by a chemical imbalance of some sort. They just don't know enough about it to say exactly what caused it.

He said anxiety and panic related disorders are about where alcoholism was 50 years ago.

He took our family history. My mother is a diabetic. My father died at 60 of a heart attack. My brother is clinically depressed—alcoholic and gay. My uncle died at 21 of epilepsy. My son is a recovering alcoholic. On examination, alcoholism runs all through the family. My maternal grandmother died of Alzheimer's disease. Not a pretty picture.

He wanted to know if I had any head injuries—yes, 2 in my teens: basketball, a broken nose; baseball catcher, knocked out by a bat for over an hour, both untreated.

I was also in an auto accident when I was 16—hit from behind. Whiplash, knocked out for a few minutes. All untreated. So there it was. I always knew it was physically caused, but no one would listen! First step in recovery, back on medication, Second step, start eating. My taste buds came back. Third step, move out of isolation, exercise, get my life back in balance, take care of Karen number one priority. Moved back to Ojai, found a competent shrink who is willing to work with me. Go to 12-Step programs. Give Anxiety Disease book and the 12-Steps of Phobics Anonymous book to everyone. Maybe they'll understand, maybe they won't. But I understand and I'm not alone anymore.

At the last A.A. meeting I went to, before the meeting started, the secretary asked me what I'd been doing all week, so I told her I was writing my story perhaps to help somebody else, to give to Marilyn, who had helped me. That I was going down to Palm Springs to see how those phobic meetings work and bring it back with me to share.

There must have been 12 women listening to this conversation. As the meeting progressed, 3 people passed notes to me. One wanted me to find out about help for Compulsive-Obsessive Disorders. Another asked for help for Post-Traumatic Stress Syndrome and another asked for help for Clinical Depression. Many suffered from panic attacks but were too ashamed to ever discuss them.

After the meeting, I got so many hugs and good wishes to bring down to you. I won't ever forget that meeting. They looked at me with hope in their eyes. It kind of scared me, but then I thought "Thy Will be Done".

I have a sponsor at A.A., Patsy W., a sister in spirit really, and this is what she always says to me: "More will be revealed", and I believe her. I think Patsy is the one person who knew, no matter what, that I would make it. Her strength and belief in me has helped me believe that there is a God of my own understanding. By his Grace I am here today.

February 17, 1992 (add on to Karen's story)

The story, from near death in January 1991, becomes more complete.

By October, we had moved from the isolation of the ranch back to Ojai. I had regained 10 pounds, I could talk again with only a slight stutter. I could walk again with a small limp.

It was now time to drive to Palm Springs and meet the people who had helped save my life.

I was nervous; I didn't know anyone, but I was determined to learn about the program of Phobics Anonymous. I had been using the 12-Step program of Alcoholics Anonymous for 14 years and I knew it worked for Alcoholics.

I arrived in Palm Springs and called Marilyn. She was glad I was there, and said she would meet me at the Phobics Anonymous meeting Saturday morning at 10:00 a.m.

When I was greeted the next morning by Marilyn, we were happy to finally meet each other. A bond had been formed. After many hugs, we went inside.

The meeting started. I sat and stared. There were a lot of people there. No more secrets, shame, no more guilt, and no more hiding. I no longer had the feeling of being on the outside. I fit in.

Marilyn introduced me and asked me to share my story. These people were me, they knew the story already; they had lived it. I felt understood and secure, after 25 years of running, I had found a safe place.

The book *The Twelve Steps of Phobics Anonymous* said it all: A meeting format that fit the disease. A belief in a Higher Power. A group of people working hard on the 12 Steps of recovery of Phobics Anonymous. The 12 Steps of P.A. are very similar to the 12 Steps of A.A., only less constrained.

The rule that makes it easier is that no one had to

talk. People don't have to introduce themselves. This makes sense...just the thought of talking in front of a group can bring on a panic attack. You can just pass; everyone understands. I felt comfortable. I enjoyed listening to other phobics talk honestly, sharing laughs, tears and hope. There was a feeling of oneness.

At this meeting, the steps of recovery from Anxiety Disease were laid out in front of me. If we were willing to go to any lengths to use these steps, we could recover. We could go on to live a life of wholeness, functioning, free of our fears. We could have a good life.

The meeting was soon over. I felt my life was just beginning.

I came home with a feeling of elation. Maybe I could do this...maybe I was enough. Could this feeling be hope?

I also brought a kit back with me, on how to start a chapter of P.A. I took one look at the kit and thought, "Patsy was right, more would be revealed!"

Then I thought, yes you can do that with the help of a Higher Power. As I worked each day toward my goal, my respect for Marilyn increased.

My first challenge was to find a place to have the meeting. It seemed I went everywhere, without much success.

I told my psychiatrist what I was trying to do and that I was having a difficult time. He suggested I try the hospital he is affiliated with.

I wanted the meeting to be on Saturday afternoons at 3:00 p.m., making it possible for people who can't drive themselves to attend. Their supporters would be welcome.

The hospital said yes to everything. They said yes to Saturdays at 3:00 p.m., they said yes to the large convention room, with lots of windows, ocean view, and plenty of doors for escaping phobics.

Next was publicity. How do you get people, (mostly phobics, who can't leave their houses) to come to a meeting? This was a dilemma.

I blanketed the Ventura County with flyers. I sent press releases to all the local radio and TV stations. I took my information about the P.A. program to Alcoholic Services and Ventura County Mental Health. I put notices in churches and bookstores. I received a tremendous amount of support from local newspapers. I found I was getting tired; all the things I was doing are not easy for a phobic.

I went back down to Palm Springs to go to some more meetings, to see my new-found friends, but mainly to strengthen my resolve to have regular meetings in Ventura County.

My friends in Palm Springs encouraged me. I also noticed the improvement in them from being able to go to so many meetings of P.A. I could actually see them getting better, gaining strength and confidence.

I came back to Ojai empowered and got started again: Get the books and pamphlets together, learn the format of the meeting, study, read, go to the hospital where the meeting would be held and desensitize myself to being there in that big room (scary).

Sometimes I would get discouraged. I would call Patsy in Paso Robles, and she would listen to me rant and rave. "Yes, it is hard, yes, it is scary, yes, you are terrified, but you can do it!" She could believe in me when I could not.

My psychiatrist was also supportive. He reinforced my goal to get a meeting started. He wouldn't let me forget my commitment to help just one person. Another tactic he used was to make me angry, saying, "Yes, maybe you're not enough...could be you're not strong".

Oh, Yeah?!

Whatever it was, it worked. My psychiatrist also did an interview on the radio, explaining the 12 Steps of P.A., bringing answers to the community of the need for a spiritual program for those who suffer from anxiety disorders. For this, I thank him.

Three weeks before the first meeting was to be held, I realized I had to go back to Palm Springs to get more help. I wanted to lead a real meeting to desensitize myself.

I am mostly a social phobic and speaking in front of a group has been impossible for me.

My friends encouraged me, saying "Progress not perfection", which helped calm my stutter and shaking hands.

I came home again filled with determination. I would like to say that I also had a support team available to me in Ojai: my Higher Power, Patsy, my sponsor, Kay, my minister, my psychiatrist, and my stuffed teddy bear, Phobic. He never misses a meeting.

The day of the first meeting arrived, January 4th, 1992, Saturday at 3:00 p.m., exactly one year after I had a gun to my head. Was it coincidence?

My body put up a tremendous battle to keep me from going. I had diarrhea, vomiting, I could not concentrate, could not stop shaking. I think terrified is the word.

I sat down and tried to calm myself. I tried everything! Finally, I told my body, "You can do anything you want to do, but I'm going to that meeting, be it on a stretcher, in an ambulance, or in a casket. I'm going, period!"

The phone rang. It was Marilyn, calling from Ventura. She had Sandy (another phobic) drive her up from Palm Springs to lead the first meeting.

Bless them!

Marilyn had her sick dog with her and Sandy had not driven outside of Palm Springs for more than 12 years, thus proving the lengths to which one phobic will go to help another.

The things I thought about driving down to Ventura to the meeting were bizarre.

"Please God, let it be OK...please give me a sign that everything will be all right." And so he did.

My 21-year-old daughter, Caroline, has always been supportive of me, even if she didn't understand what was going on.

In the past, whenever I've prayed to my Higher Power for extra help, no matter where I'm at, he plays the song Sweet Caroline. Pretty unbelievable.

I was driving to the hospital for the meeting with the car radio on full blast, hopefully to shut up the committee in my head, Her song, Sweet Caroline came blaring out. I started laughing. Everything would be all right.

At the hospital, Marilyn and Sandy were waiting for me.

We set up the meeting room and waited. Twelve people attended. A miracle as far as I was concerned.

We had a good meeting. Marilyn and Sandy had to go right back to Palm Springs, I thanked them.

Since then, I have conducted the meetings every Saturday. Each week, it gets a little easier for me. I am especially encouraged by more people attending and seeming to be helped.

I sometimes wonder if my new friends realize how much they help me. These people have been hurt so deeply, robbed of part of their lives, and now we are together helping, caring, supporting and loving each other as we work on the 12 Steps. We're not alone anymore.

After 25 years, I finally understand the Serenity Prayer: "God grant me the serenity to accept the things I cannot change, the courage to change the things I can and the wisdom to know the difference". I now have the serenity to accept my panic disorder, and the courage to go on with my life.

A man comes to the meetings. The first meeting, he sat and looked out the window. The second time, he sat at the table with the group. The third time, he introduced himself. Last Saturday, the fourth meeting, he shook my hand, looked into my eyes, and said "Thank you".

l had reached my goal: to reach just one person. I had been a channel through which my Higher Power worked.

I am grateful for my new life. I know the process will continue one day at a time.

SANDI'S STORY

The first meeting of Phobics Anonymous I attended was only because my sister, (an agoraphobic herself, who had previously attended P.A. meetings and was well on the way to recovery), dragged me in, kicking and screaming the whole way. I thought, if a psychiatrist (who one week earlier insisted I check into the psychiatric ward at the local hospital, which I refused to do) couldn't help me, if my general practitioner couldn't help me, what the heck was a meeting with people who couldn't possibly understand what I was going through going to do for me?

I sat and listened. People shared, and I related to many of their stories and experiences. Why shouldn't I? Theirs was the story of most of my life, when because of undiagnosed Panic Disorder, I thought I was absolutely going to lose my mind and was too ashamed to discuss it with my family or my friends. I was on medication for depression, my doctor said the depression was causing the panic attacks and he tried to explain to me that it was a chemical imbalance and I should treat my medication like insulin, and I might as well get used to taking it, because like a diabetic, I probably needed it for the rest of my life. I figured he didn't understand either. Something for the rest of my life, when all I was looking for was a quick fix. Little did I know he was the only person who really understood what was happening to me.

I had a severe panic attack at work and ran to the doctor next door, (not my usual doctor) who told me I was having a panic attack (gee, thanks). He said I needed psychiatric counseling. I was ready to try anything at this point, I missed three days of work; three days I barely remember because I was so heavily medicated. I went to the psychiatrist and she told me I needed to check into the psychiatric ward at our local hospital. I was terrified. I refused. I left her office in tears, and in the parking lot I thought, "My God, I am losing total control of my life". I imagined being locked up in a mental hospital. Who would pay my mortgage? Who would take care of my 17 year old daughter? What would happen to my job? How in the world would I pay for this? I got in the car and headed for home, sobbing all the way. That was probably the darkest, most depressing moment of my life. I even thought about ending it all. It was just too much to live with. I couldn't stand it any longer. I called my regular doctor and he told me to come in the next morning. My sister drove me over, (I was so drugged I couldn't drive) and my wonderful, wonderful doctor sat and talked with us and looked at the medication the psychiatrist had me on. He said, "This medication isn't going to help you". We threw it in the trash. He explained that I had only been on my anti-depressants a short time. Sometimes they took several months to kick in. He also gave me a prescription for antianxiety medication. I swear, the combination of the two medications saved my life, and I'm not kidding. He also explained that panic disorders ran in my family (my two sisters and my mother had panic attacks, we just didn't know what they were. My mother also told me her father used to have them, he called them "the shakes").

The first P.A. meeting was a revelation to me. When I found out I was not alone, and that I wasn't crazy and other people had the same problems I had and the same symptoms, I felt as if I had been reborn. I had another chance at life! I walked out of there grasping my P.A. Twelve Step book floating on air. I immediately went home and began to read. I read the whole book and that day began working the Twelve Steps. Between the power of the Twelve-Steps, the group itself, and the encouragement I received from Marilyn, the founder of Phobics Anonymous, I didn't realize it, but my life was about to change.

My boss, a local attorney, wanted me to do all the work in the office. I wanted to be so good, (I had to be the best), I had even gone to night school in another city to improve my skills. It was an hour drive and I was a driving phobic and each week night I had to drive to the other city I was in a state of total anxiety for the entire day. At school all I could think about was the drive home. Would I make it, would I have to go over a bridge or an overpass? I knew I only had to change freeways a couple of times, but the thought absolutely sent me into a cold sweat. I did this for three and a half years. Now that I look back on it, I can't believe I did it. What an incredible thing for anyone to have to go through. I did it all because I wanted to be the "best" and because I had such low self-esteem I had to prove to myself that I could do it. Even though I knew the route there and back, during the whole three and a half years I never lost my fear of the drive. I forced myself to go every week. With God's help, I managed to get through the classes, passed with a B average, and became a certified Paralegal. I continued working very hard when I was at the office, still wanting to be the "best".

Meanwhile, my boss kept making more and more demands on me. I tried to make him happy, but I just couldn't. I did everything except appear in court for him. It was a terrible time, I felt like I was a failure because my boss was not happy with me. Little did I know that no matter what I did, I could never please him. The more I did, the more he demanded. Being the perfectionist I was, the total people pleaser, I tried and tried. I was continually miserable and stressed out. I had divorced my husband who emotionally abused me only a short time before all of this began to occur. I felt like I had hit the bottom. I had.

After reading the *Twelve-Steps of Phobics Anonymous*, I started feeling better about myself.

I began to realize I was a pretty terrific person, that I had worth and value and that it wasn't me causing my problems, it was my reactions to the people around me.

I decided to do some things I had always wanted to do, but was so afraid of failing I hadn't done them. After only four meetings of Phobics Anonymous and practicing the twelve steps for about a month, I enrolled in bartending school. Believe it or not, I have a good sense of humor and I am very good with other people. I just thought I was worthless. The class was a blast (I was the only woman in the class and I was actually great at it). I passed with flying colors.

I went back to work, for the attorney, all the time thinking that perhaps I could work in the law office part time and bar tend a couple of nights a week. I was pretty excited about the prospects.

Before I had a chance to decide exactly what I was going to do, my right hand started going numb. I reported it to my boss. I saw a doctor who told me I had damaged a nerve in my elbow from so much typing over the years and I needed surgery if I wanted the numbness and tingling to go away. So I went to my boss, explained that I would like to try to work three days and rest the other two, thinking perhaps if I rested my arm it would help the nerve repair itself.

He started interviewing people to work the two days a week I couldn't. My hopes of bar tending were put on the back burner for the time being. I had to get my arm squared away or I wouldn't be able to hold onto the bottles, and mix the drinks anyway.

After a few days he called me into his office and announced that he had found someone, but she wanted more money than he had intended to pay so I had to take a three dollar per hour pay cut, in order for him to afford her. I would be making sixty-three cents more an hour than a woman who just started. I had worked for this attorney for six years, gone to school nights while working full time, and he sat there and told me about my pay cut. Also, that I was losing my three weeks of vacation, that perhaps "I could have one week" and no more sick pay or any type of benefits. I was dumbfounded. I walked out of his office and sat at my desk and it was obvious to me that I was going to have to make a decision about my life immediately. I held up my head, gathered all of my personal belongings and walked out the door - for good. I didn't know what I was going to do, but I had spent my whole life feeling bad about myself and I knew that I was being used and taken advantage of and for the first time in my life I decided I didn't have to take it, as a matter of fact, I refused to take it. If it hadn't been for the Twelve-Steps and the support of the group and realizing I had choices, I wouldn't have been able to walk out. Perhaps I couldn't control the situation, but I could control my reaction to it. It was one of the best things I had ever done for myself. Although I was out of a job, I felt wonderful. Like The Twelve-Steps of Phobics Anonymous book said, I "Let Go and Let God". I prayed for guidance and everyday gave up trying to control people and their behavior. I found the more control I let go of, the more control I had. It was amazing. The more I let go the better my life got and things just started falling into place. I began talking to people about my panic and anxiety syndrome. I decided that if they were educated about it perhaps they wouldn't think it was so strange. That allowed me not to worry about having a panic attack because all of the people I spent time with were knowledgeable about panic attacks, consequently I didn't worry about having one, I knew I was surrounded by understanding support and love. The people who couldn't or wouldn't understand started fading from my life, which was fine with me. Never again would I hide my attacks and if someone didn't like it, they didn't have to stay around me. As a matter of fact, I preferred that they didn't.

I had the surgery on my arm and entered a physical therapy class at the hospital to regain some of my strength and abilities again. It was a long slow process, but I was receiving worker's compensation benefits since my injury was work related, which provided a small source of income. As my arm became stronger, I realized that my typing speed and accuracy would never be the same. I had typed about 110 words per minute with barely any errors. Now I could type 30 words per minute with constant errors. Again, I was forced to face reality and make some decisions about my life. It was clear that I couldn't go back to what I was doing, and I really didn't want to anyway. I was so burned out, and the treatment I had received from my boss was so awful, and such a blow to my already damaged self-esteem, that I just decided my days as a paralegal were over.

I woke up in the middle of the night and I knew what I was going to do. I had prayed for guidance and I had received it.

All of my life people had told me I had a flair for writing, but I was so scared of failure I never tried to do anything with it. It was time. It was absolutely clear in my head and heart where I was going.

The next day I went out and purchased a typewriter, a desk, essential office supplies and set up a small office in my bedroom. I sat down at my desk and I wrote a book for children to help them deal with the loss of a pet. I told my family and friends what I had done. I let my family and friends critique my work and I did not receive one negative response. As a matter of fact, everyone loved my work. I showed it to Marilyn and she liked it so much she got in touch with a friend of hers who teaches Kindergarten. The teacher was excited because no one had written a book on this and they had no guidelines for helping the children in their classes when they lost a beloved pet. I was invited to read my book at the school for the young children. It was not a book about death or religion, it was a book about hope.

At this time, I had also written a short skit for television, a story about a trip that Marilyn and I took, when we went to Ventura to start a new P.A. chapter (attached), and I am writing this story about my recovery. I don't know how, but I know this is what I am supposed to be doing. I am hoping to start my own publishing company and publish children's books. I have already started another project, a series of children's books to help them cope with problems in their lives. I finally feel as if I have some direction. For the first time in my life I have confidence, I realize I am a valuable human being and I have a lot to offer. I have never felt so powerful in my life. When things begin to get crazy, I take a minute, look at what I am doing, and usually I find that I have tried once again to take control of a situation where I have no control. As soon as I let go of it, things smooth over and I am once again at peace. I thank God every day for guiding me to the meetings, for helping me practice the Twelve Steps and giving me back my life. I thank the other members of the P.A. fellowship for support, love and encouragement, and especially Marilyn who kept telling me I was worthwhile. Now it is possible for me to believe it too! Life is exciting, rewarding and I am happier than I have ever been.

I don't know where my writing will take me, but I know whatever happens is supposed to happen and I feel confident that I'm going to be all right one day at a time for the rest of my life. I still have my occasional panic attacks and anxious moments, but who doesn't? I feel that I was supposed to suffer with this so I can help those around me who suffer with it too, and are perhaps not on their way to recovery yet. The changes I experienced can happen for you, too. Keep your sense of humor and always have faith. You can have your life back.

JUST FOR TODAY

Just for today my thoughts will be on my recovery, living and enjoying life free from fear, anxiety, or panic.

Just for today I will have faith in someone within Phobics Anonymous who believes in me and wants to help me in my recovery.

Just for today I will have a program. I will try to follow it to the best of my ability.

Just for today through Phobics Anonymous I will try to get a better perspective on my life, and my insecurities that result in Anxiety and Panic.

Just for today I will be unafraid, my thoughts will be on my new associations, people who are recovering phobics and who have found a new way of life by following The Twelve Steps of Phobics Anonymous. As long as I work the Steps, I have nothing to fear.

DRIVING PHOBIA STORY

"On the road again, just can't wait to be on the road again" was not exactly what you'd call "our song", but we wanted to provide support for our fellow agoraphobic who was starting a new Phobics Anonymous chapter in Ventura, so, at one of the Tuesday night P.A. meetings in Palm Desert, three of us decided we would take that four hour drive on Saturday and offer our support. The "three of us" consisted of one generalized phobic who was only afraid to drive in the dark and two agoraphobic driving phobics who were afraid to drive much further than their own street. Dee Dee, the leader of the Palm Desert Chapter, the only one who was not afraid to drive, volunteered to take the wheel. No problem. Famous last words...

The meeting was to be held at 3:00 p.m. on Saturday, so Friday night Marilyn, herself a driving phobic, called Dee Dee, (the most functional driving phobic), to confirm the trip. Unfortunately, Dee Dee had forgotten all about it. (She is a hairdresser and since this was the height of the season in the desert, her Saturday was fully booked). It was too late to back out since we had promised that we would be there and Karen, the new chapter leader, was counting on us for support, expecting three happy, totally upbeat recovering success stories at the first meeting. We couldn't let her down. When Marilyn explained the situation or should I correctly say crisis to me over the phone, I Sandi, a major driving phobic, who had not driven out of Palm Springs in over twelve years, could see the handwriting on the wall. It slowly but surely dawned on me that if we were going to get there it was up to Marilyn and me. Marilyn was silent for a moment too, the same thought making its way up her back as goose bumps and into her hands as sweaty palms. We both said, "Oh shit" at the exact same time as it became crystal clear that one of us had to drive. The first thing we did was burst out laughing which I guess was the best thing that could have happened, because after we were able to laugh at our predicament, I felt complete calmness, and any fear I had of driving, even over bridges or overpasses (my particular panic attack triggers), seemed to disappear. We decided right then and there that nothing was going to stop us from making this trip. We wanted to go; we had promised we'd be there, and by God that's what we did! We're going to go!!!

The next morning at exactly 9:30 a.m., after filling the gas tank, checking the oil, and tires, etc., I arrived at Marilyn's house and we proceeded to put over-night bags in the car. Our "well meaning" friends had been warning us the previous evening and all morning before we left about the terrible storm forecast that was headed toward Los Angeles and that we were going to be right in the middle of it the whole time (thanks a lot guys). They weren't trying to scare us, it's just that you don't say things like that to a driving phobic. So, we were totally prepared for whatever might come up. We had both packed enough clothes for an over-night stay if the weather should turn on us, I had a triple A card, Marilyn had her MasterCard and we were all set.

I forgot to mention that one of Marilyn's dogs (she

has 3) whose name is Kojak and is deaf and blind, had been ill and having unpredictable and undiagnosable seizures, so Marilyn didn't want to leave him home alone.

Picture it - two driving phobics and a sick 14 year old poodle wrapped in a blanket, (who could do who knew what in the car), on Marilyn's lap. Start the car, fasten seat belts and take off for parts unknown and I mean *unknown*, (another favorite of phobics is not knowing exactly where we are and getting lost on the Los Angeles freeway system.) Most of the time we could take a trial run, but not for this trip...it was cold turkey!!!

Our only "map" consisted of directions jotted down on the back of an envelope containing a party invitation (I kid you not) but we were on our way. Not only did we get there in three hours (record time) despite the fact that Karen had forgotten to tell Marilyn about one little old freeway change but we were calm and even having a good time and laughing. The weather was perfect, the traffic was light (a miracle for Los Angeles), we didn't get lost one single time and the dog slept the whole trip. Talk about your divine intervention. If I ever had a doubt about a Higher Power, you can believe it was gone.

Marilyn and I found the location of the meeting (which just happened to be in a psychiatric hospital, Marilyn said they probably wouldn't let us out once they got us in there). Since we made such great time and we were almost three hours early, we had plenty of time to get something to eat. We drove down to a main highway and started looking for a restaurant, any restaurant . We drove, and we drove and we drove, nothing - so we turned around and we drove and we drove. We waved at the sign that marked the intersection we had originally come from, and still we drove. All we could find were railroad tracks, oil drills and an occasional donut shop. Oh yes, and a few liquor stores. By this time I was ready to stop at one for lunch.

Finally, a Mexican restaurant. O.K., that'll do. Marilyn was worried about leaving the dog in the car so I parked as close to the window as I could thinking she can keep an eye on Kojak from inside the restaurant. No luck. He is a tiny little dog and you couldn't see him sitting on the floor. I was starving, Marilyn was so worried about the dog that she couldn't eat and kept excusing herself every couple of minutes to go check on him and at one point had the waitress bring a "to go" bowl of water and took it out to him in the car. While all of this is going on, I'm gulping down my food, Marilyn only had a cup of coffee so I felt I should eat fast. I did, no problem.

We left the restaurant (the dog was in better shape than Marilyn) and headed in the direction of the mental hospital. Great! I was prepared to check in by this time anyway.

Karen, the chapter leader, arrived and appeared to be in control, just a little nervous (who wouldn't be) and was so glad to see us she gave us each a hug. So far so good. Still no panic attacks, no sweaty palms, no mock heart attacks (a personal favorite), all in all, everything was perfect.

Did I mention that Marilyn had decided to sneak the dog into the meeting, rather than go through a repeat of the restaurant episode?

So, here we go, two agoraphobics, a driving phobic plus whatever else I decided to be phobic about at any given moment not suitable for any occasion, and a sick dog, sneaking into a mental hospital. Not exactly what we had envisioned. I got the attention of the receptionist by asking her to throw away my used coffee cup while Marilyn and Karen tore down the hallway towards the meeting room. Kojak hidden in his blanket. GEESH. Karen just happened to be carrying her stuffed teddy bear for support. We looked like something out of the movie "The Dream Team". All we needed was the van.

People began arriving for the meeting and we did our best to put them at ease. We always remember our first meeting, don't we? There were quite a few people showing up for their first meeting. More than we expected, and it looked as if everything was going to be great. I was really excited to be at the first meeting of a new chapter, because I wanted to "make a difference" and I was hoping I could. (Does the phrase "people pleaser" remind you of anyone?)

The meeting began promptly at 3:00 p.m. with Marilyn, the founder of Phobics Anonymous, leading the meeting since Karen was having a panic attack and just wanted to listen and learn so she would be prepared to lead the next meeting. We followed the P.A. format, explained a little about not symptom swapping or discussing medication during the meeting, and then Marilyn asked if anyone would care to share anything. Karen said she would like to share her story. Unfortunately, Karen's story, like all of our stories, was rather unique. She failed to mention up front that she had slipped into a deep depression and because of it was plagued with sleep deprivation for 40 days and nights, which caused her to develop severe physical problems (which she explained in graphic detail) while seeking a diagnosis and treatment.

As I looked around the room at all the new arrivals anxious for a quick fix or cure, I could see one by one that we were "losing them". I saw faces of hope turn ashen and a feeling of gloom settled over the room like a cloud. Karen continued to share her symptoms and story in great detail, which by the way, was a horrible thing for anyone to have to go through all the years that she did and this is in no way meant to make light of her agonies. It was just that it sounded like she was telling these new members who, looking for some ray of hope, any shred of light into what was happening to them and if possible, God willing, some help, that her symptoms were what they had to look forward to.

What's that? My heart is racing? Panic Attack!! A ten on the anxiety scale! Take deep breaths, calm down, not now. I knew I had to speak or I would explode. I felt like racing out of the room but knew I just couldn't. I was going to have to ride this out. The moment Karen finished sharing and Marilyn asked if anyone else had something to say, I held up my hand, introduced myself and started talking in what I hoped was as upbeat a mood as possible. The first thing I did was admit I was nervous about speaking to a group and that I was shaking, I even held out my hands so they could see I really was, and with admitting I was nervous, I was able to let go of it. I felt myself calming down as I spoke and I tried to be reassuring and smile a lot and repeat some of the wonderful things Marilyn had said to me at my first meeting. I even made a joke about blaming a particular street in Palm Springs for my panic attacks. It was working. People were calming down, they were laughing and the "doom and gloom" in the room began to fade. I said as much as I felt needed to be said as quickly as I could and assured the newcomers that they could have their lives back, there was hope and Marilyn and I were examples. The meeting continued and a few of the newcomers began to share their stories. Before we knew it the hour was up. We all joined hands and said the Serenity Prayer and the meeting ended. Karen told everyone if they wanted to discuss medication we would go out into the yard to have a cigarette and discuss it there. All of a sudden Marilyn, who had been unusually quiet, spoke up and said she was sorry but we couldn't stay. We had to hit the road because of the long drive back. I didn't know what was wrong. Usually Marilyn is very vocal, positive, loves to share and be supportive, so it was totally uncharacteristic of her to want to leave so quickly. I didn't say anything, but I knew something was up. We quickly walked outside and Marilyn looked at me and said "I just finished having a panic attack at the meeting". I was absolutely shocked! We were both going through the exact same thing at the exact same time, yet neither one of us knew it!! We both started laughing and again, our plight was so ridiculous that our panic started to subside. I took a brisk walk around the parking lot to release some of the stress. Marilyn walked the dog and lit a cigarette, (we didn't want to stay too long, we were afraid the aides would be coming out with the white coats at any second) and took off, heading for home.

The ride home was uneventful, a couple of sweaty palm moments (give me a break, it was dark by then), and the dog was fine. Things were going so well in fact, that I kept patting the dashboard saying "Good car, Good car", when Marilyn called to my attention that I should have been patting myself, not the car, on the back and saying "Good driver, Good driver".

We arrived home safe and sound and pretty damn proud of ourselves at 7:30 p.m., in time to watch The Golden Girls, and the delay was only because the traffic was a little heavier. We still made excellent time, 3 1/2 hours.

Hopefully this story will add a little levity to your day and you can realize that if you want to do something bad enough, if you have faith instead of fear and refuse to allow fear to rule your life, you can do anything. If Marilyn and I can go through what we went through and laugh about it, you can too!

Life is a Checkerboard

Life is a checkerboard
and the player opposite you is
time. If you hesitate before moving, or
neglect to move promptly, your man will
be wiped off the board by time.
You are playing against a partner
who will not tolerate indecision.

ALAN'S STORY

My name is Alan, I am a 32 year old male and I am a recovering phobic and alcoholic. I also suffer from anxiety and panic related disorders.

Looking back at my childhood, which wasn't very happy, I can recall always feeling a little different than other kids. I was always a nervous child, afraid of elevators, closed in places, open spaces and people. I used to hyperventilate a lot. As a child I was always afraid that my bladder would lock up on me and not be able to urinate. This caused a lot of embarrassment, since I would at times, let a little urine seep out, just to be sure that my bladder was working. Then there were times I was always conscious of my heart beating. Sometimes it seemed it was beating too slow and then at times it would race out of control or even beat irregularly.

Then at age 14 all hell broke loose. I experimented with a drug called hash which my brother brought over from Germany. My brain went into total chaos. I lost all touch with reality. Things around me didn't seem real. My whole body went numb. My mind became detached from my body. I went into a complete state of panic. I didn't know what was happening to me, and no one prepared me for this. I thought, if this is what being high is all about, I wanted no part of it. Reality did finally return in a couple of hours, but only by doing some reading and praying could I bring myself out of it. This was to be a tool I used to bring me out of panic stupors in the future.

Time passed, a year maybe. At 15 I got married to a girl I

got pregnant. Then all those feelings I had experienced a year ago while in that drug induced panic, returned. I was at a local shopping center shopping, when out of the blue from nowhere, it hit me, a full blown panic attack. Here I was with jelly legs, racing, pounding heart, sweating, feeling dizzy, being detached from reality again, but how could this be happening this time? I hadn't taken any drugs, so why was this happening, I thought, and what was it? My thoughts were like the winds of a hurricane racing here and there in my mind. All I could think about was that I had to just get home, nothing else mattered as I ran out the door leaving my groceries at the checkout line. Getting into my house, I finally started to calm down and return to reality. My God, what was happening to me? I screamed. I remember saying to myself, I won't tell anyone about this, if I do they will think I am crazy and put me away somewhere, locked up in some mental institution.

I was still in school and I had to go back. I sat in class thinking about what had happened the night before. The more I thought about it, the more I could feel my heart start to gallop. I imagined it galloping right up from my throat and out my mouth. I had to get up and tell the teacher, but my legs wouldn't move. The harder I tried, the weaker they became. Just great, I thought, having a heart attack and being paralyzed on top of it all. I did finally manage to get up, stumbling to the teacher and collapsing into her arms. I finally got it out of my mouth, I think I'm having a heart attack. I was rushed to the emergency room and diagnosed as having a "nervous disposition" with "light anxiety". Cause: unknown.

Thus, started a series of panic attacks, anxiety attacks, personality disorders, suicidal tendencies, and a drinking and drugging lifestyle that would last for 17 hellish, torturing, terrifying years.

At 16 and 17, I couldn't leave my house, I was afraid to go out. Here I was just married with a child and I couldn't even work. Always fearful of when that "big one" would hit. This was my safe zone, staying here, in the house, a prisoner of my own mind. It was then that I first thought of suicide to escape the inescapable. I sat with a loaded shot gun at my head ready to pull the trigger while praying to God for relief. Prepared to hear that loud sound, the sound of the tip of the hammer on the firing pin, only to hear the tapping at the door. It was a friend of mine who came to share some feelings of anxiety that he had been experiencing recently. Coincidence or what? I don't know, but this was the first of many reprieves that was to interfere with my obsession of suicidal thoughts. Suicide, I thought, was the only control I had over my life. Suicide, I thought, was my only way out of this prison of mental torture. Thinking now about those suicide attempts, I now know that God had been intervening in my attempts, which were usually futile.

A year later I finally pulled myself out of my depression somehow, just enough to start a new job at a big name factory making tires. I thought I had finally gotten a hold of my life and things were going to be okay from there on. About 12 months into my job, it hit again, this time showing no mercy. It nearly drove me crazy, I was missing too much work because of anxiety and panic attacks, they were threatening to fire me. I broke down and went to a heart specialist thinking maybe this was what was causing all of my panic attacks. I went through tests and tests. One test, I couldn't even finish. It was a treadmill stress test. I thought I would surely have a heart attack and die if I did this one, because my heart was already racing a hundred miles an hour and this surely would end it all. I told the doctors my legs wouldn't hold up and I had to quit. It was one of many lies I would tell just to survive because no one understood this freaky disease. The result of my tests were that my heart was as healthy and strong as an ox and the irregular and racing heartbeat was the result of stresses in life. Shit, I thought, the crazy heartbeats was from some unknown disease and I was dying. I was referred to a psychiatrist. I received counseling and prescriptions for minor tranquilizers and reassurance that my problem was common and it would go away. They told me that beta blockers and tranquilizers should do the trick, but it still didn't explain the total panic and the feeling of detachment and unrealistic feelings I had had.

Well, it didn't go away, and it came back a few days later with unmerciful vengeance. I couldn't handle the panic attacks anymore. I lost my job. "What had I ever done to deserve this form of torture?" I cried to myself. Was God punishing me for something I had done in the past, or what?

I went from doctor to doctor, psychiatrist to psychologist looking for a cure, but there was none.

A couple of years earlier I had experimented with alcohol, which brought temporary relief. What if I drank constantly? Wouldn't that ease the anxiety? I rationalized this to be true. This was to be the modality of escape which I prescribed for myself and used for the next 14 years. The more anxiety I experienced, the more I slipped into the grasp of alcohol, and by drinking more alcohol, the more I was bringing a maelstrom of severe anxiety into my life. I didn't realize it at the time, but alcohol was the reason I was experiencing more anxiety and panic attacks.

The years had brought drunkenness, more suicide attempts, (six to be exact, some very close) accidents caused by alcohol, and the abuse of my family, followed by a divorce from my wife. I lost countless jobs on account of the panic attacks. I couldn't function any longer. I was labeled a being "just a lazy excuse of a human being", who didn't want to work and who used anxiety as an excuse for not working. I think panic disorders are harder on men in this respect, because society looks upon men as people who should never cry, have mental problems and who should always hold a job no matter what. I finally couldn't hold any job for long because of the panic attacks. I signed up for disability and got it. I had lost so many jobs, they figured that I really did have a problem. I soon realized later that this wasn't the answer either. It just brought on more depression. I figured I would just lay back and wait, come hell or high water I'd just drink myself to death. But it didn't work. I was slowly loosing my sanity by drinking and using drugs. Then, another suicide attempt and another trip to the psychiatric ward in the hospital. There I had finally found a name for my problem. What I had for years been trying to find out on my own was the name on this book that the psychiatrist handed me. It was called the "Anxiety Disease". I was ecstatic and relieved to finally learn what I was suffering from.

The book explained that I had a real disease. A disease that was coming from within, not just common everyday anxiety. With this information in hand, I could hold my head high and exclaim that I wasn't just a lazy, rotten human being, but that I had a real disease. Now, I knew what I had, but how was I going to bring it under control? By now, though, I didn't care, for I was being held prisoner by alcohol and tranquilizers. Tranquilizers that the doctor had prescribed to me unknowingly and without knowledge of my alcoholism, because I had earnestly hidden it from them for years. It would still take 2 more years of hell before it finally would come to a head. It all came to a conclusion in 1991, first by my getting a D.U.I. in January and my sixth and last suicide attempt in June of that year. The 17 years of hellish torment, of panic disorders and alcohol abuse had taken its toll. My health was failing. My sanity was all but gone. The doctors were talking about having me committed to an insane asylum. I was driving my family further apart from me. My depression had fallen to a new low. Life wasn't worth living, the demons in my mind were having their way.

There had to be a way out, a positive way out, I pondered. I started to feel spiritual at this time. I think God had seen that I had finally had enough. I wondered what my purpose in life had been and would be. God's presence surrounded me, I felt a fire in my heart. Not panic this time, but a glow of desire that I did have a purpose. A feeling that my 17 years of suffering had not been in vain, but that I had experienced all this suffering for a reason.

I checked myself into a substance abuse treatment center, to embark on a new journey; a new plan from God for my purpose in life. While there, I was introduced into Phobics Anonymous. I decided to put all of my effort and zeal into this program as I had never done before. While working my other 12 Step program, I worked the Phobics Anonymous 12 Step program with the same fervor. I had finally found my purpose in life. I had met others in P.A. who are suffering as much as I once did. God has brought us together to help each other with one common problem, the debilitating effects of panic disorders.

My life has had miraculous changes for the better since coming into P. A. I have been in P.A. now for 6 months and these have been the most serene and happiest times of my life. My depression is lifting. My zest for life has returned. My sanity is back. My self esteem and confidence is high. I am going back to college. I am going back to work, I am off all tranquilizers but one, which I only take as needed. I am going places I couldn't go before. I am no longer afraid of people, places and things. Life is now a challenge to me. By working through the 12 Steps of P.A., I have gotten rid of my old negative ideas and catastrophic ways of thinking.

Working the 12 Steps of P.A. has given me a feeling of control over my life, not fear. Before I would gather evidence for why I should die, I am now gathering evidence for why I should live. I am devoting myself to the practice of using techniques such as prayer, meditation, changing my diet, regularly saying positive affirmations, visualizing change, going to counseling, improving relationships. I know that a lot of my anxieties are from resentments. I am learning to forgive those that have caused me to feel resentments.

Other tools I have learned in P.A. and am now using are courage to make changes. Honesty in sharing my secrets and problems with others, realizing it's an ongoing process, learning who I am, having goals, loving myself, eliminating my addictions, obsessions, coping mechanisms, negative behavior, and self-defeating attitudes.

I know that I will experience some anxiety, but it's okay. Accepting myself, thinking positively, keeping good company, practicing love, and expecting miracles are part of my life now. To sum it up, I quote an excerpt I read somewhere "I feel that providence, nature, God, or the power of creation seems to favor human beings who accept and love life unconditionally". The universe supports me and I am worthy of that support. All I can say now is, Free at last, Free at last, Free at last. Thank God and P.A., I am Free at last.

Thank God for Phobics Anonymous.

Every Adversity
Every Failure and
Every Heartache carries with it the seed
of an equivalent or greater benefit.

Success requires no explanations
Failure permits no alibis

FRAN'S STORY

For the past 16 years, I have had agoraphobia, acute anxiety and panic attacks. My first panic attack occurred at a time in my life when I was very, very happy. I was on the interstate driving to Knoxville to see my sister, when out of the blue, I began experiencing a tremendous fear that really had no basis. BAM - it just hit me. My head started to pound, I broke out in a cold sweat, I couldn't breathe and felt like I was choking. I didn't know what was happening to me, so I pulled off the highway and called my sister, insisting that she had to come get me. My sister and her husband reassured me, saying that I was afraid because it was dark and I was driving alone, but that didn't seem right because I had previously driven and flown all over the United States without it ever bothering me.

Buoyed up by my sibling's affirmations, I returned to my car and resumed driving, but the respite was brief. By the time I got to Harriman, I had lived through a nightmare and I simply could not go on. I pulled off at a motel and called my sister again, telling her that there was something terribly wrong, even though I had no idea what it might be. She and her husband agreed to pick me up, which was a blow to my self esteem, because there I was, an independent, healthy, 28-year old woman and I really thought I was going to die.

After the symptoms of my initial attack abated, I thought no more about them. Six months later, however, they returned with a vengeance. I was at work and for-tunately, it was a setting where there were a lot of doctors in attendance. Again, for no apparent reason, I had a panic attack that resulted in my blood pressure dropping dramatically. My heartbeat, however, skyrocketed up to 250 beats a minute, so I was taken to a nearby emergency room where I was hooked up to an EKG machine for more than five hours. Even so, no one knew what was wrong and again I thought I was dying.

An intravenous drip of neosynephrine eventually lowered my heart rate while elevating my blood pressure. I was given a small supply of tranquilizers to carry me through the weekend, along with advice to consult my own physician for a complete physical examination, which proved unremarkable. Most people with agoraphobia or anxiety attacks are misdiagnosed ten to fifteen times before someone discovers the true problem. In my case, I consulted neurologists, cardiologists pulmonary specialists, general practitioners, and psychiatrists, you name the specialist and I saw him. I spent thousands and thousands of dollars trying to find out what was wrong with me. What I really wanted was reassurance that I wasn't going to die, but no one ever gave me that, so each time I had an attack, I figured I would either die or go completely crazy.

Fast and furious, the attacks struck me at all times, with no pattern of where or when. Three of the most common places where attacks commence for almost all agoraphobics are in stores, at church or while driving. I responded by avoiding those places where panic occurs. Because the attacks are so devastating, pure terror becomes associated with that place, even though there is no reason for it.

In 1976, I admitted myself to a mental hospital in Nashville. They ran a gambit of tests on me and said I could go home and there was nothing wrong with me. They gave me a multiple vitamin every day in the mental hospital - no other medication because they didn't know what was wrong with me. After three weeks I realized all they were doing for me was getting me to function and I could do that at home, so I discharged myself. I had been in the mental hospital with people who were really "disturbed" to say the least.

I was brought up in a Christian home with parents instilling "fear" as discipline, (noncommittal father, dominating mother). My father was very anxious and I never learned coping tools for emotions at home. Anger was suppressed because it wasn't "Christian like". Feelings were suppressed, especially my anger, frustrations, sorrow, joy, etc... The doctor told me I was "an emotional wreck". I was the oldest sibling and very perfectionistic, but according to my mother, "I never did anything right" (and still don't). I was taught that the consequences of something that could be positive could also be catastrophic, such as: be careful swimming, "or you'll drown", or watch crossing the street, "or you'll be hit by a car and killed". I did diagnose myself in 1978 after reading an article in *Family Circle Magazine*. I then took it to my psychiatrist, who I was seeing at the time and had been for two and a half years to no avail. I even got progressively worse and stopped driving alone. He did not want to read the article, but I insisted since I was paying him $$$$ for 50 minutes! He then said, "Well, this does sound like what you have!"

My doctor maintains that anxiety disorders may result from chemical imbalances in the brain. He also is of the opinion that people are genetically predisposed to the problem, and says that hormonal fluctuations, particularly in women, may play a part in the disorders. According to him, one percent of the general population is afflicted. Early identification and intervention are very important he emphasized. It's much easier dealing with an individual who seeks prompt attention after his or her first major attack. Some people, he noted, may demonstrate mild symptoms for some time before having a full-blown attack.

Before medication is prescribed, a course of behavior therapy should be followed. If necessary, pharmaceuticals are given, with the selection made between the benzodiazepine family, which stop anxiety attacks, or tricyclics, such as monoamine oxidase inhibitors, which suppress symptoms. "The former is very effective, but may be dependency-producing," he explained. "The latter are also good and are not habit forming, but may result in some side effects like sleeplessness, nervousness, a dry mouth and so on. In addition, the second group of drugs are anti-depressants and research has found that many sufferers of anxiety disorders also have to deal with depression."

In its earliest definition, agoraphobia meant "fear of the market place". A true agoraphobic has such severe anxiety attacks that he or she can eventually become housebound in order to avoid the places associated with the attacks. I'm aware of cases where people have become room-bound and even chairbound. No one has ever died from agoraphobia itself, but there have been instances where people have needed medical attention, but did not get it because they were too frightened to leave their houses.

When my disorder was correctly diagnosed, I was prescribed Xanax. That drug is very effective at blocking the attacks, but one must be withdrawn from the drug slowly or the ,person might have seizures. Xanax also causes a roller coaster effect, where every four to six hours, as it wears off, the person taking it may experience anxiety until the next dose kicks in. This prohibits a good quality of life. In my case, I felt "normal" until the drug wore off.

About three years ago, an accidental discovery at Boston Massachusetts' General Hospital proved propitious for me and other sufferers of agoraphobia. Quite inadvertently, the doctors observed that Klonopin, a drug that had been on the market since 1975 for petit mal seizures, worked well to control panic disorders. At present, I am on a subpediatric dosage, and that has been working well.

Since my disorder was properly diagnosed, I have become more aware of a familial link of agoraphobia. I have a male cousin the same age as I am who suffered from anxiety attacks. Neither of us even knew the other had the disorder. My sister also had bad attacks, although hers went into remission when she became pregnant.

I think that hormonal changes may well affect the frequency and duration of panic attacks. In the course of talking with many sufferers, I have found that the majority of women experienced their worst episodes during pregnancy, when they were nursing or as they stopped nursing. For example, I had a total hysterectomy when I was 38 years old and was placed on estrogen. My panic subsided at least 75 percent until those five days each month I did not take the hormones. During that time, I was in total panic. Finally my doctor agreed that I should take estrogen every day, along with my other medication, so things would remain in control.

Through my experiences I became acquainted with many other individuals who suffer from anxiety disorders, and eight years ago, Agoraphobics in Action, Inc. was born. A non-profit organization, funded exclusively by donations. Its purposes include support, education and awareness for those with the disorder and their families. Chapters throughout Nashville and other cities of middle Tennessee offer support groups and outreach programs, each held in nonthreatening and easy to escape environments. On April 15, 1991, I started the first Phobics Anonymous chapter in Nashville, Tenn....That was 40 weeks ago. My life has totally changed. Working the Twelve Steps has been the key, going to meetings, and meeting others in a program that is structured, yet casual, with no symptom swapping, or down and out tales, but good positive input and reflections. I have found my "Higher Power". As a Christian I really did not know what faith was, until I started working the Twelve Steps. Now I know. I realized my conception of God that is my Higher Power, along with my group was a conception very much unlike my parents relationship to me, which was one of fear, not trusting, not feeling, etc...I know now God is loving, feeling and all good things - not negative force.

The hardest part for me was turning the "control" over to God. I wanted to help Him. Once I "let go and let God" I learned. I work with God on a daily basis, one day at a time, sometimes a second at a time.

Through my group I have gained strength to become healthy, whole and free from fear. I am taking mini-steps and doing things during the last 40 weeks I haven't done in 16 years. Sometimes I can't believe it, then I think "All things are possible with God." It is not easy. No one ever said life would not be hard. I am blessed in some ways with the "gift of panic" because I have broadened my coping skills with life. My life will never be the same now that I have the Twelve Steps. However, it also takes time. One cannot work the Steps in four weeks. It takes months and even years. One should always return to Step One when life becomes chaotic, as it will periodically. The Twelve Steps are not a magic cure for everyone, but they are for me. I must constantly work them. As we say at our meetings "it is not for those who need it, it is for those who want it", and "keep coming back, it works, if you work it". This is something no one else can do for me. I cannot blame anyone. I must take responsibility for myself and my problems. The Phobics Anonymous Twelve Steps are God-sent and have changed my life! I am not what I was last year at this time. I am a new butterfly! Our group had gotten so big we formed Chapter Two, and as of this writing, Chapters Three and Four are in the works!

KATE'S STORY

In the wake of my first panic attack, I was left with the foundation of my life broken wide open, and two thoughts, "Why?" and "I want my life back".

My first panic attack happened while driving home from a counseling session at the Dougy Center where I had co-facilitated a group of children who had recently lost a parent or sibling by suicide. It had been a stressful day, on top of a stressful week, on top of a stressful year. I had done two massages that morning, then rushed to this group, (which caused me a lot of anxiety), then found myself rushing home to see a counseling client. It was 6:30 p.m. and all I had eaten that day was a small bowl of brown rice. As I was driving home my heart did a flutter of some kind. This had happened before, but for some reason this time my mind decided that it was lasting too long. I immediately pictured heart attack, ambulance, emergency, and who do I go to for help.

That sudden terror sent my heart into high gear. My heart was beating hard and fast and the more I tried frantically to slow it down, the more it continued to race. I got hot and my head got tingly. Determined, I kept driving to the safety of my home and my partner, who was a naturopathic medical student at the time.

Unfortunately, once I got home and had Kimberly feel my pulse I got more frightened and my heart beat even faster. Kimberly's fear added to mine. She called the naturopathic teaching clinic for help, as I paced the floors, certain I would soon pass out or die. Finally, I insisted that she drive me to the emergency room. That in itself was terrifying. I had never gone to the hospital for any health reason of my own. In addition, I didn't have much trust in traditional western medicine.

At the hospital they monitored my pulse, blood pressure, and did an EKG. The EKG was normal. The doctor told me it was probably an "adrenaline rush". I asked her if it could happen again. She said yes, but never mentioned anxiety or panic disorders.

I went home with my pulse still beating faster than normal. I fell into bed exhausted, terrified, and crying. All of the stress and loss in the last year came crashing down on my shoulders.

I stopped my practice as a counselor and massage therapist abruptly. I felt broken. I barely got out of bed for the first four days. I became afraid to do anything that would increase my heart rate. I went to my doctor, who was a Naturopathic physician. She gave me homeopathic remedies and herbs to help with my trigger happy nerves. (One scary thought could set my inner alarm blazing.) These things helped, but definitely didn't solve the problem. I got to the point where I was afraid to be alone, to drive, or to exhaust myself. I became acutely aware of every sensation in my body. I would get alarmed at any outstanding or sudden unusual feelings. I also was obsessed with constantly checking my pulse.

About a month after my first panic attack, my mother sent me a book she had gotten many years earlier when she was going through a hard time: Claire Weekes *Hope and Help for Your Nerves*. As I began to read this book, I sobbed with relief knowing I was not alone and that there was a name for what I was experiencing. I also cried from the grief that these symptoms were suddenly controlling my life.

Soon after this I planned a trip to go see my family, including my new born niece. I imagined that it would be comforting and nurturing. On the contrary, I experienced the worst and most prolonged feelings of anxiety and panic on the plane and during the 24 hours I was at my parents. Nothing felt safe, or familiar. To my surprise and sadness, my mother increased my fear and disorientation by her seeming inability to be there for me. But it was my mother that loved me enough to encourage me to fly back home the next morning. Thanks to my Nana the flight home was tolerable. It was the one and only time that I have taken anti-anxiety medication.

This trip was the single most devastating set back I have had to date. It filled me with an overwhelming fear of traveling. I have made definite progress in this area, but it seems slow. I still have not seen my niece, but I know I will soon

In my worst despair, I experienced a strong desire to be dead. It seemed the only relief. Fortunately, suicide has never been an option. About this time, I got a referral from my counselor to see a psychiatrist for a drug prescription. I went, got the prescription, and never filled it. It just wasn't worth any side effects or dependency.

Shortly thereafter, I began seeing a different counselor. She offered me a genuinely safe and gentle space to explore deep emotions at my pace. It was there that I experienced healing of some of the emotional wounds connected to my panic and anxiety. This was a major step in opening up and trusting, especially after four years of forceful, emotional work and spiritual mind control while I was involved in two separate "new age" spiritual/psychological cult groups. (It seems that this cult experience played a definite role in stripping my defenses and self-trust, leading me head-long into a panic response.)

Also, during my counseling with Dee, I relived an experience I had when I was about four years old. It seemed to be a piece of the answer to my initial question, "Why?" A baby sitter that took care of my sister and me while my parents were at work died of a heart attack while she was caring for us. While reliving this memory, I saw myself come out of my bedroom, feeling frightened and helpless as I watched this woman gripping her chest. Then I experienced the drama of ambulance, emergency and the absence of comfort or reassurance from my mother.

After a failed attempt at holding a full time job in a county park and six months of unemployment because of my panic and anxiety, I got the courage to take a job at a picture frame store doing framing. It was a humiliating adjustment from being a self-employed therapist. "Who was I, and what was I worth if I wasn't helping people?" At the same time, though, it gave me a focus, a place to go and get out of myself and rebuild my confidence to step back into the world.

I am now working full time at this frame shop, gently anticipating and actively watching for my next step towards personal fulfillment and purpose.

For the last six months I have been seeing a Naturopathic Physician, Acupuncturist. Working with

Satya has been the greatest physical and emotional support I have found. Acupuncture has had a significant effect on balancing my sympathetic and parasympathetic nervous system, blood sugar imbalance, and digestive upset. Her life, acceptance, faith and counseling has been a blessing.

Around this same time that I began seeing Satya, I read a very important book, *The Panic Attack Recovery Book*, by Swede and Jaffe. This book made me aware of the strong correlation between hypoglycemia and anxiety. I stopped eating any form of sugar, increased my protein intake, began taking supplements, and ate carbohydrate/protein snacks throughout my day. After a couple of months of these changes in my diet, my panic attacks and anxiety decreased dramatically. They still continue to diminish.

In all of my search, inner and outer, the one source of support sorely missing has been connecting with people that have experienced panic and anxiety, who are actively working to heal, grow, and recover. I have had a lot of support, but with no one who has experienced the pain and grief of this debilitating irrational fear. Therefore they couldn't fully understand the devastation.

About seven months ago, I began going to Al Anon and Co-Dependents Anonymous meetings. I went with the awareness that there were many common characteristics between co-dependents and people with panic disorders. Again, this was another step in my healing journey. The greatest gift I have received from these groups is a re-connection with my Higher Power (who I choose to call God) through working the Twelve Steps. Because there is no leader and no right way to do it, I feel safe and encouraged to truly develop my own relationship to a Higher Power within.

Last April my mother sent me an Ann Landers Column that was about people with panic attacks. It was in this column that I first heard about Phobics Anonymous. Knowing that Twelve Step programs work for other groups, I sent away for information on any existing P.A. groups in my area. There were none, so I decided I would try and start one myself. I received all of the information from Phobics Anonymous World Service Headquarters in Palm Springs, California, found a place and time to hold meetings and began putting out public notices. The response has been slow, but I have received a couple of calls. One of those people has offered to help me put the word out about the meeting. There are two of us now. I feel hopeful and see Phobics Anonymous as a positive part of my healing and recovery process. One step at a time I am regaining my life, discovering a sense of self I have never known, and developing a relationship to my Higher Power, God.

We can grow and flourish from out of the depths and darkness. I find strength in leaving no stone unturned.

Success

S ense of direction
U nderstanding
C ourage
C harity
E steem
S elf confidence
S elf acceptance

NORBERT'S STORY

I remember my first panic attack in 1974. I was 19 years old and was in the Navy. As I was taking the ferry back from Seattle to Bromington (where I was stationed) with some of my Navy friends, we were all inside the ferry when all of a sudden I felt like I couldn't breathe and I was terrified that I was going to die. I knew I had to get away from all those people inside the ferry, so I ran to the outside deck. My friends came over and asked what was wrong. I said nothing was wrong, out of embarrassment that they would find out the real truth. Afterwards, I felt like I was going crazy, going to lose control, or die, and there was something flawed in me. I had these attacks several more times while I was in the Navy. I remember going to sick bay on the ship and telling the doctor what I was feeling and he said for me to wear socks that came to my knees. To me this didn't make any sense and couldn't relieve me of my attacks. In the service, I abused alcohol to socialize and feel human. I always had this feeling of impending doom and fear. I continued to abuse alcohol in my twenties, to cut the edge and try to get rid of the fear and panic I was always feeling. I couldn't hold any jobs more than six months at a time. I was continually moving, running from fear and panic. I always hoped that when I got to a different state I would somehow feel better. I was in and out of relationships a lot. I had a hard time being alone at all. I was always in a state of panic, acute anxiety and fear. To me it became a fact of life. When it got unbearable, I'd get drunk to relieve it.

I got married when I was 28 and my panic attacks started to get worse. I was afraid to go out and socialize without my wife. I was always on guard waiting for the next attack. I was hospitalized for major depression in December, 1984. I couldn't hold a job or look for one and I wouldn't leave my house. I felt like a total failure as a man and a husband. I felt like I couldn't cope with life anymore and so I was hospitalized in the psychiatric ward. When I got out four weeks later, I had a panic attack. I tried to hold on to jobs but couldn't. My fear was so strong that I couldn't concentrate or focus on what I was doing most of the time. I ended up in the hospital again in 1985 for anxiety disorder and major depression. I stayed for six weeks and was put on anti-depressant medication. It seemed to work for awhile, but when I was released I had panic attacks, even while on medication. The doctors never discussed my panic attacks, they said it was from unresolved resentments. I went to my own doctor and he told me what was happening and he understood and he told me he had a lot of patients like me. He gave me some anti panic medication and referred me to a 12-Step self help support group, Phobics Anonymous, saying this is what really works. At this time I couldn't work. I was having panic attacks three or four times a day. I felt like I was going insane. I called Marilyn and came with my wife to my first meeting where other people with the same problem I had talked about theirs. I felt relieved that I wasn't the only one. I got all my strength from my Higher Power and these meetings with my fellow brothers and sisters. I am grateful to Marilyn and all the other people at the meetings who helped me get through this. My life has changed a lot since then. I can hold a job and function and socialize and can enjoy life and people again. I now attend Phobics Anonymous meetings to help me live one day at a time and to help my fellow phobics.

PRAYER OF ST. FRANCIS ASSISI

Lord, make me an instrument of your peace!
Where there is hatred, let me sow love.
Where there is injury, pardon.
Where there is doubt, faith.
Where there is despair, hope.
Where there is darkness, light.
Where there is sadness, joy.

Grant that I may not so much seek
to be consoled as to console.
To be understood as to understand.
To be loved as to love.
For it is in giving
That we we receive.
It is in pardoning
That we are pardoned.
It is in dying
That we are born to eternal life.

ADDY'S STORY

I got married in August of 1966. That was the beginning of the end for me. The seeds of my panic disorder had been festering for most of my life, but once I married, it took just a few short months for me to experience my first full blown panic attack.

I was teaching school and at the end of the day, while on the subway, (going into the city to attend my weekly dance class where I was to meet my girlfriend as usual), I experienced what I thought was a choking, suffocating feeling. I don't remember most of my past, but that is a day I will never forget. I felt as though I had to run and escape from the train. The panic was overwhelming. I guess my grip on reality was strong enough to prevent me from doing such a stupid thing, (since doing so would have landed me on the street in one of the city's toughest neighborhoods). I sat it out, not knowing what was happening. When I reached my destination, I was relieved to breathe air, even the dirty city air, but almost immediately I became panic-stricken again and remember feeling dizzy, disoriented, and numb. Somehow, I got to the dance class, and once there I felt better until I learned that my friend would not be taking the return trip home with me, which she usually did. Within seconds I panicked again. I had no choice except to get back on that train and go home. Somehow I found the strength to make that trip by arming myself with candy bars and magazines. From that day on, for more than twenty five years, I have been suffering with panic disorder.

For a long time I never knew what was wrong with me. I was able to continue working because I had to and also because the anxiety and panic in the beginning was very erratic. It had a life of its own and came and went whenever it wanted to. Each time I experienced an attack I, of course, associated it with the place or thing where it happened and eventually my world became smaller and smaller as I avoided places where I had my attacks. It seemed to be better when I was not alone, so I attached myself to people, often without being selective, and as a result, formed unhealthy relationships which often made me unhappy.

I struggled through my life dealing with the roller coaster ride caused by my emotions and panic attacks. Fortunately, I had two beautiful children who, I believe, kept me going all during those dark years. Their existence forced me to function every day. I had to care for them and the love I gave and received from them kept my heart from breaking and giving up on life. Those two children are still the lights of my life. They are now 19 and 23 years old.

Eventually, for a while, I became housebound. I don't know how, but with a little professional help, I pulled myself through that period and was finally able to get out. I went into therapy and continued, off and on, with different therapists, for 20 years. My confidence grew as I learned about myself, and after 13 years of a difficult marriage, I was strong enough to get a divorce, but my panic attacks were still there and I still needed to be with people to feel better, so I then began forming unhealthy heterosexual relationships, never understanding why they all ended so unhappily. I, again, was not being selective because I merely needed a support person; anyone who could help me control my anxiety!

All during those years I sought medical advice. My physical symptoms were making me anxious. I had EKG's and IVP (for kidneys), allergy tests, a colonoscopy, etc., etc., etc. You name it, I had it. But, of course, nothing seriously wrong was ever found with me. Eventually, as I corrected the negative aspects of my life, my symptoms subsided. I also tried numerous programs to eliminate my anxiety and panic attacks. I even tried a group that specifically dealt with agoraphobia. It involved desensitization training with a recovered phobic who worked with me in situations where I felt especially anxious such as driving, malls, elevators, etc. I must also mention the other modalities I tried over the years: group therapy, crisis intervention, psychoanalysis, transactional analysis, neurolinguistic analysis, and of course psychotherapy. With each method of treatment, I did gain some insights and strength, but the panic attacks still came and the devastating physical symptoms still plagued me. Finally, after about 22 years of searching, I was put on antidepressant medication, which has greatly helped. I still experience panic and anxiety attacks, but they are more controllable because of the medication. I still avoid certain situations because I don't want to feel the anxiety. I know that I must continually push myself in order to make progress.

A few months ago I read a small article about Phobics Anonymous in a newspaper. Something in me clicked. This was something I hadn't tried yet. After several weeks of communication with the founder, Marilyn, I began my own group. The need I felt was great. I always knew that I wanted to help people. One of my own therapists told me that I would make a "wonderful therapist." I was terrified, but at the same time, I found a strength I didn't know I had, and so I persevere. I found a meeting room and by word of mouth I let it be known that a P.A. chapter was being formed. I even spoke on the radio. I received many calls and presently we have a small chapter that I know will keep growing. Every time I lead the group I know I am not only helping others, but myself as well. Every time I help a group member over the phone, I feel wonderful. Every time the phone rings with a new inquiry about the group, I know I have gained something, as well as given something.

Thank you Phobics Anonymous and Marilyn.

P.S. I have been in a healthy relationship for the past five and a half years. He is a wonderful and supportive man.

YESTERDAY, TODAY, TOMORROW

When you can look at yesterday
without regret,
and at tomorrow without fear,
you're on your way to living in today.

MIKE'S STORY

In 1978, at the age of 20, I had my first panic attack. I was very ill previous to this from a case of mono. I had some very uncomfortable body symptoms that drove me to worry beyond the normal fearful boundaries prompted by illness. I was at the age where I was very sensitive about what people thought about me. I guess some of that was caused by my own insecurities, even though I was a very popular person among my friends and in my surroundings.

One night I went to Carl's Jr. fast food drive through and during my wait in line I had my first panic attack. It devastated me to the point that I drove over the curb and shrubs to flee to my parents' house, where I told my family about my devastating symptoms that soon came back. I quickly went to the emergency room at the nearest hospital (I was an employee in the engineering dept.) I was embarrassed to find my problems were related to my nerves. I was told by a doctor after a physical exam that I needed "a hobby". This came as a surprise to me because I had plenty of them. After my physical, I talked with my brother whom I confided most things in and it felt good to have someone to talk to that really listened. I discovered that the majority of people I tried to talk to about my panic attacks thought I was dealing with too much stress. After 14 years of trying to deal with my life as an undiagnosed agoraphobic, going to many doctors, taking different medications, attending stress clinics, even psychotherapy, nothing seemed to get to the core of the problem that had no "name". In desperation, I found myself really wanting to find information. I started reading books, articles, etc., anything that sounded like or described what I was going through.

In an effort to find out what my problem was I don't know where or how I heard about it, but someone told me there was a support group called Phobics Anonymous. I contacted them and when I received their information I knew that I had found the answer to my prayers. Attending their weekly meetings helped me tremendously even though I had to drive for over an hour to get to the closest one. As a result of attending these meetings, I was able to stop taking medication on a daily basis.

I guess I finally had a source of information (coping skills) that I could take with me everywhere I went. Thankfully, I was able to start a Phobics Anonymous chapter in my area which has really taken off. There is need for a self help support group for Phobics who need help and it feels good to help other Phobics as P.A. has helped me. The problem seems to take a lot of will and discipline to overcome it. I thought over the years that someday I would find a quick cure, but I found that this was false. At times I thought I would never have a normal life again. Fortunately, I've had the luxury of being self employed for 12 years which enabled me to avoid as much as possible situations and places where I would have a panic attack and so was able to make a living. In addition to attending weekly 12 Step P.A. meetings, I am working with a doctor who knows about and understands panic attacks. He's working with me on reducing symptoms, deep breathing, retraining and desensitization. I feel that the quality of my life is coming back to me. I thank God that I found Phobics Anonymous and the proper resources and people to help me get well.

A LIVING SERMON

I'd rather see a sermon than hear one any day.
I'd rather one should walk with me, than merely
show the way.
I can soon learn how to do it, if you let me see it done.
I can watch your hands in action, but your tongue
too fast may run.
All the lectures you deliver may be very wise
but I'd rather get my lesson by observing
what you do.
Though I might not understand you and the fine
advice you give.
There is no misunderstanding how you act and how
you live.

FAITH

Doubters do not achieve
Skeptics do not create
Cynics do not accomplish
Faith is the great motive and power

LORNA'S STORY

I'm not sure I remember my very first panic attack, but one of the first I remember happened while I was in the cafeteria line at the hospital where I worked. For no apparent reason, my heart started racing, I felt as though I could not breathe and by the time I was paying the cashier for my lunch, I was shaking and felt like I was going to faint.

By the time this incident took place, I had spent ten years or so abusing alcohol and other drugs off and on, mostly on. In my early 20's I was "coming out" in the gay and lesbian world and going to the gay bars. I was what I considered a "social drinker and user". Drinking, smoking marijuana, and taking an occasional upper or downer was reserved primarily for the weekends to help me feel more outgoing and comfortable since I had always been rather introverted.

When I was about 23, I began having problems with hyperventilation and was put on tranquilizers. Around that same time, I ended up in a psychiatric hospital for severe depression. When I left the hospital after six weeks, I was on seven different kinds of drugs. My drinking and drug use increased rapidly. My life is much of a blur. I know I moved around a lot, worked very little, and began to develop intestinal problems. I did not attribute any of my problems, whether they be physical or emotional, to alcohol or drugs.

In 1975, I entered into my first of several relationships with other women who basically took care of me. Although I worked, I often had to do things I either didn't like to do or felt uncomfortable doing. My drinking and using was somewhat controlled by them until they realized they could not change my character defects. This always brought an end to the relationship which would catapult me into months of serious drinking and using to make up for the time I had lost while in a relationship.

I somehow found the courage (most likely from my chemicals) to become actively involved in the gay and lesbian political community. My leadership role required me to be in the forefront quite often and I normally self-medicated myself enough to decrease my anxiety. When my self-medication, via alcohol, began to cause black-outs for me at political functions, I summoned the will to stop drinking. However, I did not give up other drugs and often dealt with my anxiety with tranquilizers or marijuana.

About a year and a half later, I began drinking again. It was worse than ever and shortly thereafter I went bankrupt, lost my apartment and moved to the desert to begin a new job and try to get myself together.

While my drinking and drug intake increased, so did my panic attacks. Soon I was avoiding grocery stores, theaters, and other places where there were lines or crowds. Whenever I was going out somewhere where there would be a lot of people, I drank before leaving home.

In July of 1986, I finally hit my bottom and entered an outpatient chemical dependency treatment program and began attending Alcoholics Anonymous meetings regularly. I got into a relationship with another recovering alcoholic and my life finally seemed to be coming together, except one thing. My panic attacks began to rapidly increase in frequency and severity.

I found I could not go to the market alone. At work I started going to lunch early enough to avoid crowds in the cafeteria and finally stopped going there altogether since I was unable to go without experiencing the panic and disorientation. I began to have occasional panic attacks at A.A. meetings and while I was driving. I had to drive in the right hand lane in case I would have to pull over quickly.

I was terrified the day I unexpectedly had a panic attack at my desk while working. A friend had to drive me home. My world was getting smaller and smaller and I no longer had the "luxury" of self-medicating myself with alcohol and drugs.

One night while driving home from an A.A. meeting that I felt the need to leave, I began to think going back to drinking would be easier than dealing with the panic. This was two and a half years after my last drink.

I sought help through therapy until my therapist suggested tranquilizers to me. I found a psychiatrist who worked in the field of chemical dependency and was convinced to go on a non-addicting drug used with phobics. He had diagnosed me as agoraphobic. Although the medication brought me some relief, I was still subjected to the panic a few times a week and I still avoided markets, the cafeteria and all lines.

In addition to the medication, I was referred to a therapist who worked with me through such things as relaxation exercises and desensitization. She also encouraged me to attend Phobics Anonymous meetings since I felt I had no one in my life who could really understand what I was going through. Phobics Anonymous is based on the Twelve Steps as in A.A. I felt it could help me as A.A. had helped me with my sobriety and my relationship with a Higher Power.

In many ways, this had been a more difficult disorder for me to deal with than my chemical dependency but finding Phobics Anonymous and recovering phobics has contributed to my sense of hope for my own recovery. I am grateful for this.

GROWING

When I was lost,
> you helped me up,
When I lost hope,
> you showed me faith,
When I was afraid,
> you shared your strength,
And so for the times you shared,
> you gave of yourself...
I'm grateful for through
> these times with you...
I have begun to grow.

ERIC'S STORY

I was a 23 year old young man in 1986 when agoraphobia deposited me into a black hole of terror, fragility and frustration.

As a boy, I was very terrified of the uncertain elements around me. My parents drank alcohol constantly, and found it necessary to use violence as a means of punishment. I was a child in constant need of attention and love, craving for a friendly word or smile. My home life was a constant battleground of angry words and angry fists. I found that keeping to myself, and staying out of the way of conflicts was the only way to survive. I found that just keeping my mouth shut, was the best way to avoid a beating, or an angry word. I was a consistent bed-wetter until I was 13 years old, suffered from painful headaches daily, and was unable to read until I was 7 years old. As a child, I never felt I was worthy of being an imperfect child. I always wanted to be 20 years older. To me, childhood was only for kids. At 15 years old, and struggling with doubts of my sexuality, I escaped a home of terror with my 23 year old girlfriend. The doubts of my heterosexuality caught up with me and I began a life of gay prostitution, alcohol, and drugs at 17 years. I thought I had finally found a way out from my fears, doubts, and tears. For many years my life was spent avoiding my true self with sex, alcohol, and drugs. I found it to be a wonderful life of irresponsibility, control and adventure.

The hidden, scared little boy was finally gone. I had washed his memory away. My years of abusing chemicals I found helped me to finally find the control I so desperately felt I needed. I could be any person that I wanted to be. I was constantly in trouble with the law for alcohol related incidents only to get out of jail and do more of the same. I was on an endless journey, looking for love and companionship anywhere it would have me. As long as I kept up the sprees of alcohol, sex and drugs, fear never entered my existence. Fear is a powerful emotion with me; lock it away for too long and it gets very angry. It will raise its ugly head before too long. That day came in 1986.

I had quit drinking about one year before. I had gotten a D.U.I. and that scared me enough into realizing that alcohol may be a problem. At this time I did not find it necessary to seek any kind of treatment for alcoholism. I felt that needing any kind of help was a sign of weakness, a sign that I was not in control. I demanded that I always be in control. I continued doing drugs, because only alcohol was a problem for me. One evening, after doing about three days worth of drugs, I experienced my first panic attack. I sensed a feeling of doom, and was sure that I was going to cease to exist. My heart was palpitating, and it was almost impossible for me to breathe. I thought that the world was collapsing, and I was going to go down with it. I excused this episode with the thought of just getting bad drugs. The next day I got into my car and drove to the beach, never giving my night of fear another thought until about three weeks later. I had been on my usual drug run, while experiencing these attacks of terror, heart palpitations and the need to run away. I refused to listen to my body, and I was sure I was just getting bad drugs. I could not sit with myself without being high. The world was so quiet - I needed noise to cover up the extreme feelings of loneliness. Around this time, I was diagnosed HIV positive. My world went black. I felt that I had no life left. I was sure that I was going to die of an incurable disease before I was 30. I hated myself for being gay, and I hated my parents for having a gay son. I did not care about myself or anyone around me. My need for running away from pain and fear continued until my body and mind could not take it any more. One night, while laying in bed, very high on cocaine, I disappeared. My sight in front of me went black, it felt as if someone had taken a hot iron rod and proceeded to run it up me from my toes to the last strand of hair on my head. I was sure that I was dying. I laid on my bed for 8 hours, unable to move for fear of the heart palpitations. Every time I tried to get out of bed, my heart would beat as if I was running a marathon. The panic attacks began to control me from then on. I was housebound. For the next few years, I tried to find relief from self help books, doctors, friends, anyone who would listen to my crazy stories. I was sure that I was destined to live my life a prisoner of my own mind. In August of 1989, it all got to be too much, and I tried to find relief again in the form of alcohol and drugs. For two weeks I was "cured". My panic attacks disappeared and I was overjoyed. But, my joy was very short term. After just two weeks of medication with alcohol and drugs, my panic attacks returned 100 fold. No matter how much alcohol I drank, no matter how much cocaine I snorted, it was not enough. The panic was there, knocking on my door as if to say, "I haven't left yet". I entered an alcohol rehab in November of 1989, after a 3 month journey of looking for relief from my fears. At the end, the panic was so debilitating, I had forgotten how to bathe or dress myself. The living room was my bed. I was unable to move or to speak. Fear had won!

Today I have been in recovery for 22 months. My panic attacks come and go on a pretty regular basis. I know that when I stray from my recovery process, my panic attacks get worse. I know that alcohol is not the answer, it is the enemy. It only gets worse when I medicate my world with chemicals. I still suffer from daily anticipatory anxiety, but it doesn't scare me as much. I still have a lot of work to do. I know today that I cannot run the show, I need people. And that is okay.

Phobics Anonymous has helped me to know that I'm not alone with my fears anymore. I have people to talk to about what is going on with me, because I know that they have all been there before. For me, just being able to open my mouth and share about Eric, is a wonderful gift. I have learned that it's okay to be me, an imperfect human being.

My endless journey with it's pot holes, is finally being repaved.

Yesterday is ashes
Tomorrow is wood
Only today does the fire burn brightly!

GINA'S STORY

I am the daughter of a Baptist minister here in Mulenberg County, Kentucky. I'm married for the second time and have two children, Candice 8, and Lane Kohl, 3. My husband's name is Jeff. I work for UpJohn Health Care Service as a Service Director and I am also a Licensed Practical Nurse. I've been suffering from phobias and panic attacks for about three years. It appears to be better now, just for today. I've started going to Phobics Anonymous group meetings that just started in Hopkins County, and we just received the book, *The 12 Steps of Phobics Anonymous* and the work sheets. The book is a big inspiration to me, just knowing that there is help and that The Phobics Anonymous program works.

The first time that I can relate to having fear was back when I was a child. I always had the fear that I was going to die or that my parents were going to die. I cried all the way up until fourth grade. My mother always had to spank me just to get me to go to school.

As I got older and married my first husband, my fear just seemed to go away. My husband at the time was a heavy drinker and drug user and I devoted my earlier years of married life trying to change him. We divorced after 6 years of marriage and the birth of our daughter.

After 6 months, I married Jeff. He was the man of my dreams. We had a good first year of marriage. After two years I became pregnant with my second child. During the birth, my fear of dying crept back into my life. I knew that I would die on the birthing table. Needless to say I did not, but this was the beginning of my hopeless

123

nightmares. Approximately 4 weeks after Lane was born, I started having severe pains at night and finally I went to the emergency room and found out that I was passing stones. This started me to click into that fear syndrome. I developed pancreatic disease and was pretty sick, mostly in my mind thinking that I had cancer of the pancreas and was waiting for them to tell me this dreadful news. Well, I did have my gallbladder removed and I was scared to death. I seemed to make it through this and returned to work in 3 weeks. After 1 week back to work, on August 25, 1988, there was one night that I will never forget. My husband and I went to the movies, no kids, just the two of us. As I was walking back to the car the worst feeling came over me. I felt a burning sensation from my feet to my head, completely burning me and tingling as if I was going to burn up. My head felt like I was going to pass out and going to die. My heart was racing and skipping beats and I started to cry and I begged my husband to take me home. We made a few other stops and I finally screamed at him, begging him to take me home. I was going to die. He finally did just that. I immediately called the surgeon who had removed my gallbladder, and told him the symptoms. He said that I was having a reaction. I was in a state of panic. Well, I didn't sleep all night. I know I called 20 people trying to see if anyone in the medical field knew anything about what was going on. But no answers. The next morning I went to a local M.D. He saw that I was in a state of panic and he put me in the hospital and hooked me up to Telemetry and ran every test he knew. All the tests came back normal. They sent a social worker in and said I was under a lot of stress and I needed to go to counseling. While I was worrying about myself, my husband was drinking heavily and was arrested for some disturbing things.

I was put on Ativan, 1 mg., and told to take this three times a day. Wow, I thought I was cured. Except at night, I would wake up from a dead sleep with the worst feeling I could imagine, heart racing, feeling of shakiness all inside and I felt just like I was going to die. I could not get back to sleep. My mind was freaking out. I went over in my head minute after minute, that I had a tumor or my heart wasn't right, or I was doomed to die. I kept going to the first M.D. week after week. He always asked me what was making me feel as if I was crazy, so I just got another doctor. The next symptom was pain in my stomach with diarrhea and dizziness. I knew this had to be cancer so, after various medications that I wouldn't attempt to take, I finally took Zantak for my stomach. I kept having these spells at night and sick all the time, not wanting to go anywhere, worrying all the time. Finally he sent me to a Gastroenterologist and he ran a series of tests, all normal, of course. Then I developed pain down my right arm and chest and I knew it was my heart and they missed something. EKG after EKG kept telling me it was just premature heart beats. By now I would only go to work and back fearing to travel and never having fun or surely not excitement. My husband's case had been dismissed so he went to a drug and alcohol treatment center for 30 days. Now I knew something was wrong with my head. My dizziness got me down and I was treated this time with antihistamine and antibiotics but it never did go away, so I was sent to an Ear, Nose and Throat specialist, only to tell me that I had nothing wrong with me. He sent me to a Neurologist who said that I had a brain tumor. I had a Cat Scan and guess what? Nothing was wrong. By this time I guess I felt as though I would give up, so I went back to the local doctor and he put me on Prozac. I would only take 1/2 of the dose.

I felt better for 2 months. My husband started drinking again and got into more trouble. I was so sick. I just couldn't believe what was happening. He went to his 2nd treatment center and followed that with 6 months in the county jail. I stopped taking my Prozac and just continued to take the Ativan. The panic became so great, I felt at times someone else was looking out of my eyes. My legs became weak; for example, walking down steps I would miss a step. I was wearing all my friends out getting them up at midnight, rushing over because I was dying. My family was getting so tired of hearing me describe the horror story, that I finally quit calling. My life was a big mix up. What was I going to do? So I filed for a divorce and started seeing another man, hoping it would take away all of my problems. Needless to say, it didn't. I told my husband about the other man, asked him to forgive me when he got out of jail and returned home. After he got home, he tried to overdose and was put in the hospital, only to be transferred to another treatment center. I was about ready to wash my hands of him. There I met a counselor who admitted him and was also sharing his problem of panic disorder and I was engrossed with his conversation. With his help I went to a co-dependency center and stayed there for two weeks thinking I was cured. They gave me several tests for panic disorders and it was there that Dr. Hall told me that I was a Phobic and that there was treatment.

I weaned myself off of Ativan at treatment, only having minor anxiety attacks while I was there, and I felt like I was ready to leave. My friends came to Florida and got me because I was afraid of flying and we traveled 16 hours back. I started having anxiety attacks coming home and panicked all the way home. I started taking my Ativan again; I had bad attacks at times but by God's power I feel I am on the way to recovery and I feel that this program will help me. I am beginning to have some fun again but it is still limited. I drove for the first time to my Phobics Anonymous meeting by myself. The support group really cheered me on. I enjoy life more just knowing that what I have, other people have and I'm not alone. I feel that I am helping others daily by sharing my story with them. I'm looking forward to working the steps but I know right now that number one, I'm powerless over this and my life is and was unmanageable. I thank you for reading this and for helping me know that there is hope for me. My husband is in A.A. and we are working together for the first time. Our love is strong, but we have to let God lead us.

There are no failures with
Phobics Anonymous
— only gradual success.

BOB'S STORY

I had to surrender to my Higher Power to begin my recovery.

Before coming to Phobics Anonymous, I never thought of myself as a phobic. I thought I was a misfit in this world. I couldn't function from day to day, I felt like checking out of this world. I was married for 28 years, but I could not find any happiness. My peace of mind was nowhere around; I carried a lot of hate for people and for myself also.

I started to get some psychological help and found out I had a "living" problem. I carried an enormous amount of guilt with me wherever I went. I had panic attacks and depression. I slept for nine months and tried to commit suicide. I hated myself and I wouldn't eat. I lost 30 pounds and was a mess. I was in such bad shape that I spent three months in the Veterans hospital with what was diagnosed as a nervous breakdown.

Being the father of two children in their teens, I realized I couldn't go on this way and I had to make some decisions.

I engaged in a counseling session with a female counselor. That's when I found out I had to end my 28 year marriage and begin a new venture in life. I attended Phobics Anonymous group meetings and by going to meetings and talking to people working the program, I also began to follow the 12 Steps. At last I had found understanding people who would help me. They understood my problems and feelings and gave me a lot of tough love. Then, positive reasoning changed my attitude by changing my negative attitude and catastrophic thinking to positive thoughts. I became able to function in this world. Previously, my method of coping was to always run away to a different city but that never helped because I would bring my troubles with me. Geographical cure wasn't the answer.

I now can make decisions that aren't destructive to my well being. I am not afraid any more and I work the P.A. 12 Step program one day at a time. I am honest about my feelings and enjoy life as it was meant to be. The world is no longer a scary place for me and I am learning to say no when I want to. I know I can cope with life and enjoy living one day at a time. The Phobics Anonymous Program gives me great strength and strong faith in my Higher Power and I am practicing the 12-Steps. I am willing to give of myself to help other people that are in the program. By giving it away, I help myself and the new people that need the help that other phobics gave me when I first found the program.

Keep coming to meetings. The program works. It will work if you want what the program offers. Give it a try. It may be just what you are looking for. Phobics Anonymous saved my life and gave me a new lease on life. It can do the same for you.

Be happy. Life is worth living.

If you live life by the inch, it's a cinch.

If you live life by the yard, it's hard.

Success comes in cans not in can'ts.

We are what we think.

CONNIE'S STORY

I was working in a bank when I had my first panic attack. I was 20 years old. For years I hated going into banks. I had no idea what was wrong, only that I was very scared. I started thinking I was going crazy. The more often they happened, the worse they got. I didn't seek help because I was ashamed and didn't know who to tell anyway. It was easier to just medicate myself with alcohol and drugs. That way I got a quick fix and felt "normal". I don't know how I raised my oldest daughter alone. But I know she suffered, too, because I was agoraphobic for several years.

After 20 years I finally quit drinking and drugs. I thought everything would change. Of course a lot of things were better but the panic attacks were still there. I would leave AA meetings because of fear. I just couldn't talk to anyone and going to the store was unbearable. I started thinking I would never get better. I talked to a psychiatrist, a therapist, counselors, pastors, hypnotists, and medical doctors. They didn't realize how bad I suffered or really know what I was talking about. I am a manic depressive and finally got some help for that. But I know the panic attacks are a big part of my depression.

I am a single parent again and the two children at home have been through their own hell because of my phobias. My oldest one is now 23 and I can see the pain in her face when she can't help me. My mother has suffered all her life and I know carries the guilt that I do.

I am working as a temporary, part time and wonder if I'll ever get a decent job. I have no benefits and have had to draw money out of my retirement savings to live on. My self confidence is so low I can't handle interviews. I get very lonely and feel like I don't fit in anywhere.

After 25 years of pain and frustration, I finally feel I can see some light. I think it's because I just got so fed up and disgusted with my life that I will do whatever is necessary. I have learned to "float" through some attacks and let them pass. Also, I am not ashamed anymore. It's an illness and I need to get better. And I've been doing some positive things lately.

I was going in the right direction when I contacted Marilyn, the founder of Phobics Anonymous, and received a lot of helpful information. Since there is no P.A. support group in my area, I started one. It would feel so good too, if I knew I was helping others in their recovery.

I know my life is going to change. I know it may take a while before I can stand in a line alone, feel comfortable eating in front of others and doing so many everyday things. But I will make it, I will get better because I can't go on like this. It's time to start living. I will not choose failure.

Failure

F rustration, hopelessness, futiliy
A ggressiveness (misdirected)
I nsecurity
L oneliness
U ncertainty
R esentment
E mptiness

LARRY'S STORY

My first panic attack occurred in 1972. I was a junior in high school and was in U.S. history when in a fraction of a second I went from being bored to total panic. My heart was beating out of my chest, I got sweaty, shaky, and the worst part was that I knew where I was but didn't know why I was so petrified. The bell rang the same time I got up to walk out of class so I didn't make a scene but I could never go back to that classroom again, which ended in my getting expelled. Later, I got my GED diploma and got accepted in college. After taking all the tests and filling out forms and swapping my new car for a used subcompact, I found I couldn't travel the 60 miles or sit in a classroom, so I never showed up for the first day. My avoidant behavior was instantaneous.

For the next nine years my avoidance gradually got worse and my drinking gradually increased until it consumed me! In 1981, sometime between Thanksgiving and Christmas, I stopped eating and collapsed from drinking so much. Twice, my wife and mother took me to the hospital. The first night seemed at least a week long. I was throwing up and had an all night panic attack. I couldn't have any tranquilizers and was coming off the alcohol cold turkey. It was a night of hell that I'll never forget and I seriously doubt I could handle it again. Sometime the next day I was told my blood-alcohol level was .38 and a few more drinks could have put me in a coma. I was also malnourished and dehydrated. I was on an I.V. for 2 days and had vitamins by the handful plus shots in the rear.

After a day or two I was given Librium for my nerves. After a week in the hospital I was released with a prescription for Ativan, which helped, and I haven't drank since. I saw a psychologist off and on for the next few years but the word agoraphobic was never mentioned. The first time I heard the word agoraphobic was on T.V. They went through all the symptoms which really caught my attention and then they had a name for it. In my case, admitting I had a problem was part of the cure, knowing it had a name was another part. I, like most people, figured if they had a name for it they had a cure for it.

I started looking for books on it and found a book by Claire Weekes called *Simple and Effective Treatment for Agoraphobia*. While it's an excellent book, treatment was far from simple. My safe area got smaller and smaller until in the fall of 1980 it got to the point that I could usually travel the two miles to work if I took my pill. On a day I felt exceptionally good, I could go four to five miles with a pill and some anxiety. I went to the Employment Assistance Program and was eventually put in a therapy group with no other agoraphobic in it. After four months of therapy, I felt I had more problems than I started with. I ended up losing 40 pounds and many sleepless nights, so I finally quit.

That was in July of 1991 and I've done more for myself than ever and I've come a long way. I came to the realization that I and only I could do what had to be done and that I had to do some research to see what had to be the best route for me. After going to co-dependency meetings, I realized that this format was what I was looking for. I wrote over a dozen letters to organizations, counselors and authors on how to start a support group. When I got the literature on Phobics Anonymous, I saw it to be exactly what I was looking for. There was no P.A. chapter in my area so I took it upon myself to start one. The first meeting is in four days and I'm excited, a little nervous, but excited. The people in co-dependency were a big inspiration as to the effectiveness of the 12 Step approach. If it's good enough for Alcoholics Anonymous, Adult Children of Alcoholics, Overeaters Anonymous, and others, it's got to be the best route for me. Of course, I now realize that I'm going to have to do the work myself and it won't be easy, but with the support I expect to get from others, at least I feel it's possible, and that is a big step.

SOME PEOPLE ARE VERY SPECIAL

Some people have a wonderful way,
Of putting others at ease...
They say and do the little things
That will comfort and will please.

They have a special kind of warmth
They're quick to understand.
And whenever there is trouble
They lend a helping hand.

This world of ours is a better place
And happier by far...
Because there are some special people
As wonderful as you are.

MARY ANN'S STORY:
TWELVE STEPS TO SERENITY

It was the night after Thanksgiving 1979, I was drunk, and had ruined another family gathering. For over twenty years I had used and abused alcohol to relieve my panic attacks. Now it had become my enemy. I was an alcoholic and drinking no longer helped. Alcohol began triggering anger. I would verbally lash out at my family. That night my husband of thirty-one years informed me I must do something about my drinking and behavior or he would.

I went to bed in the spare room and hugged the large towel I needed for night sweats. The shock of my husband's ultimatum had sobered me, and I was in a state of incredible terror. It was not the irrational fear of a panic attack. I was scared to death and realized I had to act fast if I didn't want to find out what he had in mind!

In the morning I had the usual hangover, and my fear was so overwhelming I prayed to die. To this day I don't know how or why I decided to call Alcoholics Anonymous, since it had never crossed my mind before. When I placed the call, I almost hung up, but a friendly voice answered and I agreed to go to a meeting that night. I hung up and immediately started plotting how I could avoid going but my anxiety subsided and I didn't feel the need to drink all day. Miraculously, I attended my first A.A. meeting cold sober and I have not had a drink since.

In spite of my panic and anxiety, I felt compelled to attend meetings. It took a long time for me to comprehend the meaning of "How it works". What were those steps and slogans all about? How could I ever stop projecting and "Live one day at a time"? I couldn't possibly "Let go and let God"or "Turn my will and my life over to the care of God". I finally realized I had done just that when I placed the call to A.A. The third step prayer says, "Relieve me of the bondage of self". I had been a prisoner of my own thinking for so long, I couldn't imagine freedom from panic and anxiety. I wasn't even sure I could handle it, but as I worked my way through the steps and became more involved in A.A., I found myself doing many things I had avoided for years. I was driving myself to the meetings and picking up others. Doing Twelve Step work and being on the answering service made me realize helping others took my mind off of me. The "Serenity Prayer" replaced my "Stinking Thinking". What an appropriate term that is! I went to A.A. to stop drinking, and I was given a whole new way of life by the grace of God. The Twelve Step Program works in many wonderful ways. We celebrated our forty-second wedding anniversary on January 31, 1990.

MARY ANN'S STORY II

When Marilyn first asked me to write my story for the book she co-authored, *The Twelve Steps of Phobics Anonymous*, I wrote about the twelve steps and serenity. That was in 1989, and since then I have discovered that I have something called "co-morbidity" (dual diagnosis). If I had been told that twenty years ago, it would have caused instant panic and a dash for the wine bottle.

Now I know that being co-morbid simply means that one has two or more disorders at the same time. I am a recovering alcoholic and an agoraphobic, and I must deal with both disorders to maintain my serenity.

I was born with a genetic predisposition for both disorders. My mother died at 53 of alcohol-related problems, and there are some indications that other family members led anxiety-prone lives. Since I was an only child and my father was in the Navy, we were constantly moving. I don't know a great deal about my relatives so I have no specifics.

I was an anxious child, suffering from separation anxiety, school phobia and eventually full-blown panic attacks. When I went away to college, I had to drop out of college for one semester but managed to go back and graduate. Over the years, I had sought medical help, but was always told that nothing was wrong physically: it was just my nerves.

I married in 1948 and had three babies by 1954. I functioned reasonably well, and realize now that my preoccupation with marriage and motherhood probably explains those good years. When the anxiety and panic attacks returned in the mid fifties, I turned to alcohol for relief. I functioned reasonably well using alcohol "as needed". I had two more babies in 1961 and 1963, and in 1966 my husband was transferred from Los Angeles to Chicago.

I had slipped over the line and was drinking every day. In the late 60's, I had lost my control over alcohol but the drinking still relieved my anxiety and panic. I worked part-time at a variety of jobs during the 70's, drinking only in the evenings. The cocktail hour became the focal point of my day and, as my consumption increased, so did my panic. My story in *The Twelve Steps of Phobics Anonymous* tells how I went to A.A., and not only achieved sobriety, but also freedom from my panic and anxiety.

When Marilyn decided to introduce Phobics Anonymous, I was already convinced that a 12 Step program is one of the best ways to achieve recovery from panic disorder. Recovering alcoholics talk about "working" the 12 Steps to stay sober but I prefer to "live" the 12 Step program every day of my life.

In P.A. meetings, I kept hearing "Don't project". I learned that I was constantly projecting negative thoughts. My husband would frequently ask, "What's the worst thing that could happen?". I realize now that I was always projecting the idea of having a panic attack and that was indeed the worst possible thing that could happen. Of course, it all has to do with the fear of fear itself. An important part of recovery involves understanding what your body is doing during a panic attack.

What role did alcohol play in helping me to function for years? It relaxed me and reduced the frightening symptoms. Learning coping skills to control hyperventilation and other physical symptoms is very important, and self-help books are available in libraries and book stores. That might be considered the mechanics of recovery, but what is it that motivates people to change their thinking? Those of us who are working towards recovery in any of the 12 Step programs have learned that "stinking thinking" is our main problem. Medication or alcohol can dull the thinking process, but they can't change what one is thinking. It is the responsibility of each of us to control our thoughts, and 12 Step programs teach us how to achieve and maintain that responsibility.

The twelfth step of P.A. says "Having had a spiritual awakening as the result of these steps, we try to carry this message to others and to practice these principles in all our affairs". A spiritual awakening and taking responsibility go hand-in-hand. When one has faith in a Higher Power, faith in oneself inevitably follows. Carrying the message becomes a strong motivating force in our recovery, and so Marilyn and I devote our lives to helping others to let go of all their negative thinking. After all, it is thoughts that determine what we are, and in the long run, happy thoughts are one of the best remedies for agoraphobia and alcoholism.

OUR TWO GIFTS

We all get two gifts we should use as much as possible: Imagination and Humor. Imagination compensates us for what we are not. A sense of humor consoles us for what we are.

To accomplish great things,
we must not only act but also dream,
not only plan, but also believe

DOUG'S STORY

Hi, my name is Doug. I'm 16 years old and a Drug, Alcohol and Adrenaline Addict. I'm writing my story from a residential recovery home for teenagers in California. As part of my recovery process, I'd like to share my story with you.

I, myself, like many others, have dual addictions that go hand in hand. I abused drugs and alcohol and when I had no drugs or alcohol, I got my kicks from adrenaline. In my eyes, adrenaline is a powerful drug.

I started drinking and using at age 11. The only reason I did is because I saw all my friends drinking and using and they looked so cool doing it. I thought that would make me fit in. Well, it did, but with the wrong crowd.

Soon after I started drinking on a regular basis, my grades began to drop, fights became very common, yet I thought everything was under control.

Shortly into my drinking career came my addiction to adrenaline. My booze did not cut it anymore. I needed more excitement. I started doing anything that scared me. If I was afraid to jump out of a two story window, I would do it just to get a rush of adrenaline. I would do anything you dared me to. The good feelings, the "highs" I got, masked the dangers.

At this same time I was experimenting with drugs. I soon learned certain drugs would intensify my rush of adrenaline. So I started heavily using drugs, and I was always on my quest for the biggest rush of adrenaline.

After a couple of years, I started mixing all my addictions together (drugs, alcohol, and adrenaline). I started getting in more trouble, almost every night, from something I did, not only with my parents and school, but with the law. I found this to be my biggest rush, I was scared and I loved it. It was funny, though, when I had feelings about something, I could not face them, I could only drown them with my drugs and alcohol.

Alcohol was a great cure for my feelings, and drugs and adrenaline made me feel better for a short period of time. That was my medication for feelings and low self esteem for at least five years. I thought it worked so well for me, but it didn't. Things started to become insane. It seemed that insanity ruled my life. Blackouts became real, not only when I drank, but also in rage or fear. I depended on my adrenaline rush even more now than ever. My feelings and insecurities kept building up over the years until it seemed nothing would cure this but suicide. Along with thoughts of suicide came mass depression and paranoia (for me that means fear of everything and everyone around me).

I used and used and drank and drank all day and most of the night. Nothing would overcome my fears, but I found a way to cover them. I used anger. I would jump down anyone's throat fearing that I would be hurt instead of hurting them.

I ended up deteriorating my body. I started having problems with my knees and lower back. This did not stop me in my quest for a "high". I just drank more to numb the pain. I still jumped out of two story windows, ran from the police, got in fights, anything that might cause harm to me or anyone that was around at the time. My physical problems kept getting worse and my addictions grew right along with the pain. I was in so much pain from injuries that trips to the Emergency Room became frequent. Medication was taken like candy. The medication aided me since it numbed the pain even better than alcohol. I soon was told that I might have to have artificial knees in the next year.

A couple of years passed with the same things happening over and over again. I was so burnt out on drugs and alcohol that I tried suicide again. This was my fourth attempt, but the first time I was reported to the police. I manipulated the police into believing that it was just an idle threat to scare my parents.

A few months passed and by this time I was sober. Paranoia hit me hard in my first month of sobriety. Two weeks went by and I was to be placed in a recovery home for adolescents with drug and alcohol problems. The day I was supposed to be placed was one of the worst days in my whole life. I got a call from the facility telling me that I couldn't come. My father was furious. We proceeded to argue and the argument turned into a fist fight. I pleaded with my dad not to make me angry, but he proceeded to push me around. I hit my dad a couple of times and then held him against the wall and begged him not to make me hurt him. He laughed in my face. The next thing I knew, I threw him across the room. I proceeded to throw him around like a rag doll. I left the room and he got up off the floor and chased me out. When he caught up with me he pushed me against the wall and told me he never wanted to see me again. I was scared and happy at the same time. I got my rush. I went back about ten minutes later and tried to get my sister away from there. I was only home for a short time when the police came. I was arrested and taken to the county psychiatric ward. This is when some reality hit me.

My father left at five the next morning to go on vacation so I went to my mother's house. I started attending 12 Step meetings and working a program for my drug and alcohol problems but not my addiction to adrenaline. I realized that when I fought my dad I completely lost control and I liked it. This proved to me that adrenaline had me, and the drugs and alcohol helped it go on.

I'm almost seventeen years old now and have been clean for a little over nine months. People may think I'm too young to have the problems adults do or had, but I suffered too.

Thanks to the 12 Step programs, I am currently working, I now know that I have the disease of addiction. I try my best to apply the 12 Steps in every aspect of my life. For me this isn't a battle of whether I can do it or not, but a battle for my life. I know that I will die if I live the way I did in my past, and the 12 Steps are helping me stay alive, step by step, one day at a time. I am still searching for the serenity to accept the things I cannot change, but I have gained the courage to change the things I can, and now I know the difference.

PEGGY'S STORY

How does one explain five years of hell? That's what I feel my life has been since I became filled with anxiety and fear. Actually, I've been phobic since I was a child. I was painfully shy and afraid of any social function. I blushed easily and from my head to my waist I turned bright red. Because of this I didn't like school much, I would take an "F" before I would give an oral report. Somehow I still maintained a decent grade average. I didn't even go to the painting of the "K" of the hill for our high school initiation because I was afraid. Of what, I don't think I ever knew.

My anxiety led me to be off and on tranquilizers all of my adult life. I never abused them, just needed them to function "normally". I didn't dwell too much on my anxiety until 1984. My sister died, we were facing bankruptcy, I was in a new job and my husband was out of town four to six weeks at a time, leaving me alone with our four year old son. To top it off, it was really cold and I had to drive to work on icy roads and that was always a big fear. I guess I just sort of "flipped out" and all of a sudden I started fearing everything, especially if it had to do with death, disease or pain. But, at the same time, I wished I were dead, not by my own hands, I was to afraid to do that, but hoped for some disaster that would do it for me.

My irrational fears turned into obsessional thoughts and no matter how hard I tried not to think about them, the more they would come. I think the obsessions were the worst for me. I started thinking of the worst things that could or might happen to my son and that I wouldn't be able to protect him. Then the fear changed. I worried that I would do what I feared would happen. After all, wasn't I going crazy? My thinking was totally out of whack, so I knew I had to see a doctor. He seemed to understand what was happening to me and put me on Xanax. I went back to square one. I then actively sought psychiatric help, fearing for sure they would lock me up and throw away the key. That did not happen, thank God, but I did spend three years in therapy. That didn't help. We delved into my past and present life, but never with what was happening to me. It was like taking the cart before the horse. The doctors (who changed often because it was a clinic) always wanted to take me off the Xanax (which worked) and try something different (which didn't).

Because of this disease, I have lost a lot of faith in the medical profession. Doctors just don't seem to fully understand anxiety disorders. Some do, but they are few and far between. The ironic part is, I work in the medical profession, but from it all I have learned that you must seek a doctor carefully, and see someone only if they themselves have had your disease, or worked actively with it. This year, I have been going to Phobics Anonymous and it has helped me more than even the Xanax I've learned that first we seek good medical care (and medication if necessary) and then look at our lives to see what we can do or change to alleviate some of the anxiety, thus diminishing the fear and panic. I've still got a long way to go, but I'll do it one day at a time and slowly. I feel better about myself and my future and I'm working on making changes in my life that I've been afraid to make. I feel now there is a "light at the end of the tunnel" and hope for my future.

THANK GOD FOR TODAY

This is the beginning of a new day.
I can waste it or, use it for good.
What I do today is important because
I am exchanging a day of my life for it.

When tomorrow comes, this day will be
gone forever - leaving in its place
something I have traded for it.
I want it to be gain, not loss; good not
evil; success, not failure;
In order that I shall not regret the
price I paid for today.

"MY NAME IS CHRISTOPHER, AND I'M A PHOBIC"

For those who suffer from all anxiety and panic disorders, these few words of admitting to ourselves that we are powerless over fear and need help, may very well be our first step toward recovery too!

I was 16 years old when my first anxiety attack occurred. Unfortunately, my anxieties went unnoticed and untreated for 10 years. My condition progressively worsened so severely, that I had strong suicidal thoughts associated with panic attacks. Desperately seeking relief from my emotions, my thoughts became irrational and frantic, contributing to even more fear.

1. Am I more afraid of dying or living?
2. Is feeling pain better than feeling nothing at all, or is feeling nothing at all better than feeling pain?
3. Is the cause of my distress mental or physical?
4. If I survive, will I become incapacitated mentally, physically or both?
5. Is suicide a permanent solution to a temporary problem?
6. What if the problem never goes away, and what if I am prevented from dying if I wanted to?

I was treated and released from a mental health hospital in a short time, (I was lucky). My doctor recommended that I contact Phobics Anonymous, (P.A.). What wonderful advice that became!

My feelings of fear were real, but they were not based on reality. Now with the support of P.A., I'm learning to discern what anxieties are real, and which are not.

Disturbingly, many sufferers of anxiety disorders, (and especially mental health professionals), have not yet heard about Phobics Anonymous. This 12 Step program is an excellent resource for fellowship, support, and self help materials.

You are not alone with your fears, you have a "safe place" among us!

CIRCUMSTANCES

People are always blaming their circumstances for what they are. I don't believe in circumstances. The people who get on in this world are the people who get up and look for the circumstances they want, and, if they can't find them, make them.

****

STAY IN THE NOW

I view the past as God's means of transportation that carried me to the present.

I glimpse the future as God's mystery novel to be enjoyed.

I stay in the now by refraining to turn to the last page to see how it ends.

GARY'S STORY

I'm twenty-five years old. I ran five miles a day and lifted weights every other day until I had my first panic attack in December of 1990.

One evening, while driving home from shopping with my wife, I suddenly couldn't breathe and my heart raced. We drove to the hospital emergency room as fast as we could. By the time we got there, I was hyperventilating. I thought for sure I was having a heart attack. They put me on oxygen and hooked me up to an EKG monitor, only to tell me there was nothing wrong. I was shocked to say the least. The hospital sent me home with nothing. They told me that I was just hyperventilating. My wife and I got home and I drank a beer to calm me down.

The next day I started noticing terrible chest pains while I was at work. When I went to bed that night, I noticed my heart was racing again, and I had hot and cold flashes, so at eleven o'clock that night I went to the hospital again, only to hear the same thing. This time they gave me some pills to relax me.

In all, I went to the emergency room six times and visited my personal doctor about four times. They always told me I was healthy. I just couldn't believe this. The chest pains were horrible and I would get very light headed. My heart would race at random and sometimes it felt as though someone was choking me.

My doctor sent me to a cardiologist and he ran a stress test and an echocardiogram and told me I was in perfect health. He said I had a stronger heart than most people.

I kept on those pills that the hospital gave me, but the panic attacks kept happening. I quit exercising for fear of having a heart attack, because I was not convinced my symptoms were caused by anxiety.

After about three months of total hell, I went to the Menninger foundation. My doctor has put me on Imipramine and Klonopin. Since I started those medications, my attacks have diminished. I still do not feel one hundred percent better. I was to the point of being an agoraphobic. I didn't want to leave the house until I went to the Menninger foundation for help. I have been on medication for two months now and my doctor would like to keep me on it a year or so.

I can exercise again with little fear. The medication makes me sluggish all the time though. I want to quit taking the medication, but I fear that the attacks will come back.

I sometimes feel like an attack is coming, but I just try to relax. I have spent over three thousand dollars in hospital bills and now another thousand at the foundation. When I read about Phobics Anonymous I was so excited. I hope it will help me so I can be pill free. I am so tired of drugs and feeling tired and drugged up all the time.

I know how successful 12 Step groups are for other problems, so I'm sure Phobics Anonymous can work for me.

SUE'S STORY

There were a lot of problems in my family years, fighting, violence, alcohol, and drugs. I called it "Another Tragedy Family", today it's known as dysfunctional. I was a very shy, scared, worried kid. I threw up on my first day of school. In sixth grade, the teachers called me "Silent Sue". When we graduated to Junior High we had to get up and say what we wanted to be. I worried for weeks over this. When my turn came I blurted out "psychiatrist or airline stewardess" and everyone laughed at me. I had a few girlfriends and we stuck together like glue. At home I spent a lot of time in my room daydreaming, drawing, isolating with constant headaches. When my parents' divorce came about it was no surprise.

I had a hard time talking to my mom. I asked so many questions of a big and serious nature, her answer was usually "you're having growing pains" or just plain "no because I say no". She was scared too, I guess. So, still wondering why everything I wanted to do was bad, I got sneaky and did them anyway. I hated the lying part. When alcohol and drugs entered the picture, I thought this was the help I needed, the extreme disease and crippling fears and worry went away. My solution led to 17 years of alcohol and drug abuse.

I met Mark when I was 17. He was older and very intelligent, having been through a lot of experiences, he warned me of the dangers of drinking. For many years he put up with me, patient, kind and trying to help. I was an irrational mess. I'd run off on my own wasted way and return to him again and again. His friends were very successful, nice people. I felt very strange and inferior, but I listened and watched them, trying to learn, wishing to be okay like they were. All that time I never believed his family really cared for and liked me. He had even wanted to marry me. The solution was for me to come out of the self-made prison, where I stayed trapped, lost, hiding and drunk. Instead, I chose to stay a stranger in a strange land.

I started working in graphic arts. I did pretty well. I worked a lot of overtime. I didn't have my own place for years. I stayed at friends, forcing myself to be around people. When I finally got my own place I'd go to work, then home and work on printing projects and drink until I passed out. I'd have nightmares and worry about this "life".

In 1982, I had a car accident. My mom came to the hospital and said I was going to her place. I was not happy. As soon as I could get to the liquor store I did. Then pushed into a 12 Step recovery program, I didn't last the nine months. I ran. It was a very "hard school" intense place; I see now it would have been good for me. Ten years and three hospitalized "breakdowns" later I decided I had to do something.

In 1987, I got up the nerve to get in touch with my dad. For years I was told not to. I had to see for myself. We've made amends and become friends. After 20 years my brother, my dad, and I went back east to see all the cousins, aunts and uncles. It was extremely hard and uncomfortable, fighting anxiety and facing these good people. It was very strange and hard to talk to people and have fun when they weren't afraid to leave the house, answer the phone, drive, go to the store, or "freak-out", when it came time to pay the pizza man. I had heard of such fears but couldn't even imagine them. Now, unfortunately, these horrible fears were controlling my life.

One year ago I was in a suicidal car crash. My mom enters my life again, we are talking. I see I have to sober up and start doing something to get well. On my birthday this year (1992), I saw a Phobics Anonymous announcement in the newspaper and went to a meeting. I thank God and the people who worked and struggled so hard to get this group started here.

At this point I am scared to isolate again. I know I can't get better this way, being so alone a lot of the time. It's funny (kind of) how music speaks to me. I find it a help, it's served as a reminder of what I am and helps me keep in the present. Inside, terrified, I force myself and try to get to meetings more often, to attend a class, go to a small church. I'm beginning to see there are very nice people everywhere.

I thank God for letting me exist on this planet, but to exist and live and are two different things. I pray for courage and help to do something positive each day to get around people who are understanding and share helpful things, and know a bit about this journey to recovery. I have a long way to go but I have hope and a chance, I want to join this planet and be useful. I take the good advice from people in my Phobics Anonymous groups and my doctor. I'm starting to enjoy people and things this world has, instead of being a total paranoid nervous wreck, fearfully wandering around. P.A. is helping me change for the good. Positive things are occurring in my life but I struggle to just do it. P.A. gives me the courage to go to A.A. and E.A. (Emotions Anonymous). So, I triple it and it works if you work it.

STAYING CENTERED

1. Plan three interesting things to do the following day and look forward to them the night before.
2. When someone hurts or offends you, quickly think that the person is probably tired, worried, or not feeling well. Shed the negative feeling by having sympathy for the person.
3. Join a group and be active in it. It will be a support group for you.
4. Be too busy with interesting activities to have time for depression.
5. Be with people often. It takes one's mind off self.
6. Get plenty of exercise, even walking. It makes one sleep better.

BONNIE'S STORY
RECOVERING FROM PANIC ATTACKS

I led a very adventurous life growing up. I traveled quite a bit and basically embraced life with a passion. I'd laugh at other peoples' anxieties. When I experienced my first panic attack at the tender age of 26, I was quite shaken. I wasn't laughing anymore.

I had given up a depraved lifestyle of sex, drugs and rock and roll to settle down and get married. I remember clearly my first panic attack. My child was napping and I was watching T.V. when seemingly out of the blue, a wave of panic hit me like a sledge hammer. I had no idea what had happened. When I told my neighbor what I had just experienced, she looked at me as though I was crazy.

The first doctor that I spoke to also had no idea what I was talking about. She recommended that I eliminate caffeine from my diet which I did, but by then the panic attacks had taken over my life. I did the best I could to function normally over the next few years while living in fear of the next attack. In addition to my own illness, I was trying to cope with my husband's alcoholism. My life indeed had become unmanageable.

I'll never forget the day that I picked up the newspaper and saw an article about a woman who suffered from agoraphobia. She was describing my illness! Finally, I knew what was wrong with me. My illness had a name. I was so relieved!! I wasn't crazy. Once I knew the name I began to gather as much information as I could from the libraries and book stores. Although intellectually I felt better, I could not stop the daily panic attacks. I decided to try medication so that I could calm my system. The medication blocked the panic attacks, and in conjunction with some therapy, I was able to regain control of my life. After ten months, I was able to get off the medication. Although I still kept a steady supply on hand, I very rarely needed to use it. I was never housebound, but there were many situations that I would avoid. I feared having one at night alone with the children. I have always loved flying, but still I fear panicking while in flight. Today there are times when I still have panic attacks, but they don't frighten me the way they used to. My life is 100% better.

Through the years of living with an alcoholic husband, I discovered Al-Anon. It literally changed my life. When, by chance, I saw the 12 Step Phobics Anonymous book at the library, I knew I was home. For so long I have kept my panic attacks a secret. As with alcoholism, I feel that many non-sufferers look upon our illness as a weakness, a flaw in our character.

A. A. and Al-Anon have helped thousands of people to recover. I believe that panic attack sufferers, too, can benefit from the 12 Steps. It was always beneficial to me to know that I was not alone. Now that I have found that there is a 12 Step group just for panic and anxiety disorders, I know for a fact that miracles can and do happen. I most definitely believe in a Higher Power, a positive force that is always with me, day or night, to guide me through. A power that I can lean upon when I feel that I can't do it alone. Fear is indeed the opposite of faith. With faith I can recover. One day at a time.

PATTY'S STORY -
RECOVERING MULTI-PHOBIC

In 1988, I had my first panic attack, it was shortly after my second child was born. I had no idea what had hit me but I knew it was something powerful and there was something definitely wrong. I was suddenly engulfed in blackness and I couldn't breathe. It felt like a vise in my chest and the panic that terrorized me while it was happening was overwhelming. I didn't know what it was. I thought I was dying.

My parents were living with me at the time. My mom had some Xanax and gave me one. I naturally calmed down but the attack left me devastated and exhausted. Something was changing in me and I didn't know what. I became very depressed, scared and unsociable. I stayed in my room. I couldn't take care of my two kids, not even nurse my beautiful five month old baby. I loved them, but I just couldn't feel anything but panic. My mom did everything for me. I finally went to the doctor and he said I had a severe case of post partum psychosis and nothing could be done. I kept taking my mom's Xanax. One pill once a day. I was able to function, but at a low level.

Keep in mind I'm talking about a young twenty-six year old woman who previously did everything and wasn't afraid of anything, but on that day and ever since, something was stolen from me. It was my very life, my being and my existence.

My life was on hold! I couldn't even hold my baby, let alone fix a meal. I couldn't do anything.

My heart was bothering me constantly, so I went back to the doctor. After he took some tests he told me that I had Mitro Valve Prolapse.

He prescribed more medication which included increasing my dosage of Xanax. He said the Xanax would block the panic.

I was okay for awhile but then the panic attacks returned. This time they were more severe. A ten on the anxiety scale. They struck three to five times a day and even in the middle of the night. I thought I was losing my mind. For four miserable years I was being plagued with something I didn't understand. Neither did the doctors or anybody else. Everyone said I had some deep rooted problem and kept referring me to a psychiatrist. I had no insurance so care was limited since I had no alternatives; all I could do was pray and even that was too stressful. Watching T.V., eating, or getting dressed was too hard because doing just these simple things caused attacks that were completely overwhelming. I couldn't think. Every second was taken up by conditioning my mind that I wasn't going to die. Literally, it felt like death was on hand at every moment.

Finally the doctor changed my prescription to Valium and the full blown panic attacks ceased but I was left feeling empty and incomplete. I was afraid to be in a room by myself. I would pace the floor all morning because it helped me get through those agonizing hours of fear.

My body wouldn't be still and I couldn't feel. The only feelings I had were of overwhelming fear. The mornings were the worst. I'd wake up in a panic, dreading the rest of the day and what it would bring.

My heart would race and it seemed like my body wouldn't stop shaking and vibrating. The rest of the day was just sheer terror. My body eating me from the inside out. There was no peace and believe me, I begged for it. I concluded there was just no mercy for someone like me. I became housebound and terrified of everything.

There was nobody to talk to and if there was, I was too afraid to explain what was happening to me because if I talked about my symptoms, they caused my panic attacks to return.

I had been rushed to the hospital countless times with my body in full convulsions. The tests to make sure I wasn't having a heart attack were normal and the doctors told me I needed rest. It was just my nerves. I always ended up with acute hyperventilation. Time went on, but without me, and the guilt I felt was enough to eat me alive. I worried constantly and felt guilty because of what I was doing to my family and children. All they ever heard was "no" or "I can't" or anger or crying or hiding in my room. If I did go out, it was with my husband and even that was becoming too stressful. I was still having small attacks like zappers. That's what it felt like. Unexplainable. The only place I felt safe was at home. I went to the library with my sister (one of the rare occasions that I felt semicapable). We were in the medical book section looking for a book on body aches that bothered her. She came across this book and threw it at me and said, "here, you need this". It was called *The Anxiety Disease*. I took it home and read it, front to back twice. It opened a whole new meaning to my imprisonment. I wasn't alone.

A short time later, I was with my sister in-law in Mervyns parking lot. The radio was on and the announcer said something about anxiety and panic attacks and gave a phone number to call. My sister-in-law had a car phone and we called. He said there was a Phobics Anonymous meeting and it started at 3:00 p.m. It was ten to three o'clock just minutes away. I said take me there and without question she did. Prior to this we had a deep discussion about this problem I had. She was the only one who knew about it. I started telling her because she never questioned it or analyzed it or thought anything bad of me. The anxiety book just confirmed everything I was feeling and explained why. We went to the meeting and I was terrified. I don't even remember if I talked, but I do remember everything that was said. People talking about what was happening to them. It was the same things that were happening to me. All I saw was nodding heads. They understood. I was no longer alone. It was like the book *The Twelve Steps of Phobics Anonymous* says, you will be amazed before you're half way through. Well, I've been attending the meetings regularly, and yes, it's an ongoing process but I'm being restored day by day. Sometimes I suffer a setback, but at least I know I'm not alone. I have a support system. Thanks to Phobics Anonymous, I've been reintroduced with my Higher Power whom I wish to call Jesus Christ. To Him I give all the glory for He is our healer and salvation and our hope and joy. Through Him and in Him the victory will follow and in every step I take whether small or big I'm beginning to see the victory.

Thanks to my sister-in-law and friend, Lynn, for her support and a listening ear that never criticized or laughed, who provided only compassion and support and encouragement and still never questions me when I say no or I can't.

And to my friend, Donna, for her love of the Lord and prayers. I love you and thank you for being as one with me through our Lord Jesus Christ.

Thanks to our leader, Karen, for her love of life and other people. For providing a new beginning in our lives and for her strength. God bless her.

Phobics Anonymous has restored my hope in life and that's the very thing this disease steals from you.

Thanks to my husband Jim for his unconditional love that I still have a hard time accepting. I love you Jim.

And, finally, to my children. When they grow up, we will say to each other, it was hard at times but we love you as I love them more than life itself.

<u>Matthew 11:23</u> Come to me all you who are weary and burdened and I will give you rest. Take my yoke upon you and learn from me. For I am gentle and humble in heart and you will find rest for your souls. For my yoke is easy and my burden is light.

CHRISTY'S STORY

My neighbor invites me to go bowling with her friends. I came along because she refuses to take no for an answer.

On the way to the bowling alley, I become more and more frightened. By the time we arrive, my heart is pounding, and I am shaking. Panic-stricken, I start crying in the lobby. People stare at me as I say, "I have to go home". When my neighbor asks me why, I tell her, "I just can't do this".

While my neighbor drives, I stare out the window, tears streaming down my face. I can't look at her. She probably thinks I don't like her friends. I'm too embarrassed to tell her I'm afraid to leave my house unless accompanied by my husband.

When I was a college freshman, I became depressed after discovering someone I had dated in high school was a serial killer. The world became a dangerous place.

By the time summer arrived, I couldn't go outside alone without feeling extremely anxious. I put off grocery shopping. Although I only had to walk downstairs and past four apartments to get to the laundry room, I waited until I had no clean clothes to do the wash. It could take hours, even days to walk to my mail box, which was on the other side of the complex. I blamed my strange feelings and behavior on the summer heat.

When school started in the fall, I was able to attend classes fairly regularly because I lived right across the street from the campus. Sometimes I skipped a class because I just couldn't take that first step out the door.

Weekends were the worst time. I shut myself up in the apartment while my friends were off having fun. I was so lonely.

Then I met a man I trusted. I felt safe when I was with him, so we began dating and were married about a year later. My symptoms improved for a while.

My husband didn't notice that I never went anywhere but to school alone. He was happy to take me shopping after he'd put in a full day's work.

Within six months of my graduation, we bought a house in a nearby city and I became pregnant.

I never drove unless my husband was in the car with me. But I was ashamed to ask him to leave work to take me to my doctor appointments, so I forced myself to drive to the office which was only 5 blocks from my house. I managed to do it for a while, but I became increasingly anxious and convinced him to take me. I told him I was getting so big I felt uncomfortable behind the wheel.

After my son was born, my symptoms became worse. Thinking I was going crazy, I told my husband I was afraid I might hurt our child. "You're a good mother. You'd never hurt our son," he said. I wasn't so sure. But I kept my fears to myself after that.

One evening I watched a TV news show about people who were afraid to leave their homes. One person had been housebound for decades. That was when I realized I wasn't crazy; the name for what I had was agoraphobia.

We moved to a house on a busy street when my son was two. Each time I was in the front yard alone, I felt exposed. Before I started my lawn mower, I was already drenched in sweat. I thought the people driving by were watching me.

A park was a few blocks from our home, but I couldn't take my baby there to watch him play with the neighborhood children. I couldn't even take him for a ride down our block in his stroller. The thought of opening the front door was enough to give me the shakes.

I became severely depressed. I had to drag myself out of bed every morning. What was there to get up for? I was a prisoner in my own home.

As I lay in bed, after my husband had left for work and before my son awoke, I fantasized about beating my head against the bedroom wall until I died, but I didn't try it. I thought my husband would eventually get over my death, but I wasn't sure my son would.

Two years after I saw the agoraphobia program, I found the courage to fight back and regain my life.

I was standing at the kitchen sink, staring out at the front yard. I had come to despise it because going out to take care of it caused me such agony. Then I thought, "This is enough!" I was angry. My life was a living hell. I was twenty pounds overweight, suicidal, and disgusted with myself.

I forced myself to go out. I shopped for groceries at the store two blocks away a few times. Then I drove a little farther from home. As I got used to being out alone, the anxiety faded. After a while, I enjoyed these adventures.

One day I walked my little boy, who was almost four, to the neighborhood park. I pushed him on a swing. I caught him as he came down the slide, just like any other mother. As we walked home, I felt that a weight had been lifted from my shoulders at last.

I let agoraphobia steal the joy from my life for nine years. Had I known what was wrong and gotten help, maybe I could have recovered sooner. I wish I'd had a place like Phobics Anonymous to go for support.

While I got over the worst of the disease by myself, I still struggled with overwhelming fear. I still felt anxious every day and had a full-blown panic attack on a plane a few years back.

Two years ago I joined a 12 Step Phobics Anonymous group designed specifically for people who suffer from overwhelming fear and anxiety because I know that the 12 Step program works. When I am at a Phobics Anonymous meeting, I am with people who know exactly how I feel. We support each other in our efforts to overcome our problems.

Not long ago I fulfilled a secret desire to be a dancer. My future husband and I performed with a western line dance company at the fairgrounds in front of hundreds of people grinning from ear to ear, I loved the attention.

Nobody calls me a "homebody" now. I'm not home long enough for them to call me!

Poor eyes limit ones sight
Poor visions limit ones deeds

Success is getting what you want
Happiness is wanting what you get

ROBIN'S STORY

Six weeks ago, if I were to tell you my story, I would have told the horror stories of my past dealings with fears, phobias and anxieties. I would have told of the many doctors I reached out to, but who had no clue that I was an agoraphobic. I would have described the panic attacks that seemed to come out of the blue. Personally, my favorite is the one that happened high up on a chair lift, alone while snow skiing one sunny day.

Instead, I feel it is more important to tell how recovery begins.

I realize now, but I didn't six short weeks ago, the recovery process started the day I decided to take action and responsibility for my condition. I wanted to go beyond putting myself into the hands of doctors and medicine. I wanted to take a close look inside myself, but I was afraid to do it alone.

When I was told I had a chemical imbalance in my brain I kept it a secret, being afraid people would think I was crazy. Six weeks ago I picked up the phone and I told a friend of my condition and he agreed to help me, through hypnotherapy. He also told me about a Phobics Anonymous 12 Step meeting that was going to begin in 20 minutes and to make it a point to attend. If I had more time I could have come up with a creative excuse why I just couldn't make it. I couldn't believe I was about to walk into a room with strangers to do who knows what. I was afraid, I was starting to panic, I wanted to run, but stayed and rode this one out. I left after the meeting holding the outline of the 12 Steps of

Phobics Anonymous. I kicked up my heels, I was so proud I did it! I didn't really understand the concept of the 12 Steps at first but I continued to attend the meetings. It was a whole new feeling getting to know people who have enough guts to admit they have a flaw and are willing to do something about it. I am no longer dealing with my condition alone!

My story, six weeks ago, would have been based on blame, but today, through making an effort to learn and take an honest look at my life, I admit I have a physical condition, however, I create the waves of fear and anxiety. I make the choices to give in to the fear or not. I create stressful or peaceful situations. I choose all the things around me such as my job, income, housing, friends, spouse and children, etc.

I have a choice, I can help myself using the 12 Steps of Phobics Anonymous as my guide or I can take more medicine and continue to be afraid. Personally, I find self help much more rewarding. Recovery will be an on going process. It will sometimes be fast paced, sometimes slow. Always remember fear is only a four letter word.

False
Emotions
Appearing
Real

Only if you work the program will it work for you!

JEAN'S STORY

When I think back to my childhood, I now realize that my agoraphobia was just beginning. After summer vacation, I would start to become nervous and depressed several weeks before school started. I remember crying in my third grade class, overcome with fear and the detached feeling of being at school and not at home with my mother. I would make myself physically ill from fear and would often vomit in the school yard. I avoided social activities that most children enjoyed such as birthday parties. Once I went trick or treating with the neighborhood children and one of my "spells" occurred. I was crying and scared but felt relieved when one of the parents brought me back home. I remember walking with my neighbor to the shopping center, which was not far from where we lived. When we reached our destination, I became scared and panicked. There were numerous times when I was to perform in a ballet or tap recital and would experience one of my "spells". I would try to explain how it felt but could never convey the right meaning or express the devastating feelings.

In 1975, at the age of twenty, I had undergone surgery. After surgery, I was diagnosed with mitral valve prolapse, also known as a leaky heart valve. The doctor prescribed Inderal. At the time, I was living alone in a small studio apartment, recuperating from the surgery. I would awaken in the middle of the night with a terrible panicked feeling. I had to return to work and had constant pain down my left arm. I still could not sleep at night and would walk to an understanding friend's house several blocks away, where she would try her best to console me with a cup of tea and some breathing exercises. I then went to visit my family in Northern California. My mother made an appointment with a cardiologist. After I told him my symptoms and he examined me, he said my problem was due to my work schedule. I agreed because after all, I was working two graveyard shifts, day and night shifts, and long hours. No wonder I felt panic and pain. I was very stressed.

The years that followed were relatively normal with the exception of a few reminders at a public place such as a restaurant, that I still might be crazy. I would feel faint and then retreat from the situation feeling shaken and embarrassed.

Then, in 1982, the "big one" occurred; the most memorable of all the panic attacks I have endured. It was a hot summer day in the desert and I was driving home on the freeway. I felt an overwhelmingly uncomfortable, hot sensation start in my abdomen and surge throughout my body. There was shortness of breath, sweaty palms, but most apparent was the loss of control that I felt. I rolled down the car window for some fresh air hoping it would revive me, but that wasn't too helpful since the outside temperature was well over 110 degrees. I wanted to seek help but I also wanted to rush home. Questions flashed through my mind. Was I dying? Should I stop at the highway patrol or the hospital? Could I make it home? I did make it home and went directly to my friend's apartment. I lay on her sofa describing my symptoms and trying to calm my body. She, like most friends and family, thought it was all in my head. That incident caused me to fear driving. Then I started to fear flying, going to grocery stores, restaurants, the beauty salon, etc. I even quit playing tennis because I had been playing tennis the day of the attack. I visited the cardiologist who, after examining me, suggested I seek counseling. That didn't make sense to me. There had to be something physically wrong with me. My mother made an appointment for me to see a Berkeley psychiatrist, whose expertise was in vitamin and nutrition therapy. After several blood tests and very little psychotherapy, the doctor diagnosed me as hypoglycemic and recommended a special diet, vitamin supplements and exercise. I did all but the exercise portion, scared that the activity would cause the dreaded panic attacks. I was careful to eat the proper food and snacks consisting of celery, carrots and nuts. I ate so many carrots that my palms turned orange from the beta carotene, but still the panic attacks continued.

Next, a friend drove me to L.A. to visit an internist. He told me that I didn't need a psychiatrist but my symptoms sounded like mitral valve prolapse. I was amazed that he knew I had a condition without even examining me! He said I should change from Inderal to Tenormin and had me swallow the pill right then. Of course, the "what ifs" immediately set in and after leaving the office, I experienced a panic attack. My poor, compassionate friend had to chauffeur me on a two hour drive back home, while I lay in the back seat of her car, paralyzed by fear. I arrived home and lay awake all night fully clothed with makeup on. Terrified.

By this stage, I was afraid of everything. I quit the

management job I had started in favor of a job closer to home with much less responsibility. Even though I lived five minutes from work, the drive felt like an eternity. Many days I would rush straight to the restroom to cry after experiencing an attack on the way to work. I became friends with a lady in the office who became my "support person". She was the only person at work who knew of my secret. We would take walks at lunchtime, in spite of my jelly legs and dizzy feeling.

My friend would listen to me and suggested that I call Marilyn, who had started a group called Phobics Anonymous for people like me, or that I should see a psychiatrist. During this period of my life, I was at my lowest. I was in a constant depressed, scared state. I was continuously sick with infections. I felt like a zombie. It was difficult for me to make a simple decision like turning on the heat when it was cold. As hard as it was for me, I went to see a psychiatrist. The six months of psychotherapy proved to be a positive change. My depression lifted and I began to laugh again. But my fears still remained. My mother sent me an introductory cassette from a mail order program for people with agoraphobia. I cried tears of joy when I listened to the tape. For the first time, I felt relieved. I wasn't alone. There were other people just like me. There was a name for the symptoms! I sent away for the first two sets of tapes and followed the directions. I then rationalized that I didn't need to spend any more money on tapes, now that I knew what I had. All I had to know was that I couldn't die from being an agoraphobic. Subconsciously, I thought the panic attacks would go away without my making any effort.

I continued living in a state of denial. My family and friends were telling me to "get with it", "pull yourself together". There was nothing wrong with me. This worked for a while, but only when I didn't deviate from my workaholic schedule.

Finally, in 1991, after seeing a performance at the local theater and, having experienced another major attack, I decided to face the problem head on. I was thirty-six years old. Life was not fulfilling because my world was becoming smaller and smaller by my avoidance of situations. I was becoming more and more angry, fearful, and depressed.

I again sought help from a psychiatrist who after hearing my symptoms, referred me to his wife, a counselor whose expertise was in treating people with panic disorders. With her tremendous insight and confidence building exercises, I began to see the light at the end of the tunnel. I could share my fears and progress with her and feel her genuine concern for both. I started to get in touch with my feelings and my boundaries which is something I never knew. I learned to express my feelings and not to stuff my anger. I have been driving the freeway, taking morning walks, and many other activities that I haven't done in years, especially alone. I also attended a Phobics Anonymous Group where I met Marilyn, the founder. Marilyn inspired me with her intelligence, honesty, tremendous sense of humor and sincere dedication to the group. The group is a great way to share my feelings with other people who understand. The fact that I have faced my agoraphobia has allowed me the excitement that recovery brings. I know that I must continue my meetings and concentrate on the positive.

I am at an advantage now because I have the tools which have built a stronger foundation for me to get through the adverse times. As Marilyn told me at my first Phobics Anonymous meetings, "When the student is ready, the teacher will appear". How right she was.

THE FIVE STAGES OF HEALING

1. Recognize you have been wrong.
   How, what, where.
2. Identify feelings.
   Mad, sad, glad, scared, guilt, shame.
3. Have your feelings.
   I feel sad - it's OK to cry.
4. Share your feelings.
   When you_____, I felt_____.
5. Make a decision about your relationship with the person who wronged you.

GERALDINE'S STORY

I had my first panic attack in 1965. For almost 20 years I was house bound and could only leave with my husband who I knew would get me out of a building and to a safe place like our car or our home. I was completely dependent upon him. He was my support person. Not knowing what was wrong with me, I went from doctor to doctor and was diagnosed as going through the change of life. Then after the age of the change had passed, the diagnosis was "depression". Finally I found a young doctor who had studied this problem and finally knew what was wrong. His diagnosis was anxiety disorder and agoraphobia. We started desensitization, little steps each day of going to stores and finding the exit so I could leave as soon as I began to panic. But I still clung to and was always with my husband. Each year I would have good periods and then a setback going down hill again but still I could do nothing outside my home unless my husband was with me. We came to Palm Springs in 1988 and I had a very severe panic attack. I was rushed to the emergency room and the doctor there recommended Marilyn, who founded the Institute for Phobic Awareness, and has been down this long and frightening road of Agoraphobia and panic attacks.

I started attending Phobics Anonymous self help support group meetings with people with problems much like mine. We shared our ideas and our victories each week and worked on our steps.

My husband and I came back to Palm Springs every

year and the third year I was able to go to meetings without him. I now can go to stores by myself and although I still depend on him, I can do many things without him and am able to talk about it without being ashamed if I get a little panicky.

My latest victory was riding in a car alone.

Thank God for such a loving husband and understanding family who still protect me from situations they feel might make me uncomfortable such as large crowds where it may be hard to exit but this too shall pass.

Last, but not least, I thank God for people like Marilyn who give their time to help people with anxiety and panic related disorders that are so often misunderstood and misdiagnosed even by the most knowledgeable in the medical profession.

DIFFERENT

Why should we be in such desperate haste to succeed, and in such desperate enterprises? If a man does not keep pace with his companions perhaps it is because he hears a different drummer. Let him step to the music which he hears, however measured or far away.

SEMPER FIDELIS

May 1990 and my thirtieth birthday. I was a young United States Marine platoon sergeant leading 24 of the finest and even younger marine scouts on some training exercises in the middle of the Mojave Desert in the blistering heat. We were off for the weekend of June 16th and 17th. On the 17th (Fathers day), Debi and I got married. I had to report back to duty that Monday so we made plans to go on our honeymoon as soon as my platoon finished its training in the Mojave Desert. We had been undergoing some of the most realistic combat training possible next to the actual thing.

Mid July rolled around and we had finished our training for that month. We were to return in mid August for one more training exercise so we packed our bags and headed back to the pleasant sunny weather of Camp Pendleton, CA where we were based. When we got to Pendleton I loaded my gear in my 4X4 Ford Ranger and headed east to our beautiful home in the mountains of Julian, CA (a true gift from God).

After a few days at the ranch, Debi and I loaded the ranger and headed for Rosarito, Mexico on our belated honeymoon. In Rosarito, we had a cabana on the beach - a real change after all of the training we had been doing in the Mojave.

My wife and I were spending quality time together. We had found the local Alcoholics Anonymous meeting in Rosarito. We are both sober active members of A.A. While on our honeymoon we had the opportunity to watch television. On August 2nd a news flash came that

Saddam's war machine had invaded Kuwait. A few hours later my commanding officer called and told me that they were cutting our honeymoon a few days short. He said he couldn't give any details on the phone but that I would be fully briefed as soon as I reported in. I already knew what was happening. The second I got the word on the phone, I felt a rush throughout my entire body. I felt excited that I was going to do what Marines do best and that is to win battles. I also felt some apprehension knowing that I could die in combat.

We loaded the truck and headed back to Julian, CA. All the way home and that night before I reported in, I had a million thoughts racing through my head knowing that we were heading for combat and knowing what my mission as a Marine scout was. We provide the task force with reconnaissance by operating way forward of friendly lines. We locate the enemy and report all the information we gather back to our battalion. I was also the primary forward air controller for our battalion.

The next day at the briefing from the colonel, it was confirmed. We were to pack up and prepare our men to deploy to Saudi Arabia and take on one of the largest armies in the world. The Iraqi war machine intelligence told us that we out-classed them, which we already knew but still man for man we were outnumbered. My heart was pounding as the adrenaline rushed through my body. We were to fly out in a week. We were at live fire ranges day and night firing all weapons in our arsenal, ensuring us that we were prepared.

As the days went by, the anxiety continued to build. Had I given my men the best possible training? Had I taken care of all of their needs? Did we pack all the gear we would need to accomplish the mission? Would I be bringing all of my men home alive to their families? Would I ever see my wife and family again? Had I made my amends to those people I had owed them to? Etc., etc., etc.

I continued to attend as many A.A. meetings as I possibly could for I knew that real soon I would be deprived of the fellowship that had saved and changed my life and which I had grown to love so much. God had surely blessed me. All of my A.A. brothers and sisters knew I would be leaving and supported me in every way and were there for me when I needed them.

One night we were at a machine gun range doing some night firing when one of my young marines approached me and said he had a hernia. I knew he was feeling what I had been feeling and was afraid of going to war. We had a talk and I told him that he should do what he had to do and that I wouldn't think of him as a coward or less of a man. The next day I sent him to sick-bay and dropped him from the platoon. He would not go with us or anyone else to the Gulf.

We were to leave the next morning so I drove to my mom and dad's to say goodbye to them and the rest of my family. Then my wife and I said our final goodbye.

After we mustered early in the morning, we were told that our flight had been delayed and that we would not be leaving so I went home with my wife. I called and informed my family. We went through these drills of saying goodbye several times. The anxiety level was real high by the time we finally left on Sept. 1st.

On the flight over, my emotions were running wild and I was very anxious and scared inside, but on the outside I was cool, calm and collected. I could not let my young marines see their leader show any fear. By this time the Serenity Prayer had become very repetitious. I had the best marines a platoon sergeant could have and I couldn't let them down. We would kick butt together fear or no fear. My faith in my God was definitely being put to the test.

We landed in Daharan Airport on the 1st of September. As soon as we got off of the plane we were told that they had a terrorist attack on one of the airports' gates. I wasn't sure if it was true or not but what I was sure of was that we were now in the combat zone and the rumor of war was very real and there was no turning back. It really made me nervous seeing all of these Arabs and not knowing who was who and I definitely didn't trust any of them and we hadn't been issued any ammunition for our personal weapons yet and it was night time. From Daharan we were transported on buses by Arabs with no escorts to the Port of Jubail where we would reclaim our equipment. It took us 5 days to get our ammunition and equipment loaded and head out to the Saudi desert. Our first couple of months (Sept. through Oct.) we kept extra busy trying to get as much training as possible, rehearsing different scenarios over and over. You can never train enough. At this point the average temperature was ranging between 120 to 130 degrees F. My anxiety had subsided since we were so busy and exhausted.

It looked as if we would be playing the waiting game

with Saddam so they set up one of the American oil workers' compounds to accommodate us. There we had rooms with showers, air conditioning, television and a few telephones with endless lines of marines calling home. I split my platoon into thirds so we could rotate back to the rear for R & R and still accomplish our mission in the field. My first rotation back for R & R was very nice. We were all exhausted and needed a rest. I read my A.A. books as well as my Bible every day. Prayer has always been important to me. I was also fortunate enough to attend an A.A. meeting at one of the other camps. It was surely a breath of fresh air since I believe very much in unity and attended meetings at least 5 days a week before we deployed. I had celebrated 2 years of sobriety in July prior to us leaving the good ole U.S. of A. I had become comfortable with myself and in my sobriety. Now something was happening inside of me and it sure wasn't very comfortable.

On my second trip back for R & R I had a nice dinner, telephoned my wife, had a shower and had retired to my room late in the evening for some reading before going to bed. As I lay on my bed and read a book on religions, I was feeling really relaxed. It felt great being in an air-conditioned room. It was getting late, around 11:30 p.m., when all of a sudden, wham it hit me! My chest got tight, I felt a shortness of breath, my heart was palpitating, my arms felt numb and the palms of my hands as well as my feet were tingling. I thought I was having a heart attack. I got hot and was also having to urinate a lot. I jumped out of my bed, went to the bathroom and kept splashing water on my face. I felt as if I was losing my mind. I pictured in my mind where the aid station was located. I felt as if I would totally panic and run for help but once again my mind would say to me "what will your men think about you?". I'm a leader of Marines, the world's most elite fighting force. How would I feel about myself, I would be a coward. No, I told myself, remain calm. The simple things that I had learned in sobriety saved me once again. I hung on to the serenity prayer for dear life, saying it over and over - prayer after prayer as I paced the floor and stepped outside to get some fresh air because I felt I was suffocating. This went on for a few hours. I kept saying the serenity prayer. Finally I calmed down and was able to lay back down. I feverishly read scriptures out of my Bible and prayed. I wanted back the serenity I had. I finally fell asleep sometime between 3 and 4 a.m. I woke up and got out of bed around 7 a.m. Although I was extremely exhausted, I was truly grateful that night had passed. Still not knowing what I had experienced, and concerned about my health, I went to see the doctor. They took my vitals and I explained what had happened. He simply said "that's easy, you're having anxiety attacks". He told me I described them to a tee. He also explained reasons why we get them. He asked what my mission was. I told him and he said "no wonder". He sent me back to the port city of Jubail to get a routine EKG done to insure all was okay. The test did reveal that all was well.

That night one of my team would come to pick me up to take me back out to the field. It was dark and we headed away from civilization. As we got further away, my heart started pounding once again. I told my driver that I wasn't feeling well so I had him turn around and head back to camp. We would leave the next day during twilight hours. I felt terribly afraid of the dark and the thought of dying alone raced back and forth through my head. I did not want to die.

That second night in camp I had the opportunity to call my A.A. sponsor and tell him what had happened. He said that I was realizing how precious life really is. He told me to keep my faith and trust in God and ask that His will be done in my life and just stay sober.

I eventually got back out to the field the next day. The tempo of our training continued. One day we had some down time. It was high noon and around 130 degrees. All we could do was drink water, build the best shade possible and get in it. There is nothing but sand in that country and that day my mind was yearning to see a tree or grass - anything. My mind started racing again as I felt I was losing my sanity. Once again the serenity prayer got me through.

A couple of weeks later we were rehearsing some beaching operations. One of my missions in combat would be to locate the mine fields, breach a couple of lanes through them so that the rest of the task force could pass through. I often thought about that mission a lot. It would most definitely raise my anxiety because I know that obstacles are covered by direct and indirect weapons fire.

Later in the evening, we had some mail delivered. When I was back at the camp and had my attack, I had the opportunity to call and talk to my wife and sponsor about it. Anyway, in that mail call I received a package from my wife. I opened it and there was a copy of the latest Sober Times. As I thumbed through it I noticed that there was an article on anxiety related disorders and panic attacks. I swear I read that article over and over. From what I had learned from my 12 Step program in A.A. I know that we have to take action to work through our difficulties. Well, at the end of that article there were two different addresses to get more information on these disorders. One address was in Palm Springs, CA Phobics Anonymous World Service Headquarters and the other, I believe, in Maryland. I immediately picked up a pen and paper and wrote them both requesting more information. I didn't want to feel and go through what I had already been experiencing. I took action. I wanted to know what was happening.

About a month passed. Mail took around 11 days each way. I received a package from Phobics Anonymous. My heart pounded for I knew that I would get some helpful solutions. Inside there was a hand written letter from Marilyn and the 12 Step book from Phobics Anonymous. The inspirational letter itself helped me a great deal because it confirmed that I wasn't the only one that had experienced the feeling of impending doom. I had also gotten letters from all of Marilyn's students at the teen drug and alcohol recovery center. They were very up-lifting indeed knowing that a bunch of kids who I had never met but shared something in common with were supporting me.

From that day on with Marilyn's *Twelve Steps of Phobics Anonymous* book, all the support from her and her students, all of the support from my A.A. network and most important, by the grace of God, I was able to endure my time in combat. Or maybe I should say hell for it seemed like hell with all the darkness and fire and heat. I found out that God will never abandon us. We are free agents to choose.

Once the ground war started, I realized that an adrenaline rush is sometimes needed for pure survival. I was able to cope. The war I had created in my mind was worse than the one I fought in Saudi. Sure it was tough at times but with all of the people that my God has put in my life and the books that He inspired people to write, like the 12 Step book of Phobics Anonymous, the Alcoholics Anonymous big book and, and of course the Big, Big Book, all helped me to endure one of the most trying times in my life. These fellowships, the books, and my experiences help me to cope to this day on a daily basis. As I sit and write this on this 11th day of August, 1992, a year and a half after the war, I hear news flashes on the television hearing President Bush warn Saddam that we will go in and do it again if he doesn't comply with the United Nations resolutions and also leave the Shiites alone. We are flying sorties in Iraq at this time.

I recall the time I spent there both when we were waiting to go in and the anxiety I felt and the adrenaline rush I felt when it came time for me and my platoon of young marines to do battle in the trenches.

I learned that fears are real but that I can deal or work through them through the fellowships that I have come to know and love so dearly.

If I have to go again, so be it. I would go in an instant

to do what I get paid to do (Marine Scout). I know today that I have a shield of armor to take into battle to help me survive, if I choose to pick it up.

When I was in Desert Shield/Storm, I felt like somewhat of a coward because of what I experienced within myself. I ended up getting a medal with a "V" on it for valor in combat. They tried telling me I'm a combat hero but I'm not. I'm just one of God's kids doing the best I can do one day at a time.

I send all of you my thanks and love for what you all have given me. "A peace of mind and serenity" today and in the toughest times of my life. Once again, all my love and gratitude to Phobics Anonymous, Alcoholics Anonymous, my Christian bretheran and all of the great kids that wrote me. I'm with you always in the fellowship of the spirit.

Semper Fidelis,
Jose

****

LETTERS RECEIVED FROM JOSE DURING DESERT STORM

11-21-90

My name is Joe, I'm 30 years of age. I'm also a sergeant in the United States Marine Corps. I'm in A.A. and am coming up on 3 years sobriety. I'm a platoon sgt. and am in charge of 20 Marines. We are a front line recon element and are currently deployed in Saudi

Arabia. We are way north.

My wife who is also in A.A. sent me a copy of Sober Times and I saw your article in it.

Since my new life in sobriety, I'm learning how precious life really is. I have had some anxiety problems since we've been here which is 3 months. I did go to the hospital here to have a routine EKG done. The doctors told me that it's anxiety. I also told them that I'm a recovering alcoholic. They have made me more aware of my problem which has helped. They also had me call my sponsor which also helped and I have made 2 A.A. meetings since we've been here.

I'm able to accomplish my mission but sometimes it still hits, mainly at night. I want to work through this.

I've grown a lot in sobriety and want to continue to grow. Prayer and continuous contact with God is automatic. I have no problem with that. Then I get this paper with your article so I'm asking if you can send me your book and literature. I know that it can help me work through this. I would greatly appreciate it.

I need your help.

Sincerely,
Joe (Jose)

****

2-3-91

I write this letter hoping it finds you in good health and spirits. I hope all is going well for you.

Thanks so much for having founded P.A. I did receive your letter along with your book. It has helped me a great deal to be aware of what was going on with me and now how to work through it. I really like your book. I do work the steps of A.A. I know the benefits from taking action.

I am doing much better now than I was when I initially wrote to your headquarters. I've always believed in God. I do turn to Him on a daily basis. I maintain conscious contact with God. I thank Him for all He blesses me with as the days go by. God is definitely my rock and fortress. My trust and faith in God has grown tremendously since we've been here.

We are as far north in Saudi Arabia as we can go now. We can see the flashes and thunder of our artillery and air strikes. I sit and wonder what they must be going through and how much pounding can they possibly take. I feel a lot for the Iraqi soldiers. Obviously Saddam could care less. I do pray for him too and hopefully he will have a change of heart. He is a very sick man. We are standing by in case we get called to go in. God only knows what will happen here. I put my trust in Him and hope for the best. I know that God's will will be done no matter what.

Marilyn, your book and letter have been of great help to me. I know your book and literature would also benefit my wife a great deal and I've written her of my fortune. I would like to share it with her. Would it be possible for you to send her a copy also? Please feel free to send me a bill for your expenses. I will put her address on a separate sheet of paper.

No, I don't mind that you shared my letter at one of your meetings. Yes, I have heard from some of your group. I thank God for you and the great fellowship that you have started.

Once again Marilyn, thanks so much for everything. Until next time, take care and God bless you.

Sincerely,
Jose

****

3-16-91

I write this letter hoping it finds you in good health and spirits.

I received your letter along with your group's letters yesterday.

As always, it is good hearing from all of you. You have all been very supportive of me and I thank you all from the bottom of my heart.

I write this letter (brief) to respond to your questions. First, yes I am from San Diego, CA. My wife and I live in the local mountain community of Julian. Do you know where it is? It was a mistake saying that lunch would be on you if I stopped by for I am a big eater. Also I feel very honored that you have asked me to write my story down for your book. I would be glad to start writing for you when I get home. If there is a chance that I can help another person from my experiences, that would be a blessing. I want to be of service.

I called and talked to my wife this morning and

shared your letter with her. I had also told her that some of your group asked if I could visit all of you. Upon our return to the states I plan on taking 10 days of leave. We should be home by the end of March so it would probably be in early April. Anyway, we plan on going to Palm Springs and would love to stop by and visit. If you like I will call you upon my return and maybe we can set up a date for us to stop by. I would love to share my experiences there with you all.

Yes thank God the war is over. We are at the moment back in Saudi Arabia and are awaiting a flight home. We engaged the enemy the whole way to our objective - Kuwait International Airport. We had to advance through the hundreds of burning oil wells. It was a living hell. My platoon was very successful in our mission. I have a great bunch of men. The majority of them have been written up to receive medals. Yes, it was quite an experience but with God all things are possible. I hope to be able to share this all with you sometime soon.

Well I'm going to sign off for now. It's time to get some sleep. I will leave my home address on this letter. Hopefully by the time you get this letter I will be home. Tell everyone I say hi and that I send my love.

Once again I thank all of you for your support. I couldn't have done it without you. Until next time, take care and God bless all of you .

Love, Jose

P.S. Yes your book, *The 12 Steps of Phobics Anonymous* helped me a great deal just as has my A.A. Big Book and 12 x 12. I thank God for having inspired you to put it together.

I've Done My Best

Be a little bit good and a little bit naughty
but don't go too far either way.
Say a prayer if you want to.
Say 'damn' if it helps you.
Whatever your impulse - obey!
Always try to be kind,
but if ever you find
that you've got to strike back - do it fast;
just smash out left and right;
make it one darned good fight
and then bury it all in your past.
Wear a smile when you're sad
Wear a smile when you're glad
Wear a smile when it's really a mask
Be as nice as you can be - be the best company
even when it's a helluva task.
Find your happiness where and whenever you can
and grab all the joys life can give,
make it your golden rule not to simply exist
but above all to live - really live!
Live each day of your life as if it were your last
and do something worthwhile in each one.
Live each hour so that you can shake
hands with yourself
and say to yourself 'twas well done'
May you know your reward at the end of the day.
When you lie down for your well earned rest,
as you pull up the covers and say to yourself
"I'm sure that I've done my best"

Chapter 2:
INTERPRETING
AND WORKING
THE TWELVE STEPS
OF PHOBICS
ANONYMOUS

STEP 1

"We admitted that we were powerless over fear, phobias, acute anxiety and panic. That our lives had become unmanageable".

It's not easy for a phobic to admit that we are powerless because being powerless means loss of control. This loss of control is one of our major fears and a major contributing factor in the development of the panic-anxiety cycle. Our excessive concern with control is a result of growing up in an environment where helplessness and lack of control were major issues, and a society that puts a premium on Power and Control.

Like it or not though, we found that we have no control over our anxiety and panic attacks. They come from out of the blue, in the most unlikely and unwanted places and situations, last for a variable length of time, and then disappear without regard for what we do. We are at their mercy, paralyzed by our uncontrollable thoughts and severe accompanying symptoms.

Trying to control fear is like trying to hold on to a wet bar of soap. The harder you grasp it, the more it slips away through your fingers, but the minute you relax your hold, it rests calmly in the palm of your hand.

Like the monkey that puts his hand through the fence to grasp the banana. As long as he holds it he can't get his hand back through the bars, but if he were just to let go of that banana he could get away and be free.

Do you remember the chinese finger puzzle when you were a child? You inserted your index fingers into a straw tube. Once you put them in, you really couldn't get them out. The harder you pulled, the tighter the straw enclosed your fingers. Only by relaxing and letting go, could you remove your fingers.

Through trial and error we found that we could not wish our fears away, hope them away, intellectualize them away, psychoanalyze them away, anesthetize them away with alcohol or drugs, work them away or fight them away. The perimeter of our world became smaller and smaller and our lives had no quality.

By ourselves we were powerless to do anything and finally when we had used up all of our resources, family, friends, doctors, psychologists, counselors, the clergy, etc., and when we finally stopped trying to camouflage, hide, or escape from our fears; surrendered and admitted defeat; admitted physical, intellectual, emotional and spiritual bankruptcy and accepted the fact that the motivating force in our lives, fear, had become personified. It was our enemy with a life of its own. Usually our fears become self fulfilling prophesies. What we resisted persisted. The more we tried to control and fight them, like quicksand, the deeper and deeper we sank.

It was only when we could absent ourselves from our self-centered, obsessive, fearful, negative, catastrophic thoughts, disregard our personal concerns, forget ourselves, and turn our unmanageable lives over to our Higher Power, asking humbly for intervention, that we could then find the courage to embrace life and live it with faith rather than fear. The depth of our anxiety measures the distance we are from our Higher Power.

Giving up the illusion of control is the way to true

freedom from fear. Letting go doesn't mean giving up - it means opening up to new vistas and embarking on a never-ending venture.

The very moment we surrender is the very moment we regain some of our true power.

****

ASKING PRAYER

I asked God for strength, that I might achieve,

I was made weak, that I might learn humbly to obey.

I asked for health, that I might do greater things,

I was given infirmity, that I might do better things.

I asked for riches, that I might be happy,

I was given poverty, that I might be wise.

I asked for power, that I might have the praise of men,

I was given weakness, that I might feel the need of God.

I asked for all things, that I might enjoy life,

I was given life, that I might enjoy all things.

I got nothing that I asked for,

but everything that I had hoped for.

Almost despite myself, my unspoken prayers were answered.

I am among all men, most richly blessed.

STEP ONE WORKSHEET

"We admitted that we were powerless over fear, phobias, acute anxiety and panic. That our lives had become unmanageable".

Step one is basically a two step process. In the first part, we admit that we are powerless over fear, anxiety, and panic. In the second part, we have to admit that our lives had become unmanageable. Perhaps not our entire life is out of control, but certain aspects of it are, or we would not be attending meetings.

1. What does the term "powerless" mean to you?
2. How do you view yourself as powerless over fear?
3. Write three examples of how your fear has escalated.
4. How have your fears curtailed your activities?
5. How have your fears controlled your life?
6. What are some of the defense mechanisms you've used to hide your fears from your family and friends?
7. How have you tried to take control of your fear, anxiety and panic?
    A. Did it Work? B. If so, how?
8. Have you ever pushed your loved ones away because of your fears?
9. Do you find yourself isolating from people? How?
10. Have you lost interest in things you enjoyed in the past, such as hobbies, etc.?

11. Have you ever contemplated suicide because your life has no quality due to your overwhelming fears, anxiety or panic?

12. Have your fears ever caused you humiliation or guilt? Explain.

NOW FOCUS ON HOW YOUR LIFE HAS BECOME UNMANAGEABLE.

1. What does having an unmanageable life mean to you?

2. What aspects of your life are presently unmanageable?

3. How has this affected:
   A. You?
   B. Your Family?
   C. Your Friends?

4. What physical symptoms do you experience as a result of your fears?

5. Do you experience problems with concentration or memory loss?

6. Have you ever "lost control"? What happened?

7. How have you rearranged your life style to accommodate your fears?

8. Name some of the things you've avoided because of your fears.

9. What are some of the poor choices you've been forced to make based on fear?

10. What excuses have you used to get out of or avoid "fearful" situations?

11. Did trying to control your fears work?
    A. What methods did you use?
    B. Which ones were successful?
    C. Which ones were unsuccessful?
12. How can step one help you live a fuller life?

TO FACE THE FUTURE

If we must face disappointment,
Help us to learn patience.
If we must face sorrow,
Help us to learn sympathy.

If we must face pain,
Help us to learn strength.
If we must face danger,
Help us to learn courage.

If we must face failure,
Help us to learn endurance.
If we achieve success,
Help us to learn gratitude.

If we attain prosperity,
Help us to learn generosity.
If we win praise,
Help us to learn humility.

If we are blessed with joy,
Help us to learn sharing.
If we are blessed with health,
Help us to learn caring.

Whatever the day may bring,
May we confront it honorably and faithfully:
May we know the serenity which comes to those who
find their strength and hope in a Higher Power.

STEP 2

"Come to believe that a power greater than ourselves could restore us to wholeness".

Step 2 is a Step of Trust and Hope. In Step 1 we admitted that we were powerless so there has to be some Power greater than ourselves.

When we invite our Higher Power to intervene in our lives, we disregard our personal concerns and rid ourselves of our self-centered thoughts. Spiritual support provides us with strength and serenity.

We realize that we could not eliminate our fears alone and yet because we were so disillusioned, disappointed and felt so betrayed by our previous attempts to become "normal" and whole we were skeptical about something as abstract as a Higher Power.

It's strange that we can readily accept the power of an unseen force such as electricity, and yet not accept our Higher Power and the positive energy for healing and growth.

Our Higher Power, or a power greater than ourselves, initially can be the members of the Phobics Anonymous group, a circle of friends greater than any individual in the group who provide understanding and complete acceptance, not criticism or judgement. When one attends a 12-step meeting, they can feel the positive power in the room. The power of unconditional love and trust, a feeling of connection with the entire human race.

Like pessimism, optimism is contagious and yet the

concept of a Higher Power keeps many people from attending Anonymous groups. Spirituality and the Higher Power concept are misunderstood and often confused with organized, formal religion.

Spirituality as defined in the Phobics Anonymous program is simply ones' relationship with an unexplainable Higher Power.

Spirituality is being in touch with something within that moves us to act or think another way from where we were before. It compels us to act. It motivates us to do. It ignites hope. It fuels us with the energy to start when we were stuck, and by the very action we take, we set in motion a positive flow of energy from within.

Our Higher Power does not need a name attached to it such as "God". For some, as I said before, it can be the power of the program or the goodness, caring, compassion and support of the group they are attending; for some, a force or creative intelligence; for others, some aspect of nature or a spirit of the universe.

****

"The greatest revolution of our generation
is the discovery that human beings, by changing
the inner attitudes of their minds can change
the outer aspects of their lives."
William James

STEP TWO WORKSHEET

Came to believe that a power greater than ourselves could restore us to wholeness.

Step Two is a believing step. It is something that comes from within. This step requires humility and the acceptance that there is something greater than ourselves. It is a step of Hope, Hope that something can fill the void left by step one when we admitted our powerlessness, uselessness, helplessness, and humanness. The following steps, and our ongoing recovery cannot work until we work this step. It is a process we experience within. It cannot be seen, only felt - a rallying point; an incentive to move into action that requires reliance rather than defiance. Thy will be done, not mine!

1. What does "wholeness" mean to you?
2. What do you consider to be a power greater than yourself?
3. How would you define "came to believe"?
4. Name some of the "powers" that you know exist but cannot see - (example: the wind).
5. What are the qualities your Higher Power should possess?
6. What do you think you need to make your life whole?
7. What is presently lacking in your life that is causing it to be incomplete?

8. What methods have you tried in the past to make your life complete? Did they work?

9. Do you depend on others to fill the void in your life and make it complete?

   A. If so, who?

   B. Give examples on how you depended on them.

10. How can step 2 be applied in your life to enable you to achieve healing, wellness, and wholeness?

11. How does a spiritual life differ from a religious life?

12. What negative experiences, if any, have you had with organized religion?

13. After working step two do you believe that your Higher Power can restore you to wholeness?

If you can answer "yes" to the question: "Do I now or can I ever believe there is a power greater than myself?", you are well on your way to becoming restored, renewed, made whole and ready for Step 3.

****

"Logic and cold reason are poor weapons
to fight fear and distrust - only faith and generosity
can overcome them"
Jawaharias Nehru

TO BEGIN AGAIN

What is the difference between a wise person and
a fool?
Even fools will say a wise thing now and then,
And the wisest will at times descend to foolish-
ness.
So what distinguishes a wise person from a fool?
A fool is one who never has a change of mind.
Conditions change, situations alter, and new times
make new demands,
But the fool remains the same.
What is the difference between a good and an evil
person?
There is some goodness even in the worst.
And is there a person who has not sinned?
So, what makes one person good and another
evil?
An evil person refuses to change
Doing wrong, knowing it. And yet persisting in
evil ways.
There is no sadder confession than "I know I am
doing wrong.
But it's too late now to change".
This is surrender to despair.
"If I had my life to live over..."
"If I had known then what I know now..."
But when we work The 12 Steps we learn
What will we do with the knowledge?
How will we use the gift?

STEP 3

"Made a decision to turn our will and our lives over to the care of our Higher Power, as we understand our Higher Power".

When we took the first step we admitted that our lives were out of control - unmanageable. The second step was one of hope and trust and now with the third step we admitted that we really hadn't done such a great job with our lives so far, so what have we got to lose? We've tried everything else to no avail so why not try to surrender and just let go. Our Higher Power - whatever our concept of it is - is infinite and we as human beings are limited.

It's a paradox but surrendering and becoming dependent on our Higher Power makes us more independent.

We spend most of our scattered lives conjugating three verbs: to want, to have and to do, forgetting that none of these verbs have any ultimate significance except so far as they are transcended by and included in the fundamental verb "to be". Being, not wanting, having and doing is the essence of a spiritual life.

When we turn our will and our lives over to the care of our Higher Power, we are then free to just BE - no strings attached.

Many of us have offered up some problems in our lives after we have exhausted our own abilities and failed to solve them ourselves, but turning over our will and our lives is a major commitment. It is not easy to give up self; the control and mastery of your life, after all, haven't we been told that we are the Captain of our ship, the Master of our Fate?

When you finally arrive at the realization that the management job you're doing just isn't working and you are ready to "fire yourself" for poor performance and admit to carrying this heavy burden on your shoulders, it is a relief to give that burden away to our Higher Power.

Many times when we interfered, when we meddled again by trying to manipulate and gain control because we weren't getting a quick fix and things weren't happening soon enough for us - we again become anxious and fearful.

****

LET GO AND LET GOD

As children bring their broken toys
    with tears for us to mend
I brought my broken dreams to God
    because he was my friend.
But then instead of leaving him
    in peace to work alone,
I hung around and tried to help
    with ways that were my own.
At last, I snatched them back and cried,
    "How could you be so slow?"
"My Child," he said, "what could I do?
    You never did let go..."

STEP THREE WORKSHEET

Made a decision to turn our will and our lives over to the care of our Higher Power, <u>as we understood our Higher Power.</u>
Step three is a decision we actively make to let go and release our fears: to allow a Higher Power of our understanding to take care of the problems we are experiencing in our lives-with no strings attached. It does not mean thinking "Here is my life, you fix it" without doing any of the footwork needed. It does mean, that after you have exhausted all your own problem solving techniques and tried to the best of your ability to solve your problems and failed you stop procrastinating, stop postponing and take the third step. What you resist - persists. What you release, releases you.

1. What does "Let Go and Let God" mean to you?

2. What painful events have happened in your life to require you to finally take the positive affirmative action required by Step Three?

3. What is your individual conception of your Higher Power?

4. Give examples, of methods of self will you have used to control your fears.

   A. Which ones worked?

   B. Which ones have not?

5. Are you at a point in your life where you are finally ready to stop fighting and turn your life over to your Higher Power's care?

6. When your life is out of control you may push others away.
   A. How has this hurt you?
   B. How has this hurt others?
7. Make a list of times and situations where you felt alone and misunderstood because of your fears.
8. What feelings do you experience because of the way fear dominates your life?
9. Do you at this point in your recovery have a relationship or partnership with a Higher Power of your choice?
   A. Describe it.
   B. Has it increased your confidence in yourself?
10. Define what turning your will over and surrendering means to you.
11. Is the relationship with your Higher Power strong enough to inspire trust and allow you to turn your life over?

****

The clock of life is wound but once
And no man has the power
To tell just when the hands will stop
On what day or what hour.
Now is the only time you have
So live it with a will
Don't wait until tomorrow
The hands may then be still.

We are clay.
You are the potter
Who shapes us at his will.
Mold us into worthy vessels
Even though we're only clay.
Do not smash us if we prove imperfect.
Remember we are only clay.
We are glass.
You are the craftsman
Who can form us into many shapes.
Form us into finest crystal
Even if you have to twist and turn us.
But do not smash us if we are not pure.
Remember, we are only glass.
We are silver.
You are the smith
Who molds us as he wishes.
Hammer us as you design
Even though we are not gold.
Do not smash us if we tarnish.
Remember, we are only silver.
We are the rudder.
You are the helmsman
Who steers us to the left or the right.
Direct us to the shore you choose.
Do not let us idly spin
Even if we constantly resist your grasp.
Remember that the waves are very strong.
We are the threads.
You are the weaver
Who creates the patterns that he likes.
Weave us, God, into your plan.
Make us supple, straight, and true.
And do not discard us
If we should be imperfect.
Remember we are only threads.

STEP 4

"Made a searching and fearless moral inventory of ourselves."

The 4th Step is an action step. It represents a willingness to accept responsibility for our actions. This isn't as easy as it appears and many phobics experience a great deal of anxiety while writing the 4th Step. This is normal. It's much easier to blame others for our shortcomings and mistakes than to take a critical look at ourselves with honesty and truth. To face our character defects, no matter how unpleasant and undesirable they may be. To inspect every aspect of ourselves that we have tried to hide behind the many masks we wear (you can't heal what you can't feel). Usually we will discover that fear underlies all other defects, pride, greed, lust, anger, gluttony, envy and laziness. Pride is fear of humility, greed is fear of not having enough, lust can be motivated by fear of rejection, gluttony: fear of emptiness, envy: fear of worthlessness, and laziness: fear of responsibility.

It's very painful to be honest with ourselves. This step is a direct beginning to a way of life based on the courage to replace the fear of facing ourselves, the world, or life, with Faith.

When writing our inventory, it's important to list the positive as well as the negative; the pluses as well as the minuses, the assets as well as the liabilities.

For most phobics, our inventories showed highly sensitive, creative, intelligent, people-pleasers. Perfectionistic, imaginative people who were very co-dependent, putting everyone's needs before our own. We suffered from poor self esteem, lack of confidence and our lives were motivated by worry, fear and guilt. Our self defeating, negative catastrophic thinking makes it hard for us to evaluate and admit our good qualities - - instead we continually focused on the "bad". I'd like to give as an example, someone who would be considered the most perfectly beautiful girl in the world, great hair, perfect features, a body to die for, who gets a pimple! All of her other assets are forgotten. The one small flaw unnoticeable to others, makes her miserable and is all she can focus on. So it is with us. We forget all of our good qualities and zero in on the negatives.

****

"We are largely playthings of our fears-
In one, fear of the dark,
To another, of physical pain,
To a third, of public ridicule,
To a fourth, of poverty,
To a fifth, of loneliness,
For all of us, our particular creature waits in ambush."
Horace Walpole

STEP FOUR WORKSHEET

Make a searching and fearless moral inventory of ourselves.

This fourth step basically is a step of truth and honesty. It won't be of any value if you're not completely honest. In this step you look back on your life and see how your fear and anxiety manipulated your life and took control. This step enables you to realize how unmanageable your life has been and when it first started getting out of control. It gives you a better perspective of how things have been in the past and in some cases how it still is today.

1. Define the word inventory; remember it is not an autobiography or a history, but rather an honest appraisal.

2. List some of the events in your life that preceded either positive or negative feelings. Explain the event and the feeling.

3. Are there events in your past that you have hidden or sworn to keep secret? If so, reveal them now. Remember, "you are only as sick as your secrets".

4. What does searching and fearless mean to you?

5. Do you think that you are able to be both searching and fearless when taking your inventory?

6. Have you been dishonest in the past with yourself or others? Explain.

7. Can you now be completely honest when writing your inventory?

8. Uncomfortable feelings and painful memories may surface as you write your inventory, this is only natural, list some of them.
9. Reread your inventory to make sure it is completely balanced. It must contain both your strengths and your weaknesses. The positive as well as the negative, the good and the bad. Were there any additions you wish to make?

A PROMISE - TO MYSELF

I promise from this day forward:
To accept myself... unconditionally
To love myself and cherish my existence
To always show myself respect
To not demand perfection
To stop putting myself down
To give myself the credit I deserve
To be my own best friend, someone I can depend on
To open my eyes to the beautiful promise in me
To utilize my talents to build inner security
And make a positive contribution to the world

BECAUSE

Only if I love myself can I truly love others
Only if I respect myself can I respect others
Only if I'm open to the "specialness" in me can I genuinely appreciate the uniqueness in others.
Only if I cherish my own existence, can I become the person I was meant to be!

STEP 5

"Admitted to our Higher Power, to ourselves and to another human being the exact nature of our wrongs."

We must be entirely honest with our friends and family if we are to expect recovery. We have tried to hide our fears and as a result, additional fears and anxieties surfaced from covering up and making excuses for our imperfections. We live with the ever present fear of having a panic attack and embarrassing or humiliating ourselves, but once we admit that we have a problem and accept it, allowing us the liberty of having a panic attack, we usually don't. It's trying to hide it and control it that adds to the anxiety and stress that can cause one.

One of our phobics had great difficulty riding in the car even though her husband was driving and knew of her fears. She had memorized every freeway exit, and knew where all of the hospital signs were posted, but it did no good until she was assured that her husband would stop the car immediately if she asked him to. Once he said he would she never had a problem in the car again.

Before we found the Phobics Anonymous Program, a lot of time and energy was wasted trying to act "normal" - pretending we were "just fine", when inside we were a pot waiting to boil over. When we came out in the open and admitted we had a problem rather than trying to hide our fears, when we no longer wasted our time making excuses, we could use 100% of our energy on our recovery. Of all the liars in the world, sometimes the worst are our own fears. When we finally admitted that we had fears, we took away the power and control it had over our lives.

When our lives become shallow, deepen them.

When our principles become shabby, repair them.

When our ideals become tarnished, restore them.

When our hopes become faded, revive them.

When our loyalties grow dim, brighten them.

When our values become confused, clarify them.

When our purposes grow blurred, sharpen them.

When our horizons become narrow, widen them.

STEP FIVE WORKSHEET

Admitted to our Higher Power, to ourselves, and to another human being the exact nature of our wrongs.

Step five requires complete honesty and is a continuation of step four. It consists of reading your inventory and sharing things you've never allowed anyone to know. It makes you very vulnerable. This step is really necessary for a lifetime of peace of mind. So intense though, is our fear and reluctance to do this, many phobics will try to bypass it. We search for an easier way. One less humiliating and less painful. But this step must not be avoided! The secrets we have written in step four have to be let out. Like an abscess, they must be drained if we intend to continue our recovery.

1. After completing your inventory do you feel you can risk sharing it with another person? Who?

2. How do you feel about openly discussing your faults with another person?

3. What qualities do you look for in the person you have chosen to share your inventory?

4. Do you see any value in admitting your faults to a trusted confidant?

5. What value do you see in sharing your inventory with another?

6. Do you have difficulty in admitting you are wrong? When and Why?

7. How are you feeling about yourself now?

8. Have you shared your inventory with your Higher Power?

9. After completing this step, have you experienced fear and anxiety or peace and serenity?

****

Fear is inside of you
Fear is inside of me
Fear is part of everyone
It never sets us free.

Why are we scared?
What do we fear?
Why do we always need
A support person near?

We feel so alone
We just want to hide
We're out of control
We've lost all our pride.

My fear is an aching pain
My fear is burning my heart
My fear has completely
torn my life apart!

Written by a 15-year old student at a drug and alcohol Recovery Center - Meredith.

WE WAIT TOO LONG

We often wait too long to do what must be done today, in a world which gives us only one day at a time, without any assurance of tomorrow. While lamenting that our days are few, we procrastinate as though we had an endless supply of time.

We wait too long to discipline ourselves and to take charge of our lives. We feed ourselves the vain delusion that it will be easier to uproot tomorrow the debasing habits which we permit to tyrannize us today, and which grow more deeply entrenched each day they remain in power. We wait too long to work at self-renewal. While we wait, our lives become progressively depleted of spiritual content. The estrangement between us and our heritage grows larger and more painful.

While we wait, the time for the harvest comes and we haven't even planted.

We wait too long to show kindness. We wait too long to speak words of forgiveness which should be spoken, to set aside hatreds which should be banished, to express thanks, to give encouragement, to offer comfort.

We wait too long to be charitable. Too much of our giving is delayed until much of the need has passed and the joy of giving has been largely diminished.

We wait too long to read the books, to listen to the music, and to see the arts which are waiting to enlarge our minds, to inspires our spirits, and to ennoble our souls.

We wait too long to utter the prayers, to perform the duties, to show the love that may no longer be needed tomorrow.

STEP 6

"Were entirely ready to have our Higher Power remove all of these defects of character".

The healthy person, the strong individual, is the one who asks for help when he needs it whether he's got an abscess on his knee or in his soul.

When we feel physically ill, we don't hesitate to go to a doctor. In fact, due to the nature of our problem and the confusing physical symptoms that anxiety and panic attacks caused at some point or another, we have visited every:

Cardiologist	Dermatologist
Endocrinologist	Gastroenterologist
Hematologist	Gynecologist
Immunologist	Internist
Neurologist	Opthamologist
Orthopedist	Oncologist
Psychologist	Physiatrist
Psychiatrist	Pulmonologist
Rheumatologist	Urologist
Pediatrician	Obstetrician
or family doctor	

Some of us found that we did have some physical problem such as hypoglycemia, mitral valve prolapse, or a thyroid problem, but for most of us, all test results returned normal, but still we didn't trust the diagnosis. We continued to fight and struggle, wanting an external solution.

When a drowning person panics and struggles, he also fights the rescuer and as a result they may both go under. Maybe when we finally admit that we are powerless and stop struggling and start to float, we can allow the tide to take us to shore.

Until we hit rock bottom and arrive at a state where the pain and devastation of hanging on to our fears is more intense than letting them go, we are not fully ready to have our defects of panic, fear and anxiety removed.

Sometimes this takes a long time because we have become so adept at manipulating our environment, our friends, family, etc. to conceal our fears that we do manage to survive, but we are just existing, not living the way life was meant to be.

Most of us don't know how badly we need a new way of life until the disaster of panic disorder overtakes us. It's time to have a checkup from the neck up. It is only then that we are ready to clean out the weeds that clutter our minds, the negative, fearful, catastrophic thinking weeds. Are we ready to grow and expand our horizons and go forth unafraid? The minute a tree or plant stops growing is the minute it starts to die. What the caterpillar calls the end of the world, others call a Butterfly!

Habit is like a soft bed
Easy to get into but hard to get out of

Time wasted is existence
Time used is living

STEP SIX WORKSHEET

Were entirely ready to have our Higher Power remove all these defects of character.

The sixth step is not an action step - it is a state of being, a step of willingness and honesty. We look at our reflections in the mirror with eyes wide open. We must look at our imperfections and defects, especially ones we used for survival, that are no longer necessary. We become willing to let go of them. This is a process and doesn't happen all at once. It happens when we no longer feel we need them or that they are useful.

1. What do you consider a defect?

2. How do you define character?

3. What are your character defects? List them.

4. How have your character defects helped you survive? What purpose did they serve?

5. Are you still using them today? How and Why?

6. Do you really want these character defects removed?

7. How do they interfere with your life today?

8. What would your life be like without them?

9. When your character defects or ineffective behaviors are removed, what do you think will replace them?

10. Which character defects do you feel will be the most difficult to give up?

11. At this midway point in your Twelve Step work, do you find that the program is working for you? How?

My Declaration of Self-Esteem
I AM ME

In all the world, there is no one else exactly like me.
Everything that comes out of me is authentically mine
because I alone chose it. I own everything about me, my
body, my feelings, my mouth, my voice, all my actions,
whether they be to others or to myself. I own my
fantasies, my dreams, my hopes, my fears. I own all my
triumphs and successes, all my failures and mistakes.
Because I own all of me, I can become intimately
acquainted with me. By so doing I can love me and be
friendly with me in all my parts. I know there are
aspects about myself that puzzle me, and other aspects
that I do not know, but as long as I am friendly and
loving to myself, I can courageously and hopefully look
for solutions to the puzzles and for ways to find out
more about me. However I look and sound, whatever I
say and do, and whatever I think and feel at a given
moment in time is authentically me. If later some parts
of how I looked, sounded, thought and felt turn out to be
unfitting, I can discard that which is unfitting, keep the
rest, and invent something new for that which I
discarded. I can see, hear, feel, think, say, and do. I have
the tools to survive, to be close to others, to be
productive, and to make sense and order out of the
world of people and things outside of me. I own me,
and therefore I can engineer me. I am me and

I AM OKAY

Virginia Satir

STEP 7

"Humbly asked our Higher Power to remove our shortcomings".

Steps four and five require us to take action. Steps six and seven only require us to become ready and humbly ask. This is difficult since humility is not one of our strong points. Controlling, manipulating, fighting, mastering yes, but Humility, no. Before panic attacks entered our lives, when we had a challenge, we'd work at overcoming it by our self-will and strength. As we grow spiritually, we learn that independence does not mean "going it alone" and that asking for help does not mean that we are weak!

Those of you who have suffered from panic attacks know that it's a humbling experience and many of us who never prayed before, do so now because we're sure that we are going to die. Every cell, nerve, muscle, bone and organ in your body cries out for help. The everyday activities, events and people become unimportant. No matter how much we have read about our problem, no matter how intelligent we are, no matter how we try to intellectualize what is happening to us, it's no use.

When we finally recognize that we cannot live exclusively by our own individual self will, strength and intelligence and that we need help, only then can we become humble enough to really take the seventh step. This will enable us to get better, not bitter!

STEP SEVEN WORKSHEET

Humbly asked our Higher Power to remove our shortcomings.

Although step six and step seven accompany each other, step seven is an action step. At this point we ask our power greater than ourselves to take away all of our shortcomings. Realizing that no one is perfect, we become humble and take time to pause to consider what humbling ourselves means.

1. What is your definition of humble?

2. How do you define humility?

3. What do you consider your shortcomings?

4. Which ones do you now feel ready to let go?

5. What are some shortcomings that you feel necessary to keep? Explain why.

6. Were any material things taken from you in the past before you were ready to give them up?

7. Do you agree that if you are not ready to give up your shortcomings they cannot be removed?

8. How do you think having your shortcomings removed will change your life?

9. What new qualities can you substitute for or use to replace your old shortcomings?

STEP 8

"Made a list of all persons we had harmed and became willing to make amends to them".

The most solemn of the Jewish High Holy days is Yom Kippur with its theme of Repentance and Atonement, yet Yom Kippur brings atonement only for transgressions between human beings and God. For transgressions between one individual and another, atonement can be gained only when the wrong has been righted, and the offended person has been reconciled. That's what Step 8 is about. It's an action step that deals with the restoration and reconciliation of relationships with ourselves as well as other people.

I find that the person I have harmed most is myself so I put my name on the top of my list. I have been my own worst enemy and have done to myself what I would never tolerate from anyone else.

Then, included in the list can be parents, children, friends, business associates, neighbors, etc. that we have harmed either by our actions or inactions, either intentionally or unintentionally.

As phobics, we suffer great shame and guilt because of our condition. Many of us were unable to attend social functions with our families or friends because of the fear of having a panic attack and embarrassing ourselves in public so we lied, made excuses and stayed home in our safety zone.

We must be willing to forgive ourselves for what is happening to us. We were so engrossed in our own problems and day to day survival that we became care-less about our interaction with others. Often this causes us to become full of resentment to those who appeared to be living "normal" lives, doing what we wished we could do but couldn't.

We hung on to our safe support people and this fear of separation, anxiety and fear of abandonment often destroyed our relationships.

The eighth step now offers us an opportunity to sim-ply list those to whom we feel we need to make amends.

I have learned silence
    from the talkative.
Tolerance from the intolerant
    and kindness from the unkind.
I should not be ungrateful
    to those teachers.

BREAKDOWN OF "FEAR"

"F" – for the FACT that your fear IS real.
"E" – for ESCAPE–something you want to do.
"A" – for ANXIETY–something gripping your whole being.
"R" – for RIDICULE–not letting anyone know lest you be embarrassed.

M. E. Robertson

STEP EIGHT WORKSHEET

Make a list of all persons we had harmed, and became willing to make amends to them all.

This step causes you to think back on your past and take the opportunity to thoughtfully list your past misdeeds and the names of those you have harmed. Did you ever hurt anyone physically, mentally, or emotionally because of your fears? If so, ask yourself are you now ready and willing to make amends?

1. What does the word "harm" mean to you?

2. Name the people you have harmed.

3. List ways that you have harmed others and yourself:
   A. Physically   B. Mentally
   C. Emotionally   D. Socially
   E. Spiritually   F. Economically

4. What does the word "amends" mean to you?

5. How can you make amends to yourself?

6. Do you feel you can do this?

7. How can making amends to yourself help remove some of your shame, guilt, fear, and sabotaging behaviors?

8. How do you think making amends can help release the past? How do you plan to make amends?

9. Making amends is difficult. Do you feel a reluctance at the thought of having to do this?

10. What walls are you ready to tear down and what bridges are you ready to construct?

FORGIVE

Forgive others and forgive yourself;
    mend a quarrel,
seek out a friend from the past;
    get rid of suspicion,
replace it with trust;
    write a love letter;
write a note of appreciation;
    say thank you more, much more.
Give a soft answer; encourage the young;
    encourage the not-so-young;
be loyal in your word and action;
    keep a promise;
find the time to do things you enjoy;
    give up a grudge;
forgive someone who did you harm;
    listen more;
make an apology to someone you wronged;
    try to understand more;
give up envy; examine your neighbor
Be more appreciative;
    be kinder and gentler.
Laugh more; laugh a lot more;
    be deserving of the confidence of others;
reach out and touch someone's hand
    make this a better world
We can: extend your hand to a stranger;
    give the warmth of your heart to a child; to a
    friend;
don't withhold your love - speak your
    love; speak it again;
    speak it once again.

STEP 9

"We made direct amends to such people whenever possible except when to do so would injure them or others".

In Step 8 we listed all the persons we had harmed and now in Step 9 it is time to take action. To do this requires honesty, courage and humility.

Remember the headaches, the heartaches, the shame, the remorse, the guilt, the loneliness, the pain. Remember the misery our panic attacks brought to all those whose help we so desperately sought? In making amends for our defects of the past we'll build a future where serenity shall last.

There is no set time to make your amends and no set format or rules. Whatever makes you feel comfortable. It's important to remember that apologies are not amends. Amends means acting differently. "Actions speak louder than words" and "What you are speaks so loudly I cannot hear what you say".

The very core of Step 9 is accepting the consequences of our past behavior and taking full responsibility for what we have done. It gives us a chance to put aside the past and its excess baggage and get on with our daily living and recovery.

Those for whom we hold resentments live in our heads rent free.

There are basically three major areas of amends:

1. <u>MATERIAL</u> - These are tangible wrongs done to others involving material things such as borrowing money

and not returning it - not paying bills, abiding by contracts, damage to property, and in the case of most phobics, lack of productivity on the job, being absent or being late.

2. MORAL - Not being able to provide the guidance for our friends, family etc. and setting bad examples by our anxious, fearful conduct, or being so pre-occupied about our own physical symptoms, that we manipulated, controlled, and used other people for our own selfish needs, paying no attention to theirs. We hurt the ones we love.

3. SPIRITUAL - Being inattentive to others in our lives because of our irrational fears. Not being able to fulfill our obligations to family and friends. Being so wrapped up in our own lives that we forgot special occasions and neglected our self-development. We reached a point in our lives where we felt like a lost cause. We had no self worth, we were imperfect and flawed, failure had become our way of life and our self esteem was nonexistent.

When we got sick and tired of being sick and tired and made our amends, we're ready for Step 10.

****

"They can conquer who believe.
It is he who has done the deed once who does not shrink from attempting it again."
Ralph Waldo Emerson

Robert Muller, former assistant secretary general of the United Nations, wrote this lovely piece especially for International Forgiveness Week.

DECIDE TO FORGIVE

Decide to forgive
For resentment is negative
Resentment is poisonous
Resentment diminishes and devours the self.
Be the first to forgive,
To smile and to take the first step.
And you will see happiness bloom
On the face of your human brother or sister.
Be always the first
Do not wait for others to forgive
For by forgiving
You become the master of fate
The fashioner of life
The doer of miracles.
To forgive is the highest,
Most beautiful form of love.
In return you will receive
Untold peace and happiness.

****

FORGIVENESS, by George Roemisch

Forgiveness is the fragrance of the violet that clings fast to the heel that crushed it.

So, if perchance you are the "heel" that crushed a violet, this is the time to seek forgiveness.

EACH OF US IS AN AUTHOR

Each of us is an author.
Writing, with deeds, in life's Great Book.
And to each You have given the power,
To write lines that will never be lost.

No song is so trivial,
No story is so commonplace,
No deed is so insignificant,
That you do not record it.

No kindness is ever done in vain;
Each mean act leaves its imprint;
All our deeds, the good and the bad,
Are noted and remembered.

So help us to remember always,
That what we do will live forever;
That the echoes of the words we speak,
Will resound until the end of time.
May our lives reflect this awareness;
May our deeds bring no shame or reproach.
May the entries we make
Be ever acceptable to you.

STEP NINE WORKSHEET

Made direct amends to such people whenever possible, except when to do so would injure them or others.

Step nine, an action step requires courage. It is a continuation of step eight and instructs you to make amends to all people you have harmed, except if making amends would injure them or others. The importance of this step should be obvious. It enables us to eradicate past concerns. To remove excess baggage we've been carting for years, and allows us to start living in the now!

1. How do you interpret "make direct amends"?
2. What risks are involved in taking this step?
3. What is the difference between an apology and an amends?
4. How do you think you could injure someone by making an amends?
5. Are you able to swallow your pride and show or say you are sorry?
6. If so, what feelings does it produce?
7. Do you feel a resistance toward making amends?
8. How do you feel that making amends will help you?
9. How can you make amends without causing harm?

STEP 10

"Continued to take a daily inventory when we were wrong — promptly admitted it".

A person trying to recover must clearly see that our present methods do not succeed and can not succeed. When meeting any situation in life only one of two things can happen:
1. The situation takes charge of you.
2. You take charge of the situation.

Anxiety breeds anxiety and fear feeds upon fear. Our old course across life's sea has taken us nowhere so it's time to set sail in a new direction.

Step 10 helps you monitor your progress on a daily basis and catch mistakes early before they become major problems. It allows you to know yourself and be honest. It enables you to live one day at a time and keep short accounts.

Since we are human it's very easy for us to fall back into our old habits; old ways of thinking and behavior. It's been said that the price of freedom is eternal vigilance. A business that doesn't take a regular inventory usually goes bankrupt.

We can no longer allow ourselves the luxury of hanging on to useless, harmful thoughts, activities and behaviors. We must clean house on a daily basis.

Our irrational fears are cunning, baffling and powerful and the emotional pain is the "interest" we pay on our long term accounts and it is just too high.

We must constantly watch for signals that re-activate past experiences and trigger fears. A daily inventory is invaluable as a means of keeping in touch with where we are and how we're behaving and also the progress we're making.

****

A little less impatient with those we deem too slow.

A little less arrogant because of all we know.

A little less conceited since our worth is slight.

A little less intolerant even when we're right.

A little more forgiving and swifter to be kind.

A little more desirous the word of praise to find.

A little more eager to help others to rejoice.

A little more careful to speak with a gentle voice.

A little more effort to see another's view.

A little more determined to be grateful for what we do.

A little more willingness to extend a helping hand.

A little more commitment to our people and our land.

A little more eagerness to listen and understand.

A little more readiness to respond to God's Command.

A little more resolve to do what must be done.

And a greater understanding that truly "we are one".

STEP TEN WORKSHEET

Continued to take personal inventory and when we were wrong promptly admitted it.

When a store takes inventory of its merchandise, it does not include stock that has been sold; so it should be with your personal inventory. Your inventory is not a history, it is fluid and changes from day to day and should be kept one day at a time.

1. How has working the steps enabled you to take responsibility for your actions today?

2. What ineffective behaviors have been changed as a result of working the steps?

3. Which area in the first nine steps do you feel you need to continue to work?

4. Are you ready to try again in that area?

5. How do you know when you are wrong?

6. Why is promptness important when admitting your wrongs?

7. Have you gained the courage to admit when you are wrong?

8. To whom do you admit your wrongs?

9. If you still have not learned to appraise or inventory your actions on a daily basis, how can you begin to do so?

10. In what areas do you continue to slip into your old patterns of behavior?

11. What painful or destructive patterns would you like to leave behind?

12. What methods can you use to change those habits?

13. Are you continuing to take the daily risk of growing and changing?

****

Believe in yourself and in your dream
No matter how impossible it may seem
Someday, Somehow, you'll get through
To goals you have in view
Mountains fall and seas divide
Before the ones who in their stride
take a hard road day by day.
One day at a time, sweeping obstacles away
Believe in yourself and in your plan
Say not, I cannot, but I can
The prizes of life we fail to win
Because we doubt the power WITHIN.

STEP 11

"Sought through prayer and meditation to improve our conscious contact with a Higher Power of our choice, praying only for the knowledge, the will and the courage to carry that out".

Step 11 requires that we improve our conscious contact with our Higher Power. Two of the most effective methods are prayer and meditation. It is really a combination of the Second and Third Step on a daily basis and calls for faith and persistence.

When we stop trying to control and manipulate our lives, the best methods for meeting our needs will always be made clear to us. When one door closes, another opens and what may appear to be defeats can and do turn into successes. Everything happens for the best.

Prayer is a way of talking with our Higher Power, asking for what we want. Meditation is designed to drive everyday concerns and thoughts from our minds and quietly listen for an answer.

Prayer is at the heart not only of great religion, but of significant living. Without prayer, we cannot scale the heights of compassion, or attain the peaks of love of our fellow man of which we are capable.

Prayer has been an enduring and universal phenomenon of human life, not because a priesthood ordained it, nor because tradition hallowed it, but because man is ever seeking to probe into his own depths and bring to light his hidden yearnings.

Prayer is a step on which we rise from the self we are to the self we wish to be.

Prayer affirms the hope that no reality can crush; the aspiration that can never acknowledge defeat.

Prayer is not an escape from duty. It is no substitute for the deed.

Prayer seeks the power to do wisely, to act generously, to live helpfully. It helps to reinforce the act rather than to replace it.

Prayer is the search for silence amidst the noise of life.

Prayer takes us beyond the self. Joining our little self to the selfhood of humanity, it gives our wishes the freedom to grow large and broad and inclusive.

Our prayers are answered not when we are given what we ask, but when we are challenged to be what we can be.

****

MEDITATION

Meditation to me is talking (to) my Higher Power. I try to find a serene awareness of my feelings. I ask for help and look for the answers throughout the day. Meditation is serenity. You have to trust the process even if you don't believe, willingness is the key. It can be a very spiritual process if you want it to be.

Written by: Pablo G.

TO BE PRAYER

Oh Lord, I ain't what I ought to be,
And I ain't what I want to be,
And I ain't what I'm going to be,
But Oh Lord, I thank you
That I ain't what I used to be.

When we improve our contact with our Higher Power through prayer, we are challenged to examine our heart and thoughts. Prayer demands that we ask ourselves:
Have we been silent when we should have spoken?
Have we been selfish when we should have been responsive to the needs of others?
Have we been thoughtless when we should have been sensitive?
Have we pursued that which is hollow when we should have reached for that which can hallow our lives?
We do not ask our Higher Power to do our will - we accept the challenge to fulfill His will

THY WILL—<u>NOT</u> MY WILL BE DONE.

STEP ELEVEN WORKSHEET

Sought through prayer and meditation to improve our conscious contact with a Higher Power of our choice praying only for the knowledge, the will and the courage to carry that out.

There is a difference between prayer and meditation, yet both of them are our principal means of conscious contact with our Higher Power.

This is the step where our spiritual awakening should occur. Previously we may have had numerous spiritual experiences but in this eleventh step we come to know, not only believe, there is a Power greater than ourselves.

1. Do you now, after working the first ten steps have a better perspective of your understanding of your Higher Power? Explain.

2. How do you feel prayer and meditation improve your conscious contact with your Higher Power?

3. How does it feel to ask your Higher Power for help?

4. In what areas do you still have difficulty turning to your Higher Power for guidance?

5. In what ways do you still cling to fears and anxieties?

6. How does this interfere with your relationship with your Higher Power?

7. Do you feel that you still concentrate on and exercise your own self will, rather than of your Higher Power?

8. Has prayer or meditation revealed some solution to you unexpectedly?

9. Explain what you feel your relationship with your Higher Power is today.

10. How do you think this relationship could be improved?

****

COMMITMENT

Commitment is what transforms a promise into reality. It is the words that speak boldly of your intentions. And the actions which speak louder than words.

It is making the time when there is none. Coming through time after time after time, year after year after year.

Commitment is the stuff character is made of; the power to change the face of things.

It is the daily triumph of integrity over skepticism.

STEP 12

"Having had a spiritual awakening as a result of these 12 Steps, we sought to carry the message to others and practice its principles in all our affairs".

The paradox of any 12 Step Program is that to keep it for ourselves, we must give it away. The more we give, the more we receive. It's a never ending cycle.

The awakening of spirituality does not come in one all-enveloping flash. It's an ongoing, never ending process. A journey that is gradual, progressive and healing. A journey that we take one step at a time, one day at a time.

When we try to carry the message, we don't try to convince, coerce or reform anyone. We cannot change anybody but ourselves. We can only share our story, our experience, faith and hope and use the 12 Steps toward our recovery. If someone has a hole in the soul, we can't repair it for them. Whenever we tried to fix other people we usually failed. You don't have to be a loser to become a winner. We must not focus on the destination but rather the journey.

We have found the best way to get stronger and get our minds off our own troubles is to try to help someone with theirs. As an old Chinese proverb says: "When I dig another out of trouble, the hole from which I lift him is the place where I bury my own."

STEP TWELVE WORKSHEET

Having had a spiritual awakening as the result of these steps, we tried to carry this message to others and to practice these principles in all our affairs.

This step requires action. It is now time to share what you have learned with the newcomers, in addition to continuing to practice the principles in all your affairs. This, however, does not put an end to your recovery process. The process will continue for the rest of your life. The twelfth step allows you to return what you have taken so that others may have the chance to share your experience, strength, and hope.

1. What changes have you experienced as a result of working the Twelve Steps?

2. How do you apply these steps in your life on a daily basis?

3. What does spiritual awakening mean to you?

4. What spiritual experiences have been the most meaningful for you?

5. In what areas can you continue to grow spiritually?

6. Have you noticed any change in your personal relationships since you started working the steps?

7. How do you feel you can share your experiences with others?

8. What is the recovery message you plan to share?

9. Explain how sharing your experiences with others can be a gift and further your recovery.

10. How do you plan to share your message?

11. Why is it so important to remember when carrying the message to others that actions speak louder than words? How do you plan to continue working these steps in your daily life?

****

If you care to write your experiences to be included in the next edition of our book so that others can relate to your life story and realize they are not alone and help is available (use first name, age, and geographical location), we would really appreciate it. Please write us a signed release and mail it to: The Institute For Phobic Awareness, Phobics Anonymous World Service Headquarters, P.O. Box 1180, Palm Springs, CA 92263

Extremes

The vast potential of your life
Your wildest dream exceeds
But if unvisualized, you're doomed
to mediocre deeds.

Life is a game of chance
and each must take his fling
The coward ventures not
The brave risk everything

The high souls take the highway
The low souls grope the low
While in-between on the misty flats
drift the others to and fro
for every man decideth
the way his soul shall go

So

Give me a life of intense emotion
Give me the joys of extremes
Life with the breath and the depth of the ocean
I crave a fullness, not dreams
Don't waste my time with a part of the story.
I want it all here and now
Peace and slow plodding may lead to glory
My fate is different somehow
Let me be classed with the highest or lowest
Only with these will my senses be keen
You'll find me either the fastest or slowest
I'll never rot with the dull in-between.

Chapter 3:
HOW PHOBICS ANONYMOUS WORKS WITH THE PROFESSIONAL COMMUNITY

HOW PHOBICS ANONYMOUS WORKS WITH THE PROFESSIONAL COMMUNITY THROUGH COOPERATION, UNDERSTANDING, REFERRAL AND RESPECT.

We'd like to introduce our Phobics Anonymous twelve-step, self help fellowship to those in the community who deal with persons suffering from the number one mental health problem in the world today: Anxiety and panic related disorders, which affect roughly 10% of the population. It is our desire to promote understanding, communication, cooperation, and respect, as well as facilitate the exchange of information between us, so that together we can achieve our common goals:

1. The diagnosis of the problem. (77% of phobics don't receive treatment because they are undiagnosed). Untreated anxiety can lead to the exacerbation of serious medical complications.

2. Aiding the recovery process of those persons to whom fear, phobias, acute anxiety, and panic attacks have become a controlling, debilitating entity in their lives, eliminating much of the joy and productivity, and substituting instead chemical and alcohol abuse, sadness, dejection, isolation, despair, and suicidal depression.

3. The encouragement to pursue some form of treatment for their anxiety disorder. Most phobics fear the stigma of mental illness (that is reinforced in our society) and therefore resist treatment.

The twelve step movement is sweeping the country as an adjunct therapeutic approach to a variety of compulsions and addictions.

Alcoholics Anonymous - more than 50 years of success. Overeaters Anonymous - more than 30 years of success. Narcotics Anonymous, Emotions Anonymous, Gamblers Anonymous, Debtors Anonymous, et. al. and now Phobics Anonymous, that specifically addresses fear, anxiety, and panic, which we have found to be the common underlying denominator of all 12 step groups.

Phobics Anonymous is intended to be a helpful supplement, not a threat to the professional community. It is an ongoing process for breaking the bondage of fears, phobias, acute anxiety, and panic attacks. To enable the suffering phobic to achieve wholeness, our program incorporates the spiritual aspect of recovery generally omitted by the other current treatment modalities.

Many of you who read our literature may balk at the idea of "spirituality" and the concept of a "Higher Power", so please before you tune us out and consider us a bunch of religious fanatics, read on. Then make an educated decision.

To those who have no faith in the existence of a "Higher Power" as a source of additional help that we as phobics need, ours may appear to be a rash claim, but it needs only a willingness and a fair trial. Our "Higher Power" does not need a name attached to it such as "God". Our conception, however inadequate, is sufficient to make an approach and effect a contact. Many of us were, and still are, suspicious and skeptical because of disappointments we experienced with organized religions. Some of us are Agnostics and Atheists, but still there is a spirit or an energy that can be felt at our Twelve Step meetings. We are a fellowship, and all of our members are free to choose the concept of a Higher Power that works best for them. For some the concept of a Higher Power can be the power of the program they are working. For others a Higher Power represents the goodness, compassion, caring, and support of the group they are attending. For some a force of creative intelligence, for others some aspect of nature or spirit of the universe.

We have found while working with phobics there must be a joining of resources: The best approach is a Multimodal-Integrated Treatment Approach. The intellectual, physical, emotional, and spiritual aspects are all related and relevant. They must all be addressed for the body to achieve and maintain balance. Recovery needs a program of effective therapy plus a 12 Step Support System.

It is only recently that we have seen the mainstream of scientific concern and The 12 Step programs merge closer. To enhance and further this relationship is one of our goals. When one can answer "yes" to the question "Do I now, or can I ever believe there is a power greater than myself?" When one is ready to admit that they are powerless over fear, anxiety, and panic. When one is ready to give up control and admit their lives are unmanageable, they are then ready to begin working the 12 Step program of Phobics Anonymous. Our program is not for everyone! We have no quick fix or cure. Just a process for improving the quality of life enabling the phobic to cope and become functional, thriving not just surviving "one day at a time". Phobics Anonymous is not intended as a substitute for, or to replace medical care and/or supervision. It is in no way intended to conflict with any form of treatment or therapy.

We strongly agree that professional services are essential in assisting, diagnosing, and treating the symptomatology presented, and for some phobics, medications are indispensable in the treatment of these devastating anxiety and panic related disorders.

At some point however, formal therapy can and does come to an end. Involvement in Phobics Anonymous is a much longer commitment which has proved effective and successful both as a continuous process of recovery and in prevention of relapse and setbacks.

The nature versus nurture controversy is moving closer to the Nature *Plus* Nurture.

Phobics Anonymous World Service Headquarters maintains a positive working relationship with the professional community in the Palm Springs area. We encourage and strive for that relationship to exist whenever Phobics Anonymous chapters are formed. We are not in conflict with any current treatment modality, such as, but not limited to:
*Psychoanalysis *Counseling *Cognitive Therapy *In Vivo Desensitization *Relaxation Techniques *Mental Imagery *Meditation *Positive Affirmations *Bio-Feedback *Nutrition *Vitamins *Exercise *Goal Setting *Behavior Modification *Stress Reduction *Assertiveness Training *Anti-Panic, Anti-Anxiety or Anti-Depressant Medication. "Different strokes for different folks". Whatever Works!

We are continually researching the latest findings on Anxiety and Panic related disorders, and searching for answers - Genetics? Physical? Hormones? Chemical Defects? Environment? Diet? Brain Abnormality? Mental? Emotional? Biological? Behavioral? or a Predisposition of the body that is triggered by stress?

We know the How, but not the Why. We also, unfortunately know that anxiety disorders continue to be disregarded as a serious health concern despite their widespread occurrence.

We know that people grow and improve much easier being around others who have had the same experiences.

There is a unique brand of conversation that occurs at meetings providing emotional companionship which can not be matched by the most highly trained caring professional who has not suffered, and thus has no personal insight into the condition.

Our only role is providing support and the spiritual component missing in other forms of therapy in a self-help support group setting; a setting which serves as an antidote to loneliness, isolation, and ridicule by providing an instant network of possible friends and support people. Through meetings and telephone contact, the group provides a safety net which is vital to someone in a crisis or panic state.

We are a fellowship of peers and are not an organization in the usual sense of the word. There is no bureaucracy and no intimidation. Anyone is welcome to walk through the door.

Each group is autonomous and without elected or appointed officers. Recovering phobics volunteer to serve as leaders on a rotating basis.

There is no cost to join (we have already paid a very

high price for membership and "paid our dues" by the devastation of our lives). We pass a basket at meetings and voluntary donations are used to pay our bills. We have no paid staff. After you give us a try, if you're not satisfied, your misery will be cheerfully refunded.

Before jumping to any conclusions regarding our effectiveness, we urge you to read our book *"The 12 Steps of Phobics Anonymous"*, send for our literature (enclose a legal self addressed stamped envelope and a small donation to help defray printing costs) or attend a 12 Step meeting. Speak to our members and ask any questions you may have. We welcome your comments and suggestions. We always encourage our members to seek outside assistance whenever possible.

We are a unique complement to, not a replacement for, therapy, medical treatment, medication, etc. Our program of self-help support groups are ideally suited for those who cannot find or afford local resources.

In conclusion, let me emphasize that our primary function and goal is to follow the Twelfth Step of the Phobics Anonymous program, which states: "Having had a spiritual awakening as a result of these steps, we tried to carry this message to others and to practice these principles in all our affairs."

"The largest room in the world is the room for improvement."

Choices

Choose to love rather than hate
Choose to laugh rather than cry
Choose to create rather than destroy
Choose to persevere rather than quit
Choose to praise rather than gossip
Choose to heal rather than wound
Choose to give rather than take
Choose to act rather than procrastinate
Choose to grow rather than rot
Choose to pray rather than curse
Choose to live rather than die

My Choice

My higher power moves within me
There is happiness ahead
No looming thoughts of trouble
Imagination instead
The small decisions that I make
When taken all together
Form the tapestry of my life
Woven tightly strong as leather

I can choose the good
That I want to fill my life
I can make the choice each day
Be it happiness or strife
I can choose in tranquil confidence
and select with serene trust
Fearless, calmly, positive
my attitude to adjust.

Chapter 4:
GUIDELINES
FOR ESTABLISHING
A PHOBICS
ANONYMOUS
CHAPTER

INITIATING A PHOBICS ANONYMOUS CHAPTER

If you are considering joining us, and establishing a Chapter of Phobics Anonymous, we welcome you to our fellowship. Here are some useful hints to help you get started.

1. Make sure you have sufficient time and are well enough along in your own recovery to get a Chapter launched because in the beginning although very rewarding, it can be a very time consuming and anxiety producing project.

2. Select a meeting place and decide on a convenient time (meetings should be held a minimum of once a week). Phobics prefer to meet at some "safe" place so they don't have to confront a new location each time the group meets. Try to have ample parking and a ground-floor meeting room (many phobics fear elevators). Recommended places are a private home or office where anonymity and privacy can be assured, churches, hospitals, bookstores, and banks are often willing to provide facilities. Make sure the room is equipped with comfortable chairs and a table to display literature and refreshments.

The room should be free from telephone calls and other disruptions or distractions. The temperature should be comfortably controlled and have an atmosphere of privacy with access to restrooms.

The room should be set up and in readiness before the meeting starts.

3. Your biggest obstacle after starting a chapter will be

to find additional group leaders. Phobics tend to shy away from leadership roles so be prepared to serve as leader for at least four weeks.

4. As soon as your chapter is formed, advise the Phobics Anonymous, World Service Headquarters of the name and phone number of the organizer with an appropriate contact and the meeting particulars. Each Phobics Anonymous Chapter should supply at least one contact and one backup contact. Please advise Phobics Anonymous, World Service Headquarters by mail of any changes in writing.

5. Have sufficient copies of *The Twelve Steps of Phobics Anonymous* and *From Anxiety Addict To Serenity Seeker* books on hand so that each participant can refer to portions of the books. A chapter of the book is read at every meeting and then discussed in terms of your groups needs. Photocopy The Anxiety Scale and the Phobics Anonymous Symbol (about one dozen of each to hand out at the meetings.)

6. Compose a press release to meet the particulars of your group. Send a copy to all local media (newspapers, radio, and television stations), mental health associations, public health organizations, churches, and Twelve Step (Serenity) bookstores, etc. This must be done a minimum of two weeks before your meeting.

7. You will be getting numerous phone calls in response to your publicity. The first telephone contact is extremely important!!!! Expect it to be a lengthy one since phobics are so excited and relieved to find someone who understands them, someone who can relate to their problems and offer help, they think they can get "instant ther-

apy" over the phone. Try to avoid this, but since we phobics are so sensitive, avoid cutting them off and rejecting them. Instead, encourage them to attend the first meeting with a support person (friend, family member, etc.). It will relieve the anxiety of going to an unfamiliar location, walking into a room full of strangers, being fearful about what will be expected of them, questioning their ability to relate effectively, and wondering about being accepted as they are and for what they are!

They must be assured that you and all other members of the group are people (phobics) like themselves who all share the common denominator of fear!

Stress the fact they will not be called on or forced to speak. They will not even be required to introduce themselves and are free to leave the meeting at any time their anxiety level peaks!

Explain that Phobics Anonymous is not a "Fix-it" group. Each member is responsible for his or her own recovery by attending meetings and taking the action necessary to get well.

Emphasize that Phobics Anonymous is neither a duplicate of, nor replacement for professional treatment and that we stay neutral on all treatment issues and most important, we have no religious affiliations.

Most of all stress that whatever is shared at meetings is strictly confidential as are the names of those who attend.

THE MEETING GUIDELINES/ ROLE OF THE LEADER

This is to be read by the group leader, either silently before the meeting to gain understanding or may be read aloud and shared:

The reason a Phobics Anonymous group works for some people when other forms of treatment have failed is because the support of the group gives each member the inner strength to confront their fears and phobias and overcome them.

"You alone can do it, but you cannot do it alone".

The primary purpose of a Phobics Anonymous group is to carry its message, of experience, strength, and hope to the phobic who still suffers. We are open to all persons experiencing fears, phobias, acute anxiety, and panic disorders. We must make it very clear that we are a unique complement to, not a replacement for medical care, therapy, or any other treatment modality.

Many of us have been, or still are consulting doctors, psychologists, therapists, psychiatrists, counselors, etc., and that is O.K. However, in addition to whatever else we are doing, we find the group experience is successful because it eliminates the feelings of social isolation so common to phobics. It encourages communication, the expressions and sharing of feelings with others who have experienced similar problems. In addition, the group may lead to friendships and of course mutual aid. Due to the support and encouragement of its members, experimentation with new behaviors, changing old unsuccessful patterns, and motivation for different experiences can be attained.

Personal problems lose some of their intensity when they are shared, and being able to help others makes it easier to accept help from others when it is needed. As a member of the group, we gain strength from the group. Our members attain goals they never could achieve alone.

A successful Twelve Step group relies on mutual aid and support. Everyone must contribute to help one another. Leaders of meetings are servants of the meeting. Inconspicuous and non-controlling, they don't "carry" the meeting. They merely <u>facilitate</u> it. Leadership is rotated weekly to avoid dominance by one individual thus offering all willing participants a chance to lead.

<u>Important Ground Rules for Meetings:</u>

1. There should be no symptom swapping or graphic details describing your condition. Instead refer to numbers on the Anxiety Scale to tell the way you feel.
2. There is no "cross-talk". We don't interrupt others. We are not here to "fix" problems.
3. Sharing should be limited to 2-3 minutes per person and sharing is strictly on a voluntary basis.

REMEMBER:

"I will not expect a whole meeting to
     give ear to my woes.
I pray that what I bring to it will help
     and inspire others, or pose a problem on which
     we can all sharpen our understanding"

4. Stick to the problem of phobias, fears, anxiety, and panic attacks. No other issues should be dealt with.
5. Avoid politics, religious dogma, and other divisive or controversial issues.
6. Avoid blaming and dumping on others, and self-pity.
7. Try to be completely honest and transparent, taking the risk which accompanies total self-disclosure, secure in the knowledge that nothing said will leave the meeting. Confidentiality and anonymity are safe-guarded.
8. Speak in terms of I, not we, or you. We don't give advice, nor do we tell others what is wrong with them. We are not a replacement or replica but rather a complement to other forms of therapy or treatment.

Refreshments should be available but keep in mind that most phobics find caffeine and sugar induce panic attacks. Therefore, we suggest: fresh fruit, vegetables, cheese, crackers, decaffeinated coffee, tea, or soft drinks. Fresh cold water must always be handy since anxiety and some medications cause dry mouth.

Make it perfectly clear that if someone feels trapped or anxious, it is acceptable to retreat or leave the meeting and return when the anxiety level drops to a comfortable zone. Always leave a door open (if possible) during meetings and point out locations of rest rooms.

Confidence

C oncentration on a stronger self-image
O ffer it full partnership in your life
N ever let it disappear
F ullfill yourself with your self image
I nfuse your self image with compassion when
you suffer setbacks.
D evelop it early every day - only your true sense of
self can make you strong
E levate yourself with your self image so that you need
not fear anything
N ourish it - it is basic to your happiness
C reate a climate in which it can grow
E njoy it - continually reactivate the success instincts and
the success mechanism within you.

Creative Day

C oncentration with courage
R eturn to yourself - look inward
E ars for others - hear what is being said
A ffirmations to reprogram negative thoughts
T raining in self-discipline
I magination
V ictory over fears
E agerness for recovery

D aily growth and progress
A djustment
Y earning for improvement

Chapter 5:
SUGGESTIONS FOR CONDUCTING A PHOBICS ANONYMOUS TWELVE STEP MEETING

THE ROLE OF THE LEADER

1. The primary role of the leader is to provide focus and direction for the group: to keep things moving smoothly and on schedule. The meeting should begin on time and end on time - no exceptions.
2. The leader should explain the purpose for which the group was established, since a group experience may be new to some phobics.
3. The leader's job is to help make the members comfortable and encourage a friendly, informal, supportive atmosphere.

**NOTE: The leader must clarify that the primary purpose of the group is to help members help each other. Therefore, a feeling of "groupness" must be established as quickly as possible.

4. The leader is the custodian and dispenser of the money received by passing a basket at meetings. Detailed accounts of group finances should be kept after the money is counted.

**NOTE: Phobics Anonymous, World Service Headquarters is entirely self-supporting. Therefore, members and group contributions make up our total support. It is suggested that each Chapter send regular contributions payable by check or money order to: Phobics Anonymous, World Service Headquarters. All groups are urged to develop some policy and means of contributing a share of excess funds after paying all group expenses in order to expand Worldwide Phobics Anonymous Twelve Step work. All contributions support the work of Phobics Anonymous, World Service Headquarters and are tax deductible.

5. The leader should receive prior written approval from Phobics Anonymous, World Service Headquarters for all literature displayed at Phobics Anonymous meetings. A list of suggested readings and books will be sent upon receipt of a stamped self-addressed envelope and a small donation.
6. The leader should have a sign-in sheet handy at each meeting so that contacts can be made between members.

**NOTE: Encouragement of using this list is essential so group members can receive additional support when needed. This enables them to break out of the loneliness and isolation. THIS LIST CONTAINING NAMES AND PHONE NUMBERS MUST NEVER BE GIVEN OUT. THEY ARE STRICTLY CONFIDENTIAL. Group members may exchange phone numbers if they wish.

7. After attendance at a few meetings when trust is established, the leader should point out how beneficial it is to seek out a fellow phobic who has progressed in recovery to act as a support person or sponsor.

**NOTE: This book gives directions for participation meetings, dependent on the leader and the group. There are other types of meetings which you might want to try after a while.

1. Speaker Meetings
2. Twelve Step Book Reading Meetings
3. Goal Setting Meetings
4. Practice Session Meetings
5. Combination of Speaker-Participation Meetings
6. Educational Meetings (to discuss some of the latest research, or newspaper articles on the subject of phobias).

WHICH BONE ARE YOU?

Any group is made up of Four Bones

1. There are the "wishbones" who spend all of their time wishing someone would do the work.

2. There are the "jawbones" who do all the talking - and very little else.

3. Next come the "knucklebones" who knock every thing that everybody else tries to do.

4. Finally there are the "backbones" who carry the load and do all the work.

GROUP GUIDELINES FOR PHOBICS ANONYMOUS MEETINGS

1. A feeling of confidentiality is extremely important to group work. What is discussed in the group stays in the group.
2. Speak with the first person "I". Do not speak for others.
3. Speak directly to individuals, not just to the group leader.
4. Speak from your honest feelings, thoughts and experiences.
5. Talk about what you are seeing, hearing and feeling in the group as it is happening in the here and now.
6. Do not have side conversations or whisper to others during group.
7. Be aware of your roles as they relate to the group.
8. Talk about how persons in this group remind you of other significant people in your past or your present life.
9. Try to have genuine interaction with others. Tell a person how he, or she, appears to you.
10. Expect periods of silence. Remember that growth will happen faster and in a deeper way in an atmosphere of trust, openness, and unconditional love.
11. Listen actively.
12. Give each member the chance to talk. If someone is dominating the group and taking up all of the time, be aware that you are allowing this to happen. It's okay to tell them how you feel about this.

**NOTE: Being in a group can be a very emotional experience; therefore, feelings, awareness, and anxieties may arise following a session. These are normal feelings and will decline as more meetings are attended and friendships and trust are established.

HOW TO COMMUNICATE AT MEETINGS

1. HEAR - What was said - concentrate on what is being said - Don't tune out.
2. ACCEPT - Wait to give verbal response.
3. CHECK OUT - Ask, don't assume! "What I hear you saying is_____?"
4. UNDERSTAND - What was said exactly.
5. AGREE-DISAGREE - after you have checked out:
    a. What am I feeling?
    b. What am I doing or responding - body language.
    c. If necessary, delay your response.
6. USE "I" MESSAGES.
7. TALK ABOUT YOUR FEELINGS - not about the other person. "When this happens, I feel_____ because_____".
8. BUILD SELF-ESTEEM - Your feelings count, be firm, assertive, not aggressive.
9. DON'T PEOPLE PLEASE - You just get angry at "them" and at yourself - then feel guilty for feeling angry - <u>BE HONEST!</u>

THE MEETING FORMAT

Leader introduces herself/himself.
1. Leader reads "Our Symbol"
2. Leader reads "Welcome"

    Hi everyone, my name is _____ and I'm a recovering phobic. Welcome to this meeting of Phobics Anonymous. Our meeting is for those desiring freedom from fear, anxiety, and panic who feel they can benefit from group support and self-help techniques.

    We have found that fear of public speaking, reading in front of a group, or even introducing oneself can be a traumatic experience for a phobic. Thus, causing a suffering phobic to stop attending meetings or to come late to avoid the experience of mandatory participation. Therefore, I must stress that nobody will be called on at any time. If you desire to speak, just raise your hand.

    Think back to when you were a child at school and the anxiety which mounted as either the teacher called on you or you went around the table or circle in reading groups dreading your turn. For this reason, Phobics Anonymous groups never "go around the circle", or unexpectedly call on people. We always allow someone to "Pass".

ALL PARTICIPATION IS STRICTLY VOLUNTARY.

3. Readings: Leader asks for a volunteer to read, "Who is a Phobic".
    Leader asks a volunteer to read "The Twelve Steps of Phobics Anonymous".
    Leader asks a volunteer to read "The Promise".

**NOTE: These should be put in plastic "jackets" and handed out individually to those who volunteer to read before the meeting begins.

**NOTE: The leader must be prepared to fill in when necessary if there are no volunteers. Suffering phobics are extremely sensitive. Just the physical act of getting the body to the meeting is a major accomplishment and the first major step in recovery.

4. Introductions: Leader: Let's take a minute to introduce yourself by first name only if desired. It is perfectly acceptable for a suffering phobic to decline introducing himself. Due to the nature of our problem, we are sensitive to the fact that even this act of speaking aloud in front of a group can precipitate a panic attack. Therefore, no one will ever be called upon.

5. Group sharing: Leader: The leader shares his or her own story, experience, strength and hope. The leader then reminds the group to limit individual sharing to a courteous time span of about three minutes and stresses all discussions are respected and confidential as is the anonymity of each phobic.

**NOTE: The attention of the total group should be channeled to the subject, fact or feeling being discussed (which is fear, anxiety, panic, or phobias). If members are unable to identify or relate to the problem, they are not inclined to participate in the discussion and probably will not return to future meetings.

Participants are encouraged to keep their sharing as positive and uplifting as possible, using numbers on the Anxiety Scale to describe their symptoms. This will alleviate the panic often caused by graphic symptom swapping.

All are encouraged to share any crisis, tears, or pain. The group is here to offer love, compassion, encouragement, and support.

6. Discussion: The leader picks a topic for discussion. In the beginning we suggest using *The Twelve Steps of Phobics Anonymous* and *From Anxiety Addict To Serenity Seeker* books for the 12 Step Interpretations and Worksheets. At future meetings, a theme such as honesty, powerlessness, surrender, denial, co-dependence, etc. can be discussed. The leader asks volunteers to share their feelings and related experiences. (Try allowing everyone who desires ample time to participate).

7. Donations and Announcements: At the conclusion of participation, the leader announces that we pass the basket to help defray costs of literature and help support Phobics Anonymous, World Services Headquarters. We do not have any dues or fees. Phobics Anonymous is entirely self-supporting and relies on your contributions.

While the basket is being passed, ask if there are any

announcements. This is the time to also ask for a volunteer to lead next week's meeting. When the basket is returned to the leader, it is time to make the closing statement.

8. Closing Statement: Anything you have heard at this meeting is strictly confidential. We are an anonymous program, so please keep the name or any information concerning our members private. What we say here stays here!!!

9. Close with Serenity Prayer, affirmation, or prayer of your choice.

SERENITY PRAYER

God grant me the serenity
to accept the things I cannot change,
The courage to change the things I can
And the wisdom to know the difference.

THE WELCOME (Read by Leader)

We welcome you to our Phobics Anonymous meeting. We are a group of people who share the common denominator of irrational fears or phobias accompanied by acute panic and anxiety attacks. We are here to share our experience, strength and hope.

Through following the Twelve Steps of Phobics Anonymous, we are on a journey to wholeness, wellness, and a life based on faith not fear.

We are pleased that you are here. We ask that you come here with an open mind and a willingness. Take what you want from our group dialogue and leave the rest. Please respect the confidentiality and anonymity of what's said in this room as we share and grow together in the unity of the Spirit.

We have found that fear of public speaking, reading in front of a group, or even introducing oneself can be a traumatic experience for a phobic, thus causing a suffering phobic to stop attending meetings or to come late to avoid the experience of mandatory participation. Therefore, I must stress that nobody will be called on at any time. If you desire to speak, just raise your hand.

Think back to when you were a child at school and the anxiety which mounted as either the teacher called on you or you went around the table or circle in reading groups dreading your turn. For this reason, Phobics Anonymous groups never "go around the circle", or unexpectedly call on people. We always allow someone to "Pass". *All participation is strictly voluntary.*

THE PHOBICS ANONYMOUS SYMBOL

THE EIGHT-SIDED OCTAGON is recognized as the universal stop sign. We in Phobics Anonymous chose this symbol to serve as a constant reminder that we must STOP catastrophic, negative, fearful thought processes and behaviors. We must STOP blaming people, places and things for our problems and begin looking at our own reflection in the mirror.

THE BUTTERFLY at the top of the octagon symbolizes the freedom we experience upon working the 12 steps of Phobics Anonymous. It is the most human of all insects for the pain of its metamorphosis most closely resembles the pain experienced in human growth and the struggles which the Butterfly undergoes to emerge from its chrysalis is what gives the Butterfly the strength to live.

THE INITIALS "P. A." of Phobics Anonymous also serve as a devastating reminder of Panic Attacks which have given birth to the fellowship of Phobics Anonymous.

THE SOLID DOUBLE LINE around the octagon symbolizes the fact that we cannot do it alone. When we change the "me" to "we", we gain a sense of connection with the help of our Higher Power, to gain strength, become healthy, whole and free.

Who Is A Phobic (Anxiety Addict)?

We are a group of individuals who found that we are powerless over fear, phobias, anxiety and panic. We experience irrational fears often accompanied by acute anxiety and panic attacks. At times we experienced the following physical symptoms (refer to Anxiety Scale) to such an extent that they made our lives unmanageable.

Our fear of fear - of being trapped in our emotions, made us feel we were either going crazy, going to lose control, or die. The perimeter of our world became smaller and smaller and we avoided situations, people and places, such as markets, restaurants, theaters, social functions, driving, job related activities, etc.

We sought help from physicians, clergy, psychologists, psychiatrists, nutritionists, hypnotherapists, family and friends. Many of us self-medicated with alcohol, excess food and drugs. All of these provided temporary relief. They addressed the physical, emotional and intellectual part of man. Yet, there was a missing link. We found the recovery process was incomplete without addressing the spiritual aspect of man.

THE TWELVE STEPS OF
PHOBICS ANONYMOUS

1. We admitted that we were powerless over Fear, Phobias, Acute Anxiety, and Panic*, that our lives had become unmanageable.

2. Came to believe that a power greater than ourselves could restore us to wholeness.

3. Made a decision to turn our will and our lives over to the care of our Higher Power, <u>as we understood our Higher Power.</u>

4. Made a searching and fearless moral inventory of ourselves.

5. Admitted to our Higher Power, to ourselves, and to another human being the exact nature of our wrongs.

6. Were entirely ready to have our Higher Power remove all these defects of character.

7. Humbly asked our Higher Power to have our shortcomings removed.

8. Made a list of all persons we had harmed, and became willing to make amends to them all.

9. Made direct amends to such people wherever possible, except when to do so would injure them or others.

10. Continued to take a daily inventory and when we were wrong, promptly admitted it.

11. Sought through prayer and meditation to improve our conscious contact with a Higher Power of our choice praying only for the knowledge, the will, and the courage to carry that out.

12. Having had a spiritual awakening as the result of these steps, we tried to carry this message to others, and to practice these principles in all our affairs.

*The words "phobias", "acute anxiety" and "panic" have been added to the original version of the "12 Steps Of Phobics Anonymous" to make them more inclusive.

THE PROMISES

- Recovery is an ongoing daily process that requires commitment and dedication that will lead to continuous progress and growth.
- We will be amazed before we are halfway through. We are going to experience a feeling of freedom and newly found happiness.
- We will not regret the past nor wish to shut the door on it but will use our painful experience as a stepping stone for growth.
- We will comprehend the word serenity, and we will experience calmness and freedom from fear.
- No matter how high on the anxiety scale our fear has peaked, we will see how our experience can benefit others, and in helping them, we will aid our own recovery.
- We will no longer fear or be anxious about how others respond to our feelings. Our need to be perfectionistic and people pleasers will diminish.
- We will no longer fear rejection nor being hurt by others.
- We will no longer respond in fear to other peoples' actions and attitudes.
- What we say and how we act will no longer be determined by our fear of others' feelings.
- We will no longer have difficulty expressing our feelings.
- Our serenity will no longer be determined by how others are feeling or behaving.

- That feeling of uselessness, rejection, abandonment, and self-pity will disappear.
- We will no longer be the nucleus of our own world but will gain an interest and understanding of our fellow phobics.
- Our self-will and compulsion for control will leave us.
- Our catastrophic and negative thinking and attitudes will change.
- Fear of people, places, things and situations will be replaced by faith.
- We will learn how to accept, cope with, and float through situations which previously panicked us.
- We will come to accept our Higher Power and realize our Higher Power is doing for us what we could not do for ourselves.
- We will gain the inner direction to stand and face our fears rather than retreat.
- Our shame, bondage, and self-made prison walls will crumble.

Are these extravagant promises? We think not. They are being fulfilled among us, sometimes quickly, sometimes slowly. They will always materialize if we work for them. A man would die of thirst if he failed to open his mouth to receive the water, even though there were gallons of fresh water surrounding him. So it is with the Twelve Steps - one must open up to receive them. Since even a thought, even a possibility, can shatter us and transform us. This is not the end. It's a new beginning.

THE ANXIETY SCALE

FUNCTIONAL

1. "Butterflies", a queasy feeling in stomach, trembling, jitteriness, tension, uneasy feeling.
2. Cold or clammy palms, hot flashes and warm all over, profuse sweating, shivering and chills.
3. Very rapid, strong, racing, pounding or irregular heartbeat, tremors, muscle tension and aches, chronic fatigue, exhaustion.

DECREASED FUNCTIONAL ABILITY

4. Jelly legs, wobbly, weak in knees, unsteady feelings, shakiness, need to sit, lean or lie down.
5. Immediate desperate and urgent need to escape, avoid or hide, inability to concentrate, focus or make decisions.
6. Lump in throat, dry mouth, choking, muscle tension, difficulty with swallowing.
7. Hyperventilation, tightness in chest, shortness of breath, smothering sensation, racing thoughts.

LIMITED OR COMPLETELY NON-FUNCTIONAL

8. Feelings of impending doom or death, high pulse rate, difficulty breathing, palpitations, change in eating habits.
9. Dizziness, visual distortion, faintness, headache, nausea, numbness, tingling of hands, feet or other body parts, diarrhea, frequent urination, sleep disturbance.
10. COMPLETE PANIC, non-functional, disoriented, detached, feelings of unreality, paralyzed, fear of dying, going crazy, or losing control, depression.*

*Frequently people experiencing their first spontaneous "panic attack" rush to emergency rooms convinced that they are having a heart attack.

STEPS TO A HEALTHY SPIRITUALITY

1. Clarify your purpose for living. We do better with our lives if we have a "why"?
2. Clarify your personal faith, search out parts of your religious tradition which speak of a spiritual being who will love and empower you to work for your own well being. Choose the path of peace and love.
3. Seek avenues of spiritual cleansing of bitterness or forgiveness.
4. Choose joy in life. Be in touch with all of the reasons to give thanks each day. Give yourself and your gifts to others because of who you are, not because it is something you "should" do.
5. Develop a method of prayer that fits your personality.
6. Involve the body in your personal time. Develop relaxation skills and don't forget to take deep breaths as part of your prayer and personal time.
7. Use your imagination. Visualize yourself reaching your goal of good health. See your immune system fight off disease.
8. Restructure your negative belief system. Get in touch with the unconditional love in your life which helps you think positively about how all things have a purpose in your personal and spiritual development.
9. Begin a regular, common-sense exercise program which becomes an important part of loving the gift of your life.

10. Use good judgement in your diet, partaking in those foods that truly nourish you. Use good judgement in your use of reading and the media, partaking in those cultural and artistic events that truly nourish your spirit. Fast from what does not nourish; feast on what nourishes mind, body and spirit.

****

SIGNS OF A SPIRITUAL AWAKENING

- An increased tendency to let things happen rather than make them happen.
- Frequent attacks of smiling.
- Feelings of being connected with others and nature.
- Frequent overwhelming episodes of appreciation.
- A tendency to think and act spontaneously rather than on fears based on past experiences.
- An unmistakable ability to enjoy each moment.
- A loss of ability to worry.
- A loss of interest in conflict.
- A loss of interest in interpreting the actions of others.
- A loss of interest in judging others.
- A loss of interest in judging self.

****

TWELVE TECHNIQUES FOR A BETTER LIFE

1. Positive Affirmation. Stating positively to yourself, who you are and what you can do.
2. Descriptive Technique. Describe the kind of person you want to be. The better you describe the route to your goal, the greater your chance of believing the positive affirmation and behaving accordingly.
3. Fear Technique. The better we understand the negatives we will experience if we do not achieve our objectives, the more we will be motivated to strive until we succeed.
4. Benefits Technique. The more we sell ourselves on what we will gain if we succeed, the more likely we are to persevere.
5. Vivid Imagination. The subconscious mind follows what you believe to be true, whether real or imagined.
6. Reward. Decide on the gift that you will give yourself if you succeed, or are in the process of achieving your objectives.
7. Honesty Technique. Your defense mechanisms may be so strong that, while protecting you, they may also be blocking you from your objectives. By being honest with yourself and determining what your defense mechanisms are, you have to push yourself to strive forward.
8. Forced Scheduling. Create a schedule that forces you to perform, but set realistic goals.

9. Commitment To Others. Here you reverse the fear of rejection and have it work for you by obligating yourself to someone who is important to you.
10. Competition. It often challenges us in a way that makes us operate at peak effort.
11. Leadership. By helping someone else accomplish something of value, you can often accomplish something for yourself.
12. Challenge Thinking. Instead of viewing an obstacle as a problem, think of it as an opportunity to prove how good you really are. Nothing is a problem unless you make it one.

****

TWELVE REWARDS TO THE TWELVE STEPS

1. Hope instead of desperation.
2. Faith instead of despair.
3. Courage instead of fear.
4. Peace of mind instead of confusion.
5. Self respect instead of self contempt.
6. Self confidence instead of helplessness.
7. The respect of others instead of pity and contempt.
8. A clean conscience instead of a sense of guilt.
9. Real friendship instead of loneliness.
10. A clean pattern of life instead of a purposeless existence.
11. The love and understanding of our families instead of their doubts and fears.
12. The freedom of a happy life instead of the bondage of fear, panic and anxiety.

Be A Winner

A Winner respects those who are superior to him
and tries to learn something from them.

A Loser resents those who are superior and rationalizes
their achievements.

A Winner explains, A Loser explains away.

A Winner says "Let's find a way"

A Loser says "There is no way"

A Winner works through a problem.

A Loser tries to go around it.

A Winner says "There should be a better way to do it"

A Loser says "That's the way its always been done here"

A Winner shows he's sorry by making up for it

A Loser says "I'm sorry" but does the same thing next time.

A Winner knows what to fight for and what
to compromise on.

A Loser compromises on what he shouldn't and fights for
what isn't worth fighting for.

A Winner works harder than a Loser and has more time.

A Loser is always too busy to do what is neccessary.

A Winner is not afraid of losing.

A Loser is secretly afraid of winning.

A Winner makes commitments.

A Loser makes promises.

Chapter 6:
GETTING RID OF "STINKIN THINKIN"

GET RID OF "STINKIN THINKIN" WITH THE FOLLOWING "FOOD FOR THOUGHT"

Each can be used as a topic for discussion at a 12 Step meeting or interpreted as a written exercise, or used to open or close the meeting. Also see to which step they would apply.

- Each day is a gift to you. Make it blossom and grow into a thing of beauty.
- A person who aims at nothing has a target he can't miss.
- Behind the idea that one calls one's own are the thoughts and efforts of many.
- When you're through changing, you're through.
- It is good to let a little sunshine out as well as in.
- Time flies; but remember, you are the navigator.
- We see through others only when we see through ourselves.
- The nice thing about teamwork is that you always have others on your side.
- Those who are ashamed of the past and afraid of the future don't find the present so hot either.
- We are like trees; we must create new leaves, new directions, in order to grow.
- Don't let life discourage you; everyone who got where he is had to begin where he was.
- Great Visions often start with small dreams.
- Most worries are reruns.
- The beginnings of all things are small.

- The best and most beautiful things in the world cannot be seen or even touched. They must be felt with the heart.
- You keep on getting what you've been getting when you keep on doing what you've been doing.
- Friendship is like a rainbow between two hearts.
- You won't strain your eyes if you look at the bright side of things.
- Incomplete termination interferes with new beginnings.
- It is what we are that gets across, not what we try to teach.
- When I do good, I feel good. When I do bad, I feel bad. That's my religion.
- We can't all be shining examples, but we can at least twinkle a little.
- There is no greater loan than a sympathetic ear.
- Treasure is not always a friend, but a friend is always a treasure.
- Loneliness expresses the pain of being alone and solitude expresses the glory of being alone.
- Live to make the world less difficult for each other.
- To dream of the person you would like to be is to waste the person you are.
- Life's a pretty precious and wonderful thing. You can't sit down and let it lap around you. You have to plunge into it; you have to dive through it.
- If you don't know where you are going, you may miss it when you get there.
- Long range planning is based on the premise that change is the order of the day.

- An optimist may see a light where there is none, but why must the pessimist always run to blow it out?
- If you don't enjoy what you have, how could you be happier with it?
- Each day slowly shapes our lives, as dripping water shapes a stone.
- Nature is filled with restorative processes that can heal all the wounds we have inflicted, if we will only give her a chance.
- Faith has to do with the basis, the ground on which we stand. Hope is the reaching out for something to come. Love is just being there and acting.
- One thing is sure. You can't have darkness and light in the same place at the same time. The cure for a gloomy outlook is a lighted mind.
- Who bravely dares must sometimes risk a fall.
- Whatever I have passed on has come back to me in word or deed. Whatever I have given I have gained and now still start the cycle again.
- The real voyage of discovery consists not in seeking new lands, but in seeing with new eyes.
- The great victories of life are often won in a quiet way, and not with alarms and trumpets.
- The day will happen whether or not you get up.
- Only in quiet waters, things mirror themselves undistorted. Only in a quiet mind is adequate perception of the world.
- A man must have his dreams, memory dreams of the past, and eager dreams of the future. I never want to stop reaching for new goals.

- Sorrows are like thunder clouds: In the distance they look black, but overhead they are hardly gray.
- The faults of others are like headlights on a passing car. They seem more glaring than our own.
- Our dilemma is that we hate change, but we live it at the same time. What we really want is for things to remain the same but get better.
- It takes as much energy to wish as it does to plan.
- Things turn out best for the people who make the best of the way things turn out.
- Man's mind stretched by a new idea never goes back to its original dimensions.
- Maybe the search is over and the journey has begun.
- We couldn't conceive of a miracle if none had ever happened.
- Vision isn't enough - it must be combined with venture. It is not enough to stare up the steps - we must step up the stairs.
- We are surrounded by insurmountable opportunities.
- It is not because things are difficult that we do not dare; it is because we do not dare that they are difficult.
- I have always been delighted at the prospect of a new day, a fresh try, one more start, with perhaps a bit of magic waiting somewhere behind the morning.
- Those who wish to sing, always find a song.
- A hard stretch of road is always made easier by a good traveling companion.
- What I do today is important because I am exchanging a day of my life for it.

- Your mind is a sacred enclosure into which nothing harmful can enter except by your permission.
- It is only with the heart that one can see rightly; what is essential is invisible to the eyes.
- Life does not require us to make good; it asks only that we give our best on each new level of experience.
- The miracle is this.... the more we share, the more we have.
- If you get some hard bumps, it at least shows you are out of the rut.
- It is not hard to find truth. What is hard is not to run away from it once you have found it.
- The farther backward you can look, the farther forward you are likely to see.
- We are so much accustomed to disguise ourselves to others, that at length we disguise ourselves to ourselves.
- Nothing is really work unless you would rather be doing something else.
- The doors we open and close each day decide the lives we live.
- In every winter's heart is a quivering spring and behind the veil of each night there is a smiling dawn.
- We are not put on earth to see through one another, but to see one another through.
- A candle loses nothing by lighting another candle.
- All the flowers of tomorrow are the seeds of today.
- Life is a measure to be filled, not a cup to be drained.

IRRATIONAL IDEAS
WHICH INCREASE ANXIETY

1. I should be thoroughly competent, adequate, and achieving in all respects.
2. It would be terrible if I were to make a mistake. (oops!)
3. I must meet my goals. If things do not go the way I want them to, it will be awful, terrible, or catastrophic.
4. When I am faced with a difficult reality, I must remain worried and upset until it is fully resolved.
5. My early childhood experiences must continue to control me and determine my emotions and behavior.
6. It is easier to avoid responsibility and difficulties than to face them.
7. There is invariably one right, precise, and perfect solution to a problem and it would be terrible if I don't find it.
8. I should become upset over other people's problems and I am obligated to solve their problems for them.
9. I cannot even tolerate feeling anxious. I should never be upset or angry.
10. I have a right to be dependent and someone should be strong enough (and willing) to take care of me.
11. Unhappiness is caused by other people or events and I cannot control my own happiness, (unless I control the other people).
12. A real friend will always know how I feel, and I shouldn't have to tell him or her what I want or need.
13. The world, and especially other people, should always be fair. Justice and mercy must triumph.

WE PHOBICS HAVE MANY STYLES OF DISTORTED THINKING

1. <u>FILTERING</u>: We take the negative details and magnify them while filtering out all positive aspects of a situation.
2. <u>MIND-READING</u>: Without their saying so, we know what people are feeling and why they are acting the way they do. In particular, we are able to know how people are feeling toward us.
3. <u>PERSONALIZATION</u>: Thinking that everything people do or say is some kind of reaction to us. We also compare ourselves to others, trying to determine who's smarter, looks better, etc.
4. <u>CONTROL FALLACIES</u>: When we feel externally controlled, we see ourselves as helpless, as victims of life. The fallacy of internal control has us responsible for the pain and happiness of everyone around us.
5. <u>SHOULDS</u>: Life should be fair. We should be rewarded for our sacrifices. We have a list of ironclad rules about how we and other people should act. People who break the rules anger us and we feel guilty if we violate the rules.
6. <u>EMOTIONAL REASONING</u>: We believe that what we feel must be true automatically. If we feel stupid and boring, then we must be stupid and boring.
7. <u>POLARIZED THINKING</u>: Things are black and white, good and bad. We have to be perfect or we are a failure. There is no middle ground.

8. <u>OVER-GENERALIZATION:</u> We come to a general conclusion based on a single incident or piece of evidence. If something bad happens once, we expect it to happen over and over again.

9. <u>BLAMING:</u> We hold other people responsible for our pain, or take the other track and blame ourselves for every problem or reversal.

10. <u>BEING RIGHT:</u> We are continually on trial to prove that our opinions and actions are correct. Being wrong is unthinkable and we will go to any length to demonstrate our rightness.

****

GOD GRANT US;

Gratitude to look backward and be thankful,
Courage enough to look forward and
be hopeful,
Faith enough to look upward and be humble,
Kindness enough to look outward and be helpful,
Strength in the days of weariness,
Trust in times of trouble,
Keep us slow to anger. Quick to forgive,
Eager to speak words of praise and endearment
Grant us,
Health of body,
Peace of mind
and Serenity of Spirit.

"BELIEVE YOU CAN SUCCEED AND YOU WILL"

1. Believing the "I'm positive, I can" attitude, generates the power, skill, and energy needed to do. When you believe "I can do it", the "how to do it" develops.
2. The "how to do it" always comes to the person who believes "he can do it".
3. Belief, strong belief, triggers the mind into figuring ways and means and how to.
4. Belief in success is the one basic, absolutely essential ingredient in successful people.
5. Believe, really believe, you can succeed and you will.
6. The "Okay I'll give it a try, but I don't think it will work" attitude produces failure.
7. Disbelief is negative power. When the mind disbelieves or doubts, the mind attracts "reasons" to support the disbelief. Doubt, disbelief, the subconscious will to fail, the not really wanting to succeed, is responsible for most failures.
8. Think doubt and fail... Think victory and succeed.
9. Belief is the thermostat that regulates what we accomplish in life. A person is a product of his own thoughts. Adjust your thermostat forward. Launch your success offensive with honest, sincere belief that you can succeed.
10. Believe in yourself and good things do start happening.
11. Think success, don't think failure. Thinking defeat conditions your mind to think other thoughts that produce failure.
12. Success isn't based on luck.

13. The size of your success is determined by the size of your belief.

14. Success is arrived at over time and is based on belief in ourselves, our abilities, and our worth.

15. With a strong and healthy belief in oneself, we can go out and survive the stress of day-to-day living and reach worthy goals. You as a person are always valuable, while your actions are learning experiences, not to be repeated if negative, and to be reinforced constantly if positive.

16. We are what we see, what we do, and most important... what we think.

17. When we look in a mirror, there are three reflections: the child of our past, the person we are today, and the person we will become. With the right role models and self-talk, we can change the perceptions that have twisted and colored our image of who we really are.

18. Successful people make life happen *for* them, not *to* them.

19. Success is the journey, not the destination.

20. The only difference between stumbling blocks and stepping stones is the way we use them.

21. How well you are actually doing is not the main issue; it's whether you perceive that you are doing well that counts.

22. Successful people learn from the past, live in the present, and set goals for the future.

23. Successful people make commitments to themselves and to others and keep both.

24. Successful people seek a solution in every problem rather than a problem in every solution.

HUGS

It's wondrous what a hug can do.
A hug can cheer you when you're blue.
A hug can say, "I love you so"
Or, "I hate to see you go."
A hug is "Welcome back again,"
And brings a rainbow after rain.
The hug, there's just no doubt about it
We scarcely could survive without it!
A hug delights and warms and charms,
It must be why God gave us arms.
Hugs are great for fathers and mothers,
Sweet for sisters, swell for brothers;
And chances are your favorite aunts
Love them more than potted plants.
Kittens crave them, puppies love them;
Heads of states are not above them.
A hug can break the language barrier,
And make travel so much merrier.
No need to fret about your store of 'em;
The more you give, the more there's more of 'em.
So stretch those arms without delay
And give someone a hug today!

HUGS

There's something in a simple hug that
always warms the heart;
It welcomes us back home and makes it
easier to part.
A hug's a way to share the joy and sad
times we go through,
Or just a way for friends to say they
like you 'cause you're you.
Hugs are meant for anyone for whom
we really care,
From your grandma to your neighbor
Or a cuddly teddy bear.
A hug is an amazing thing - It's just
the perfect way
To show the love we're feeling but can't
find the words to say.
It's funny how a little hug makes
everyone feel good;
In every place and language, it's always
understood.
And hugs don't need equipment, special
batteries or parts
Just open up your arms and open up
your hearts.

THE ADVANTAGES OF HUGGING

Hugging is healthy: It helps the body's immune system, it keeps you healthier, it cures depression, it reduces stress, it induces sleep, it's invigorating, it's rejuvenating, it has no unpleasant side effects, and hugging is nothing less than a miracle drug.

Hugging is all natural: It is organic, naturally sweet, no pesticides, no preservatives, no artificial ingredients and 100 percent wholesome.

Hugging is practically perfect: There are no movable parts, no batteries to wear out, no periodic checkups, low energy consumption, high energy yield, inflation-proof, non-fattening, no monthly payments, no insurance requirements, theft-proof, nontaxable, non-polluting and, of course, fully returnable.

Have you had a hug today? Have you given any hugs away? Never underestimate the value of a hug!

DO IT NOW

I expect to pass through this world but once. Any good thing, therefore that I can do or any kindness I can show to any fellow human being let me do it now. Let me not defer nor neglect it; for I shall not pass this way again.

JUST FOR TODAY

Just for today I will try to live through this day only, and not tackle all my problems at once. I can do something for twelve hours that would apall me if I felt that I had to keep it up for a lifetime.

Just for today I will be happy. This assumes to be true what Abraham Lincoln said, that "Most folks are as happy as they make up their minds to be."

Just for today I will adjust myself to what is, and not try to adjust everything to my own desires. I will take my "luck" as it comes, and fit myself to it.

Just for today I will try to strengthen my mind. I will study. I will learn something useful. I will not be a mental loafer. I will read something that requires effort, thought and concentration.

Just for today I will exercise my soul in three ways: I will do somebody a good turn, and not get found out; if anybody knows of it, it will not count. I will do at least two things I don't want to do - just for exercise. I will not show anyone that my feelings are hurt; they may be hurt, but today I will not show it.

Just for today I will be agreeable. I will look as well as I can, dress becomingly, keep my voice low, be courteous, criticize not one bit. I won't find fault with anything, not try to improve or regulate anybody but myself.

Just for today I will have a program. I may not follow it exactly, but I will have it. I will save myself from two pests: hurry and indecision.

Just for today I will have a quiet half hour all by myself, and relax. During this half hour, sometime, I will try to get a better perspective of my life.

Just for today I will be unafraid. Especially I will not be afraid to enjoy what is beautiful, and to believe that as I give to the world, so the world will give to me.

DON'T QUIT

When things go wrong,
    as they sometimes will,
When the road you're trudging
    seems all up hill,
When the funds are low,
    and the debts are high,
And you want to smile,
    but you have to sigh,
When care is pressing you
    down a bit,
Rest if your must,
    but don't you quit.
Life is queer with its
    twists and turns,
As everyone of us
    sometimes learns,
And many a failure
    turns about,
When we might have won
    had we stuck it out,
Don't give up though
    the pace seems slow,
You may succeed
    with another blow.
Success is failure
    turned inside out,
The silver tint of
    the clouds of doubt,
And you never can tell
    how close you are,
It may be near
    when it seems so far,
So stick to the fight
    when you're hardest hit,
It's when things seem worse,
    that you must not quit.

THE DIFFERENCE

I got up early one morning and rushed
right into the day.
I had so much to accomplish
that I didn't have time to pray.
Problems just tumbled around
and heavier came each task.
"Why doesn't God help me?" I wondered.
He said, "But you didn't ask."
I wanted to see joy and beauty
but the day tolled on, gray and bleak.
I wondered why God didn't show me.
He said, "But you didn't seek."
I tried to come into God's presence.
I used all my keys at the lock.
God gently and lovingly chided,
"My child, you didn't knock."
I woke up early this morning and
paused before entering the day.
I had so much to accomplish
that I had to take time to pray.

PERHAPS

Perhaps the reason prayer works is that God doesn't give advice or try to fix things.
God doesn't trample on our feelings by telling us we shouldn't feel that way.
Irrational as they may be, we sometimes have them in order to understand what's behind them.
We may be discouraged and faltering, yet God does not see us as helpless, so He continues to do what He does best - He listens.

****

After awhile you learn the subtle difference between holding a hand and chaining a soul.
And you learn that love doesn't mean leaning and company doesn't mean security.
And you begin to accept your defects with your head up and your eyes open, with the grace of an adult, not the grief of a child.
And you learn to build all your road on todays because tomorrow's ground is too uncertain for plans.
After a while you learn that even sunshine burns if you get too much.
So plant your own garden and decorate your own soul instead of waiting for someone to bring you flowers.
And you learn that you really can endure, that you really are strong and you really do have worth.
And you really are a child of God.

THE GAL IN THE GLASS

When you get what you want in your
      struggle for self
And the world makes you
      queen for a day,
Just go to the mirror and look at yourself
And see what THAT gal has to say.
For it isn't your husband
      or family or friend
Whose judgment upon you must pass;
The gal whose verdict
      counts most in your life
Is the one staring back from the glass.
Some people may think you
      a straight-shootin' chum
And call you a person of place
But the gal in the glass
      says you're only a bum
If you can't look her straight in the face.
She's the gal to please,
      never mind all the rest.
For she's with you clear up to the end,
And you've passed your most
      dangerous, difficult test
If the gal in the glass is your friend.
You may fool the whole world
      down the pathway of years,
And get pats on the back as you pass.
But your final reward
      will be heartaches and tears
If you've cheated the gal in the glass.

GOD, FORGIVE ME WHEN I WHINE...

Today, upon a bus, I saw a lovely girl with golden hair,
I envied her... she seemed so gay... and wished I were as
   fair.
When suddenly she rose to leave, I saw her hobble down
   the aisle.
She had one leg, and wore a crutch
   But as she passed... a smile!
OH, GOD FORGIVE ME WHEN I WHINE,
I HAVE TWO LEGS. THE WORLD IS MINE!
I stopped to buy some candy.
   The lad who sold it had such charm.
I talked with him he seemed so glad.
   If I were late 'twould do no harm.
And as I left he said to me:
   "I thank you. You have been so kind.
Its nice to talk with folks like you.
   You see," he said, "I'm blind".
OH, GOD FORGIVE ME WHEN I WHINE,
   I HAVE TWO EYES. THE WORLD IS MINE.
Later, while walking down the street
   I saw a child with eyes of blue.
He stood and watched the others play.
   He did not know what to do.
I stopped a moment, then said,
   "Why don't you join the others, dear"?
He looked ahead without a word,
   and then I knew he could not hear.
OH, GOD FORGIVE ME WHEN I WHINE.
I HAVE TWO EARS. THE WORLD IS MINE.
WITH TWO FEET TO TAKE ME WHERE I'D GO,
   WITH TWO EYES TO SEE THE SUNSET'S GLOW,
WITH EARS TO HEAR WHAT I WOULD KNOW...
   OH, GOD FORGIVE ME WHEN I WHINE.
I'M BLESSED INDEED. THE WORLD IS MINE.

This Is To Have Succeeded

To laugh often and love much;
To win the respect of intelligent persons
and the affection of children;
To earn the approbation of honest critics and
To endure the betrayal of false friends;
To appreciate beauty
To find the best in others;
To give of one's self;

To leave the world a bit better,
whether by a healthy child, a
garden patch, or a redeemed soul;
To have played and laughed with
enthusiasm and sung with exultation;
To know that only one life has breathed
easier because you have lived-
This is to have succeeded.

- *Ralph Waldo Emerson*

A NEW DAY HAS BEEN GIVEN TO ME TO EXPERIENCE THAT WHICH I DESIRE

How did I wake up this morning? With a heavy feeling wondering how I was ever going to get through today? Or did I wake up relaxed, ready for anything, and expecting only the best to come to me? If I awakened full of stress and tension, it's time to change my attitude now. Not another moment will go by with my thoughts still attuned to yesterday's problems and dilemmas. I have no desire to drag the old behind me into the new day.

I see that I can make or ruin the day by the way I approach it. At this moment, I wake up to the fact that I have free choice, and I will exercise it consciously. I will use this day carefully, knowing that time is precious. Enough time has been wasted in self blame, rigidity, and remorse.

If I have problems that need solving, I will keep myself open to all possibilities. With this attitude, I will find the help I need, possibly right before my eyes. I have much to learn today, and I am ready for wonderful things to unfold.

TEN COMMANDMENTS OF HUMAN RELATIONS

1. Speak to people. There is nothing so nice as a cheerful word or greeting.
2. Smile at people. It takes 72 muscles to frown, and only 14 to smile.
3. Call people by name. The sweetest music to anyone's ears is the sound of their own name.
4. Be friendly and helpful. If you want friends, you must be one.
5. Be cordial. Speak and act as if everything you do is a joy to you.
6. Be genuinely interested in people. You can like almost everybody if you try.
7. Be generous with praise and cautious with criticism.
8. Be considerate with the feelings of others. There are usually three sides to a controversy: yours, the other person's and the right side.
9. Be eager to lend a helping hand. Often it is appreciated more than you know. What counts most in life is what we do for others.
10. Add to this a good sense of humor, a huge dose of humility. This combination will open many doors and the rewards will be enormous.

SLOGANS

Face the fear and the fear will disappear.
Face, Accept, Float and let time pass.
Others need to help me, just as much as I may
    need their help.
FEAR is False Emotions Appearing Real
Courage is fear that has said it's prayers
Easy Does It
When the eyes can't weep, the organs will
Bring the body and the mind will follow
If you fail to plan, you plan to fail
First Things First
Live and Let Live
One Day at a Time
Let Go and Let God
K.I.S.S. - Keep It Simple, Stupid
This Too Shall Pass
Expect A Miracle
I Can't...God Can... I think I'll Let Him
If It Works...Don't Fix It
Keep Coming Back... It Works, If You Work It;
It Won't If You Don't
Stick With The Winners; Win With The Stickers
Identify Don't Compare
Recovery Is A Journey, Not A Destination
H.O.W.= Honesty, Open-mindedness, Willingness
Live in the NOW
Turn It Over
Utilize, Don't Analyze
We Are Only As Sick As Our Secrets
Be Part Of The Solution, Not The Problem

Keep An Open Mind
Willingness Is The Key
Don't Quit - Surrender
No Pain...No Gain
Go For It
Principles before Personalities
N.U.T.S. = Not Using The Steps
Before You Say: I Can't...Say: I'll Try
Don't Quit 5 Minutes Before The Miracle Happens
Gratitude Is The Attitude
H.A.L.T. = Don't Get Too Hungry, Angry, Lonely,
    Or Tired
E.G.O. = Edging God Out
Wherever you go, there you are
Stay in recovery for yourself
Look for similarities rather than differences
Try not to place conditions on your recovery
When all else fails follow directions
Count your blessings
Share your happiness
Respect the Anonymity of others
Let go of old ideas
Try to replace guilt with gratitude
What goes around, comes around
Change is a process, not an event
Sick and Tired of being Sick and Tired
To keep it, you have to give it away
Remember happiness and serenity are an inside job
Help is only a phone call away
Anger is but one letter away from Danger
Courage to Change
Easy Does It, But Do It

AFFIRMATIONS

Today I reward myself with thoughts of praise. I forgive myself and others.

I am always there to catch myself when I fall.

I will attain and maintain my goals with speed, ease, comfort and joy.

I see positive opportunities in everything I experience.

I encourage myself to conceive, believe and achieve my goals.

My enthusiasm spurs me on to success and prosperity.

I release and dissolve self-critical thoughts, feelings and images.

I now clear negative beliefs and accept positive influences in my life.

Today I am filled with new visions, dreams and inspirations.

I balance my feelings, my body and my thoughts each day.

I choose the contents of my mind, of what I think and feel.

Beginning now, I have all it takes to create and achieve my goals.

I give myself permission to be all that I can be. I deserve the best in life.

I restore myself and heal from my past. I no longer believe in old limitations and fears.

Now I release fears, barriers, and imbalances.

Today I approach myself with softness and gentleness.

I love life for the things it teaches me.

I see the world differently by changing my mind about what I want to see.

I express myself freely. It is safe to ask for what I want in life.

My mind encounters a problem as an adventure in a positive and centered way.

My heart sings and soars. Today I release feelings of burden.

I take charge of my life by maintaining positive attitudes.

I have many inner gifts worth unwrapping.

Today I support and respect all my feelings, thoughts and actions.

I face the future with confidence because I will achieve my goals.

My mind has complete control over my body.

My body relaxes at my command.

I meet my experiences today with courage, hope and confidence.

I am committed to recovering from my past wounds.

All difficulties I experience are perfect for my growth.

I have an energy for living and love of life today.

Each day is a new moment. I move forward with confidence and ease.

What I see without is a reflection of what I first see within my own mind.

I now dissolve barriers today.

I constructively use money to benefit myself and others.

I value and respect who I am because I like myself.

****

When thoughts enter my mind uninvited,
I do my best not to let them get comfortable there.

GOODBYE PANIC ATTACKS

Goodbye to the one I thought I was going to spend my life with. The one I had to take for better or worse. The one with whom I was going to share my anger, resentment, self pity, and self-centered egotism. The one that caused me the pain of rejection, the feelings of worthlessness, and the memory of the hurt I caused myself and others. You appeared out of the blue but now I can do the things you made impossible. I bought into your lie. With you gone, I can start the emotional and spiritual growth that you stopped when you controlled my life.

Goodbye, Panic

****

WITHOUT RECOVERY

Without it, I could not laugh. I only cried.
Without it, I could not trust or be trusted.
Without it, I could not love, I only hated.
Without it, I could not sleep. I only lay awake in fear of nightmares.
Without it, I could not smile, I only frowned.
Without it, I could not be me.
Without it, I could not live. I only wanted to die.

****

DEAR PERSON LETTER

Dear

I need to tell you something about myself. I have a problem caused by a little known condition called Agoraphobia. This is not a form of mental illness but a kind of anxiety which causes self defeating avoidant behavior to avoid having a panic attack.

I have found help for this problem by attending Phobics Anonymous meetings and am making progress. I still have some physical reactions and symptoms but at this point I am doing more things and want to do even more. However I still need to know that there's a way out of situations that are frightening to me.

Not many people have heard of Agoraphobia and very few understand it even though as many as 24 million people are affected by it. It is difficult and embarrassing to talk about a problem that prevents me from doing many things others can do, and that makes me appear different, but I need to share information about my problem with you.

You have probably heard of claustrophobia where people suffer a severe anxiety or panic attack in confined areas. Agoraphobia is very similar except that the attacks are triggered by many things such as crowds, distance from home, freeways, bridges, doctors, airplanes, supermarkets and so forth. I cannot control these attacks. I cannot anticipate when or where they will occur. It is not my fault I have them. But they cause me to avoid situations which might arouse this extremely uncomfortable and embarrassing reaction.

I have found that when I have permission to leave an uncomfortable situation and feel people understand, I can do better and it helps me in my recovery.

I don't ask that you understand my condition but I

would appreciate you understanding my predicament. I need you to allow me the privilege of leaving any given situation at any time when and if I need to.

Few people, other than those who suffer can relate to or appreciate the terrible, devastation of being imprisoned by irrational fears, depression and turmoil caused by the problem - being unable to do things others can do, unable to go where others can go, unable to participate in things outside a small area, enduring criticism, making excuses, being misunderstood, being blamed for troubles they didn't cause and over which they have no control (and being criticized for having a condition they don't understand and can't do anything about.)

In telling you this I am not soliciting your sympathy but I would like your understanding, compassion and moral support as I work toward recovery. I realize that the way I confront the problem may confuse you and even seem inappropriate but be assured that I have desperately tried other ways and am convinced the process I am using now is the only one that works, as it has already proven itself to other sufferers and to me.

Signed_____

LETTER TO MY FAITHLESS FRIENDS

Dear Fear, Anxiety, and Panic,

We haven't spoken for a while now and I feel the need to say some things to you. Our relationship has been going on and off for too many years, and it's time I bid you adieu.

You've lied to me so much and for so long that I had come to believe in you. The truth is, you stole away my deepest desires. You invaded all areas of my life and you were physically, spiritually and mentally abusive to me. You twisted my mind until you nearly wrung it dry, distorting every thought, feeling and emotion. You battered me so badly that I almost died. Believe me when I tell you now, I refuse to allow you to do those things to me ever again!

You've stolen from me on a daily basis, affecting my health and my mind. You stripped me of self-worth, self-confidence and happiness. You ran off with the respect of my family and friends.

Sure, you gave some things too. You showered me with loneliness, despair, feelings of unworthiness. You taught me to lie without guilt, to run away from responsibilities, to hide my emotions (even from myself).

Well, I don't want any more of your "gifts" so I'm returning as many as I can. We can no longer have anything to do with each other. Show up on my doorstep and I'll slam the door in your face, just as you slammed the door of my life. I'll be doing all I can to help others fight back against you .

Not that I won't be thinking of you; we've been together far too long for me to ever forget you. I know you'll get along fine without me - - unfortunately, there will always be someone waiting for you.

The damage you've done will be hard to repair, but one day at a time, with the help of my Higher Power, friends, the 12 Steps, and attendance at and participating in Phobics Anonymous meetings we will conquer you.
Goodbye!!!

****

A WINNER'S CREED

If you think you are beaten, you are.
If you think you dare not, you don't.
If you'd like to win, but think you can't,
It's almost a cinch you won't.

If you think you'll lose, you're lost.
For out in the world we find
Success begins with a person's will,
It's all in the state of mind.

Life's battles don't always go
To the stronger or faster hand,
But sooner or later, the person who wins
Is the one who thinks "I CAN!!!"

TERMINATION NOTICE

Dear Mr./Ms. Phobia:
This letter is to inform you that your services are no longer required.

When you came into my employ, you significantly implemented your services in eliminating my zest for life and relegated my feelings of fear, anger, frustration, depression, joy and happiness to your complete control. I have made the decision that I will not allow you to take control. I am the boss and therefore, I have decided that your employ is no longer required. You have bankrupted me physically, intellectually, emotionally and spiritually.

Your services which were once useful in disguising my real feelings, have been replaced. I have now employed (<u>Insert name</u>) to take over your position. I am much more qualified to make decisions as to what is good for me. I have begun to enjoy the benefits and good feeling, knowing that I am a worthwhile human being. As yet, I do not know how far I will go, but I do know that I am no longer alone and I will continue to grow and not remain rooted in the rut you created. I know that I can now accept and cope with my problems without your assistance. We have had a long personal relationship but I do not regret your termination.

Sincerely,

IT BECOMES A HABIT

I could handle things myself, and that became a habit.

I didn't face my problems, and that became a habit.

I started to be the problem of my family, and that became a habit.

I started to procrastinate, and that became a habit.

Except to bargain, I rarely prayed, and that became a habit.

I became sick, guilty and hopeless, and that became a habit.

I came to meetings, and that became a habit.

I started to work a program, and that became a habit.

I started to pray, and that became a habit.

I began to have hope and gratitude, and that became a habit.

I started to love you, my family and myself and that became a habit.

We can change our habits. H.O.W.?

Honesty, Open mindedness, Willingness,

"One Day At A Time".

****
THE SAME OLD CHOICES

When I got up this morning I was faced with
the same choices that I face every day of my life.
Is the day going to be a bore and a chore
or will it be an adventure?

LETTING GO

To let go doesn't mean to stop caring;
    it means I can't do it for someone else.
To let go is not to cut myself off; it is the realization that I
    can't control another.
To let go is not to enable, but to allow learning from
    natural consequences.
To let go is to admit powerlessness, which means the
    outcome is not in my hands.
To let go is not to try to change or blame another; I can
    only change myself.
To let go is not to care for, but to care about.
To let go is not to fix, but to be supportive.
To let go is not to judge, but to allow another to be a
    human being.
To let go is not to be in the middle arranging outcomes,
    but to allow others to effect their own outcomes.
To let go is not to be protective; it is to permit another to
    face reality.
To let go is not to deny, but to accept.
To let go is not to nag, scold, or argue, but to search out
    my own shortcomings and to correct them.
To let go is not to adjust everything to my desires, but to
    take each day as it comes and to cherish the
    moment.
To let go is not to criticize and regulate anyone, but to try
    to become what I dream I can be.
To let go is not to regret the past, but to grow and live for
    the future.
To let go is to fear less and love more.

Here is a list of words to help you get in touch with your feelings. Make copies and check how you feel on a daily basis. Feel free to make additions.

HAPPY
festive
enthusiastic
restful
relaxed
calm
complacent
satisfied
serene
comfortable
peaceful
joyous
ecstatic
inspired
glad
pleased
grateful
cheerful
excited
cheery
lightheaded
buoyant
carefree
surprised
optimistic
spirited
vivacious
brisk
sparkling
merry

generous
hilarious
exhilarated
jolly
playful
elated
jubilant
thrilled

DEPRESSED
anxious
cold
injured
proud
offended
distressed
pained
suffering
worried
unhappy
melancholy
gloomy
somber
dismal
heavy-hearted
quiet
mournful
dreadful
dreary

flat
blah
dull
in the dumps
sullen
moody
sulky
out of sorts
low
discontented
discouraged
disappointed
concerned
sympathetic
compassionate
choked up
embarrassed
shameful
ashamed
useless
worthless
ill at ease

EAGER
keen
earnest
intent

HURT
pathetic
desirous
excited
isolated

SAD
afflicted
sorrowful
aching
crushed
heartbroken
despair
tortured
lonely

ANGRY
bewildered
awkward
confused
belligerent
resentful
irritated
enraged
furious
annoyed
inflamed
provoked
infuriated
offended
sullen
indignant

irate
wrathful
cross
sulky
bitter
frustrated
grumpy
boiling
fuming
stubborn

AFRAID
fearful
frightened
timid
wishy-washy
shaky
apprehensive
fidgety
terrified
panic
tragic
hysterical
alarmed
cautious
shocked
horrified
insecure
impatient
nervous
dependent
engrossed
pressured

worried
doubtful
suspicious
hesitant
awed
dismayed
scared
aggressive
distrustful
petrified

PHYSICAL
taut
uptight
immobilized
paralyzed
tense
stretched
hollow
empty
strong
weak
sweaty
breathless
nauseated
sluggish
weary
alive
repulsed
tired
feisty
anxious

FEARLESS
encouraged
courageous
confident
secure
independent
reassured
bold
brave
daring
heroic
hardy
determined
loyal
proud
impulsive

INTERESTED
concerned
fascinated
intrigued
absorbed
excited

AFFECTIONATE
close
loving
sexy
tender
seductive
passionate
appealing
warm

DOUBTFUL
unbelieving
skeptical
cowardly
threatened
appalled
dubious
uncertain
gutless
questioning
evasive
wavering
perplexed
indecisive
hopeless
powerless
helpless
defeated
pessimistic
hesitant

MISC.
cooperative
torn
mixed-up
envious
jealous
preoccupied
cruel
distant
bored
hypocritical
phony
two faced
humbled

Chapter 7:
THE PHOBICS ANONYMOUS PERSPECTIVE CONCERNING MEDICATION

PHOBICS ANONYMOUS PERSPECTIVE CONCERNING MEDICATION

We in Phobics Anonymous believe that good health, be it physical, emotional, intellectual or spiritual is primarily a matter of taking responsibility for yourself and your actions. Nobody else, no matter how concerned, husband, wife, teacher, parent, friend, clergy, physician, therapist, etc. can do that for you. The choice to use or not use medication depends on your individual needs. Many members of our fellowship for whom antianxiety medication or antidepressants have been prescribed express fear over the possibility of physical addiction or physiological dependence, especially when well meaning but uninformed acquaintances or physicians criticize and urge them to "throw away the pills" and "stop using a crutch". Such negative attitudes and misconceptions toward the use of medication does nothing more than produce additional fear, anxiety and guilt.

The last decade has provided new powerful scientific evidence that anxiety and panic related disorders have a biological and chemical basis. Since environmental factors clearly play a role too, it makes sense to make available to phobics effective treatment modalities that address both biological and non-biological factors.

Before the use of medications for the treatment of anxiety and panic related disorders began in earnest, little practical progress was made. The vast majority of people received ineffective therapy or "snake pit" confinement. Recently however, dramatic progress has occurred, but there is still much room for improvement. While nonmedication approaches have accounted for much of that progress, medication must be credited for most of it.

We in Phobics Anonymous have seen how panic disorders can disrupt or even destroy life. It is imperative that phobics receive the most effective treatments. If medication helps, great; if it is not needed, fine. All medications are capable of producing side effects as well as benefits. Focusing on just the side effects without due attention to the benefits or rewards, is a disservice to medicine and to phobics. Non-medication treatments for anxiety disorders have disadvantages too, such as high cost, duration, uneven geographical availability and inconsistent quality. They often, unlike medications, have not been tested scientifically. They can sometimes, just like medications, do harm, rather than good.

Unless one argues against the use of all medication (which raises entirely different issues), it is intellectually difficult or indefensible to deny their use to those with anxiety and panic related disorders. It is also cruel. Widespread misinformation exists about medications for anxiety disorders. One of the most damaging, is the claim that these medications produce "mind control". That makes about as much sense as claiming other medications produce "body control". Both, when they work correctly, help the body or brain function more efficiently. If they do not provide benefits that outweigh their disadvantages, they should not be used. Only a phobic working with a physician can decide what their reward-risk value is.

To put the matter differently, a person with diabetes might need a medication like insulin to normalize biochemistry, while another person with depression or any other chemical imbalances might need a medication to normalize or adjust the brain's biochemistry. It makes little sense to refer to these processes as either "body control" or "mind control". No one would say that a person who needs insulin is the victim of "body control"; it is equally ridiculous to say that a person with depression or an anxiety disorder who used medication is victimized by "mind control". People who use these medications can tell you they do not "control" the mind any more than insulin "controls" the body.

A second claim is that the medications used to treat anxiety disorders, particularly antianxiety medications, frequently lead to "addiction". That is false. On the other hand, they usually don't but they can produce dependence. It is important to understand these terms and relate the issue of dependence to everyday life. People who worry about "addiction" fear being victimized by a substance. They worry they will crave more and more of it and focus their life on maintaining a supply of it; they worry that when they stop taking it, they will feel compelled to start again and get caught in a vicious cycle. That is a rational fear especially when dealing with a substance like cocaine, heroin, alcohol, nicotine, or caffeine, none of which has any positive value.

"Dependence", on the other hand, means that the body's chemistry has become accustomed to a substance and adapted to it's presence. When that happens, and the substance is removed, especially if it is removed suddenly, the body must go through a period of readjustment. For a typical patient, that readjustment is usually uneventful, but it can be difficult, depending on how sensitive the person is to the substance.

For an occasional person who drinks a lot of coffee or smokes heavily, for example, stopping can be tough. Difficult withdrawal effects can occur for a few days or weeks. Dependence can develop with many substances though for most people it does not become a problem.

The truth is then, that medications have positive medical value for people. Phobics rarely get caught up in "addictive" behavior. They rarely take more and more medication or end up struggling to secure a steady supply. Ask those who use them. Just the opposite is true. Phobics typically take no more than their doctors prescribe; they often take less. When they stop taking these medications, few people start up again compulsively. They may start again because they feel they still need the medication. Dependence can occur, but for most phobics it does not. When it does occur, it can usually be managed without difficulty.

Furthermore, the same dependence "problem" can occur with most other medications, but this fact is typically overlooked.

The medications people take for diabetes or high blood pressure often produce dependence. When their use is discontinued, withdrawal symptoms may occur. This is not evidence they are "bad" or "addictive" medications, but rather evidence that the body adapts to many substances after a while, and must readjust when those substances are withdrawn.

Because dependence should be a concern when taking any medication, particularly those used to treat anxiety disorders, it is considered proper medical practice to discontinue them gradually. With gradual tapering of the dose, under a physician's care, which can take weeks or even months, few phobics experience significant difficulty. According to a recently published University of Pennsylvania study, done under the guidance of Dr. Karl Rickels, some symptoms do occur when medication is discontinued. However, the symptoms were considered to be of mild to moderate intensity, not severe. The major symptom reported was the feeling of anxiety accompanied by restlessness and agitation. Others included loss of appetite, nausea, light headedness, increased awareness of sounds and smells, difficulty concentrating, feelings of weakness, tremors and insomnia. (It's interesting to note that all of these withdrawal symptoms are the same symptoms that people suffering from anxiety disorders experience before entering treatment. We must then ask ourselves when the medication is discontinued does it cause symptoms or is there only a return to the previous anxiety symptoms that were being suppressed by the medication?)

Phobics who have learned coping skills and have an understanding of how to deal with anxiety and panic attacks have a much easier time discontinuing medication than those who have relied on it to treat their symptoms exclusively. One is much less fearful of dying, going crazy, or losing control when one knows and understands what the body symptoms mean.

When you take a shot of penicillin for the first time, you risk a serious reaction or even death. But death is so unlikely and the benefits are so great, that society feels it's worth the risk. What the Food and Drug Administration looks at in deciding if a medication can be approved is, is it safe and effective enough to justify the risk involved in its use? In the case of medications used for anxiety disorders, it is clear that the benefits far outweigh the risks.

It should be noted that people with a history of substance abuse may be at increased risk of developing dependence with these medications, particularly the antianxiety medications called benzodiazepines. That does not mean these people should not use them at all. It does mean that the doctor and patient should carefully evaluate benefit/risk considerations. It also means such patients and dosage should be monitored closely. All of these concerns about benzodiazepine dependence and abuse can be put into their proper perspective by quoting a recent report from one of the country's foremost experts on substance abuse, Professor Roland Griffiths of Johns Hopkins University: "Benzodiazepines are among the safest, most effective, and widely prescribed of all psychotropic drugs (i.e., drugs used to treat emotional disorders). During the past decade, increasing concern about benzodiazepine misuse and physical dependence, often fueled by intense media attention, has sparked the erroneous impression that benzodiazepines have relatively high abuse liability. In fact:

1. patients who take benzodiazepines medically do not generally become abusers, except when they have a coexistent drug or alcohol abuse problem;

2. the incidence of nonmedical use of benzodiazepines is very modest relative to their widespread legitimate medical use; and

3. non-medical benzodiazepine use represents only a small fraction of a large and serious drug abuse problem in the United States." (Journal of Clinical Psychopharmacology, vol. 10, page 237, 1990.)

Unfortunately, there is an enormous stigma associated with having an anxiety disorder . A major need of those who are afflicted and whose lives are devastated by fears, phobias, and panic attacks is to be freed from that stigma. Criticizing those who need or benefit from medications only increases their anxiety and drives many away from useful treatment. The decision to use, and not abuse medication rests with the individual. Consultation with a physician or other professional is strongly recommended and medication should only be used <u>in addition to, and never in place of some other</u>

treatment. Modality such as a Phobics Anonymous or any other self-help support group, behavior therapy, exposure therapy, cognitive therapy, psychotherapy, etc. The phobic's right to make that decision should be respected and not interfered with nor discouraged.

****

Nothing in life is to be feared. It is only to be understood.

A habit cannot be tossed out the window. It must be coaxed down the stairs one step at a time.

Many of our fears are paper thin and a single courageous step would carry us clear through them.

To live well we must have
A faith fit to live by
A self fit to live with and
A cause fit to live for.

Worrying is stewing without doing.

Knowledge is the antidote to fear.

Chapter 8:
WE
GET
LETTERS...

Dear Phobics Anonymous:

Hi! My name is Steve and I'm a recovering phobic. I am interested in receiving information on how to start a 12 Step self-help support group. I currently live in the South Bay area of San Diego. I began my ordeal about eight and a half years ago. I had been working as a field supervisor for a general contractor in San Diego. I helped move people out of their homes due to fires. I also was on call 24 hours a day for emergency water losses. The work was very stressful. One of the first times I began to experience some panic was when I had to do some emergency roof covering. There had been some leakage at a house overlooking Mission Bay and one of the guys I worked with was already on top of this house and I was just about to climb up to join him. I was near the top of the ladder when I started to feel like something was wrong. I thought I was going to fall, so I got off the ladder and tried to assist my partner from the ground. He knew something was wrong but said very little about the incident. A few weeks later, I was driving back from a job site by myself, when I began to feel like I was going to lose control and just die! I started to breathe rapidly. I drove onto the shoulder of the freeway to get off. I managed to pull into a parking lot of a store, so I could try to calm myself down. I thought maybe I'm just hungry, so I ate some food I had with me. It seemed to help, but I began to develop an incredible fear of going places. I even went to doctors to see if there was anything wrong with me. Not a thing was found! One doctor said I might be working too hard and prescribed some kind of medication (Visteral I think). I had trouble keeping awake at work and a lot more difficulty going on jobs so my boss said to get some more help or I'd lose my job.

I went to a doctor not far from where I lived and was told not to return to work since he said I was suffering from nervousness, depression, and anxiety. He also put me on a prescription pill called Ativan. That was October, 1984. I spent a lot of time going to doctors trying to find a cure for what I had. I took a lot of pills. Even after I was diagnosed as being an agoraphobic, I was using the same type of medication for the panic attacks. I had attacks every day! Some doctors tried other pills but the Ativan was the only pill I was able to tolerate.

In March of 1988, I decided to try to get off the pills. I went to a drug rehab and was there 34 days. I was released to go to an empty apartment with terrible withdrawals. I rarely got out. My panic attacks continued. I finally went to a doctor who prescribed more pills and I was back to where I started.

After almost two and a half years, I decided to try again. This time I went into the rehab with a more positive attitude. I went to meetings and groups every day, exercised, walked and talked recovery. Sure enough, I began to feel like I could do it! I've been to various types of recovery meetings and have been making some progress. I try to keep active doing work on my folks' property planting, painting and other forms of handy work. I also write for a couple of environmental groups (volunteering my time so far). I have also been on a train to and from Los Angeles. I try to get out of the house as often as I can. I feel my best when I'm out doing some physical work outside in the sunshine. Last year I had foot surgery, so I'm doing the best I can getting around while experiencing some pain. I have been chemical free for two years and four months. The phobic group I had been attending on Monday nights was discontinued due to lack of a meeting place several months ago. I would like to get another group together, but don't know how to get started. So, that's where I'm at. I would appreciate any information from you on how to get going.

Thank you.
Steve

****

Dear Sir,

I am an economist cum company director, 54 years old, married with 2 children, and have suffered with anxiety disorder and agoraphobia for 12 years. I am currently doing my self help support exposure therapy (a cognitive behavioral treatment package mainly based on Dr. M. Zane's contextual therapy and other cognitive approaches) regularly which has helped me greatly in returning to the normal functioning of my mind and body for the last 15 months. At present, I am still not able to travel by air and/or enter a large and extensive enclosed shopping mall or a crowded underground commercial center normally without fear.

I shall be much grateful if you will help by sending me some of your pamphlets, newsletter and/or any other printed materials providing the latest information about prevention and cure of anxiety disorder and agoraphobia so as to enable me to work on my self help therapy more effectively. At present, the majority of the medical and health care practitioners at home are still very conventional and dominated by Freudian view. They mainly use conventional psychopharmacologic treatments in dealing with anxiety disorder and agoraphobia. I am interested and planning to organize a Phobics Anonymous self help group in Kuala Lumpur, aiming at assisting my country's increasing fellow agoraphobics by educating them with modern and effective self help knowledge and skills. As a recovering agoraphobic, my last 12 year devastated phobic life has really made me know how desperately the agoraphobic wants correct diagnosis and proper treatment to help return his/her normal life again apart from his/her dire desire of banishing the trivialization and stigmatization of this mental illness or disorder in our society, East and West.

I look forward to your support and assistance.

Yours sincerely,
Peter
Selangor, Malaysia

****

Dear Marilyn,

I hope it's O.K. for me to write to you. My name is Aine (sounds like Anya).

Tonight my boyfriend announced that he'd bought our tickets to L.A., to spend Thanksgiving with his family. The familiar headache and stomach upset following the news compelled me to write this.

For the last six years, social situations - be they family dinners, a cafe with a good friend, class room for staff meetings - all have produced in me the same situation. I am mentally crippled by the fear of blushing (which has frequently occurred) and then my feeling of being totally embarrassed and then being utterly confused and uncomfortable. I got through the University by avoiding brightly lit student areas, arriving late and using back entrances and keeping a low key. I would shop after dark. Basically isolating myself to "protect". I've missed out on so many good times - relationships. Others have suffered, as I couldn't be a consistent friend. I would find excuses to leave or not turn up all. They all sense my unease and naturally it rubs off on them, making them feel uncomfortable in my presence. I am so sorry!

I am hidden away in San Francisco. Returning to my family for Christmas (in Ireland) would be too difficult for me.

At 22 years old with a reasonable education, I chose house maid in a Yuppie hotel as my career, since it requires minimal interaction with others.

I laugh at the sheer craziness of it all and how far it has actually gone. But more often I cry for my lost youth, my burned talents and my deep pain and loneliness as I struggle through life every day in a constant state of fear and frenzy. I am a bad sleeper and have memory loss. I am sure this mental disorder has physical side effects.

Please send a copy of your book, *The 12 Steps of Phobics Anonymous*. Please, please, please send it immediately and if you can write me a note of advice or anything. I would love to meet or talk with someone who is currently experiencing this "social phobia" or who has recovered. Perhaps I'm a first...?

Thank you for reading,
Aine

Phobics Anonymous,

I am 28 years old. About 10 years ago I experienced my first panic attack while away at college. It was during final exams after my first semester of school. After returning home for Christmas vacation, the panic attacks continued and I found myself unable to return to school. The panic attacks continued and little by little I found the world closing in on me. I became unable to travel outside the confines of my hometown. Traveling a couple of miles to the beach, ski trips, vacations, all activities I had always loved, I was now terrified to do. I thought I was going crazy.

After about a year, when my life was becoming unbearable, I finally went for help. I saw a psychiatrist for about 5 years. I grew up in a family with two alcoholic parents and most of our sessions focused on the difficulties of my childhood. While I don't feel that these 5 years of therapy were a waste of time (I was unable to sort out a lot of my confused feelings pertaining to my parents drinking problems) the sessions did not "cure" my panic attacks. I did feel more in control of my life. I had been taught some relaxation exercises which help. I began going outside of my hometown. I took small vacations and ski trips, but very often it was a struggle to keep my anxieties under control.

A couple of months after I was married, however, the panic attacks returned in full force. I once again found my world crumbling!

A family friend recommended a psychiatrist. At my first visit with this psychiatrist, he told me that more and more research is being done in this area and that a growing number of professionals believe that anxiety attacks, such as the ones I was suffering from, were caused by a chemical imbalance. He recommended that I try a drug called "Imipramine". It took a little over a month to determine the correct dosage and I must admit I had severe anxiety attacks during this month over whether or not the drug would work and whether or not I should be taking any drugs at all. Little by little, however, I felt like a big black cloud of anxiety and despair was being lifted. Since taking Imipramine during the last 3 years, I have not suffered from one single anxiety attack! I feel like the old adventurous, outgoing me that was lost over 10 years ago. I feel very angry when I think of the pain I went through for almost 10 years ago.

I stopped taking the drug for about a year to become pregnant and give birth to a wonderful little boy. I didn't have any trouble with anxiety while I was pregnant (although I consciously avoided situations which I know in the past had brought on panic attacks). A couple of months after giving birth I felt the beginning of anxieties returning and along with the consent of the psychiatrist, decided to go back on the Imipramine. I feel great!

I feel very angry when I think of the pain I went through for almost 10 years before finding a doctor who knew how to help me. I don't understand why the psychiatrist I had seen when the panic attacks first occurred did not at least give me the option of taking medication. I got your address today from an article that discussed panic attacks. In this column they recommended support groups, Dr. Clair Weekes' book, a physical exam to rule out a problem such as low blood sugar, but nowhere does she discuss the possibility of a chemical imbalance. I wonder how many people out there are suffering as I did for so long who could also be helped by a drug like "Imipramine". Thank you for your time and help.

Marcie

Dear Sirs:

I am very interested in joining a Phobics Anonymous group.

I'd like to explain a situation to you for which you could be very helpful to me.

For the last 15 or so years I drank excessively to mask my phobias. During this period, in approximately 1984, I was arrested for distribution of cocaine. In 1985 I was sentenced to 5 years in prison. I was released after serving 17 months to the parole office in San Diego, California. After only 7 months I had violated a condition of my parole by being arrested for driving under the influence of alcohol. I was released after serving one more year. In June of '88 I again had violated a condition of my parole, served another 13 months, and again in January of 1991, I was arrested for D.U.I. and again my parole was violated.

This problem is all a direct result of a neurotic mother, which manifests itself usually when I'm tired and causes these panic attacks. For the past 14 months I've been working very hard to learn more about my problems, but have yet to find a way to conquer them. I have been seeing counselors and a doctor on occasion.

At present, I am again incarcerated at the Federal Prison Camp in Duluth, Minnesota, awaiting a parole revocation hearing. They will, no doubt, revoke my parole for the remainder of my time unless I can show them an alternative or give them a very good explanation, as I am trying to do with you, why I continue to drink excessively. It is a way of self-medicating myself to relieve the panic and anxiety but no one believes me.

I became aware of your organization through an article in the newspaper. I have always had hope to some day, God willing sooner or later, be able to again regain confidence in myself and to enjoy life. What a release, what a relief this would be without that God ugly fear of having one of those very intense panic attacks.

Thank you very much,
J.

****

I am 33 years old and suffer from panic attacks and more predominately, a fear of being the center of attention/public speaking. I shake uncontrollably.

I have been examined by medical doctors and there is nothing neurologically wrong. My psychiatrist states there is a chemical imbalance and I have been on Xanax for about four months.

I do not like drugs and would love to find a self help group of people who suffer from the same type of problems.

Do you know of any 12 Step programs in my area?

Thank you for your help,
Diana

Hi! I very much need the information on phobias. I am in prison and here you are forced to be around a lot of people and large crowds. For me it's a problem and I'm sure that I suffer from agoraphobia because of this. I do not eat any meals in the dining room here, because of the noise and people. I don't go in there at all so I eat off my canteen. Also, for 90 days I only came out of my room to shower once a day and to shop in the canteen once a month so it is very difficult and I need to know more about my fears and overcome them. Hoping to hear from you soon.

Thank you,
Beverly

****

My daughter, eleven and a half, has suffered from panic attacks for years. We have sought the help of a therapist. I think her aid from a support group would be significant rather than meeting with just a therapist.

I know she feels very alone with this problem.

My daughter was to spend the night with a friend last night. The first call for help came at 8:30 p.m., only one and a half hours after arriving at her house. The next call came at 9:00 p.m. She was sobbing, pleading with me to come "save" her. I reassured her, calmed her down and told her because I love her I would not bring her home, that I knew she would be okay. She was able to stay the night. It's indescribable just how it feels when your child is terrified, reaching for your hand and you have to let her handle it alone, not truly alone but to her, it feels that way. Please send me anything helpful. I need to know if I'm managing this appropriately.

My daughter will call soon when she wakes up at her friend's house. She will sound calm, glad she was waking up there, but aware that this monster, this fear will be back again. She does not talk about these issues unless she is in the midst of an attack. She acts like everything is okay and she can manage social situations. A support group and information would be life-saving.

Thank you,
Fran

****

I have been suffering from panic attacks for almost 20 years. In 1975, I was diagnosed as having a chemical imbalance and manic depressive illness. I take Lithium for this. However, even though I have been receiving professional treatment for my condition since 1975, I still have the panic attacks. It is very embarrassing and also limits me in trying to further my career because I get these attacks when I am in class, in meetings, in church, in movies, or in general, in a group of people in a controlled setting. I had to quit going to all of these, except I have to go to occasional meetings. These attacks, as a matter of fact, have gotten worse over the years. They also occur when I:

- am standing in line at the grocery store
- am driving in lots of traffic, traffic gets stalled, or sometimes when just riding in a car
- am on escalators (sometimes even elevators)
- am in crowded restaurants
- am in concerts, etc.

Now, these attacks occur even at pleasurable outings. I love to fish but sometimes it hits me when I'm in a boat. I have been suffering with this for so many years and nothing has cured it. The sad part is that it has seemed to get worse over the years. My world is becoming smaller because of my fear of doing things for fear of having a panic attack. Please send me information on how to combat this problem and also if there are any cures for this problem. Also, if there are any support groups in my area for this type of problem please let me know how to contact them. Thanking you in advance for your assistance. I remain.

Sincerely,
Linda

****

Please help direct me to a panic-attack support group. These attacks are affecting the quality of my life and destroying my mental health. I am currently seeing a counselor, but it is proving to be ineffective. I have been under a great deal of stress for the past year and I feel that I am near the end of my rope. My brother served in Operation Desert Storm and my father was killed almost three months ago in an automobile accident. Needless to say, these events have greatly affected and changed my life. Certain places trigger my attacks but the fear has invaded all aspects of my life. I live in a small town and I can't seem to find other people who share this problem. Please help me.

Sincerely,
Lisa

I have suffered from an anxiety disorder for the last fifteen years. I'm 24 years old now. My symptoms are: rapid heart beats, nerves, tense up, I secrete a lot of saliva. I am conscious through the attacks. I can't drive, walk, run, ride a bike, etc. The attacks last 15 seconds to two minutes. Can you send me some information?

Thank you,
Doris

****

I am 40 years old and I had my first anxiety attack on 4/1/91. It happened on my way to work. I was driving and I thought I was dying. I somehow managed to go back home and then went and saw my doctor. He prescribed some antibiotics to take but by the time I started them I already had three more attacks. I went on the antibiotics and hoped that would cure my problem. I was fine while I was on them and after a week of finishing them, I got another mild attack. Now I am really scared and I am afraid of driving because every time it's happened, I have been driving the car. I don't understand this since I have been driving in L.A. for almost 13 years.

I know I have to learn to deal with these but I'd like to be able to talk to someone who's had similar experiences.

I would appreciate it very much if you let me know how and where I can join such a group.

Thanks again,
Asmita

I came down with this disease in November of 90! I would like to hear from someone first. I'm a Christian woman for six years now, 28 years old, my word is good. This disease is terrible and I praise God that he has helped me this far, but need to talk to other people who understand what I'm going through!

Thank you for caring,
Pam

****

I would like to receive more information about your organization, Phobics Anonymous. I suffered from panic attacks four years ago, which eventually went away with medication and some counseling. They are now back and I am unable to drive for fear of passing out. Medication is not helping and I am very frustrated. We are new to this city and have no family or friends here.

Thank you,
Paula

****

Hello, I am interested in joining an anxiety support group or phobic support group. I am now seeing a psychiatrist for attacks of anxiety. I was nervous all my life. I am 39 years old. I had my first attack in May 1990, which I suffered at work since I had problems in the job. If so many people have anxiety attacks how come I only found a few at work who have experienced something like them, but their feelings are not ongoing?

I have had clusters of attacks for three straight months. I have feelings of them when I am nervous and now I am working two jobs so I feel nervous and anxious but I try and stay calm.

Will I ever be cured? It seems like a curse. Please send information on support groups and hurry.

> Thanx,
> Shellie

****

A few weeks ago I noticed a clipping in my local paper on your organization. I am a 46 year old white male who has had agoraphobia since 1966. Somehow, I was able to finish my schooling and land a good paying job and worked at this plant for almost 18 years. Because of the agoraphobia and work stress burn-out. I ended up with a nervous breakdown. I ended up on disability and am still on disability. I am seeing a local psychiatrist. I've also had some medical problems in the past five years but they seem to be subsiding. The pattern of the agoraphobia has not. It is the same, if not worse. I believe my local doctor is very frustrated with my progress. He has me on Xanax which seems to be help-ing, but it is not an over-night solution to the problem. The problem seems to run in my family, but I've just learned that recently. Obviously, my income is limited, but will enclose a S.A.S.E. along with this letter. I sin-cerely doubt if I could start a chapter but any informa-tion you may have would be greatly appreciated.

I wasn't diagnosed as having agoraphobia until 1987

and even that was after I was already approved for disability. Before that time I really just thought I was crazy or just strange.

Sincerely,
Thomas

****

I've suffered from panic attacks and agoraphobia since 1973, and I am very happy for anyone nowadays as there is so much information available and help. It took me until 1978 to find a therapist who understood what I was dealing with, and help me start putting my life together again. I'm assuming from the name that you are a twelve step organization, if so, I'm glad as I have belonged to one of the programs for five years now and have found it to be quite useful when I'm having a rough day with the anxiety.

Sincerely,
Cathy

****

I am interested in finding a support group in the area in which I live. Although no one has clearly defined for me that I do have a phobia, I have had several medical checkups and no physical defects have yet been found.

On July 20, 1990, as I approached the Baltimore Harbor Tunnel, I felt a rush of hot air. I felt as if I were going to faint. I pulled over to the side with a dull thudding headache and a general feeling of dizziness and nausea. I rested, then I tried to proceed through the tunnel and I felt as if any moment would be my last. There was a tingling in my left arm and numbness in my fingers. I felt light headed and the lights of the tunnel seemed to fade fast. I got out of the tunnel, but I have only driven a car twice since then. The chest pain, light headedness and headaches have now lasted almost a year. I have had an EKG, and EEG and several chest x-rays. I have had several blood tests among them a painful blood gas test.

Yesterday, I saw an ENT. He told me that my inner ears appear to be in good shape. Last month I saw an ophthalmologist and he gave my eyes a thumbs up. I saw a neurologist last summer and he said I should see a physiatrist, because he believed that my problems were being caused by stress. Personally, I think my neurologist was a quack himself. How much stress is involved in having a vacation, the first one in four years! Well, the more bits and pieces that I read about phobias I am seemingly convinced that perhaps that is where my problems lie. So any referrals that might help would be greatly appreciated.

Sincerely,
Yolanda

****

My first panic attack was four years ago. It came from nowhere, when I was driving on a major highway going to the doctors. Needless to say I never drove that highway alone again. After that first experience of panic my life changed right before my eyes. Before I knew it I was avoiding grocery stores, restaurants, stores, churches, and on and on. Then at age 24, 5'5" and 128 lbs I got down to 98 lbs and looked like hell. I never felt more alone in all my life.

Finally two years later was when I got my first help. I was accepted in a group at a local hospital for an eight week program dealing with panic attacks. It helped quite a bit. I also started to read Dr. Clare Weekes books and sent for her tapes. They are great. They came to me from Australia along with some information.

Today I've come a long way since my first attack. I just want you to know that we need some more groups and information out there for people.

Today now with three children I've come a long way since my first experience. I'm writing this letter to you because if I can help anyone who has this disorder it would make me feel great. I also would be helping myself.

Thank you,
Shawna

****

I began having panic attacks almost two years ago. I remember the first one I had, like it was yesterday. Even though it has been less than two years, I can hardly remember what my life was like before the attacks began. My panic attacks occur when I go to take a trip. As a business person, that opportunity occurs frequently. I live in dread of seminars. I have a family physician who did tell me that waiting it out is about all I can do. He said that counseling would probably be beneficial, but I live in a rural area and he knew of no one in our area that he would refer me to. In order to make it through trips, I have to take Xanax, an anti-anxiety medication. It makes me sleepy, so I have to take low, frequent doses to be able to concentrate. What misery!

My husband is very understanding and patient, thank God. It is so very distressing and frustrating to have the desire to go places but know that I can't. It is embarrassing to have to explain to family and friends why I don't go like I used to. Before the panic attacks began, I loved to travel and did every chance I got. When I look back on the trips I've taken in the past, I can't begin to imagine how I did it.

I don't really know what type of information you may want to send me, so I'll leave it with just the brief background I have provided above. I want, more than anything, to work through this and get it behind me. Any help you can provide me with will be sincerely and deeply appreciated.

Sincerely
Cathy

****

My name is Bob. For many years I have been scared to travel very far from my home. It seems I can travel up to 60 miles or less, but anything further I get seized by panic attacks. I have been sober in A.A. for almost 14 years and before A.A. I couldn't drive more than 10 or 5 miles away from home without a panic attack. The program (A.A.) has helped me some, but I don't seem to be getting anywhere. This problem has deeply affected my social life and I have had problems in personal relationships. I have been to counselors, but I don't seem to be getting anywhere. I read about Phobics Anonymous in the paper and it gave me hope. I live in Santa Barbara, CA. I don't know if there are any Phobics Anonymous meetings here or not. Please send me the information I need.

Respectfully,
Bob

****

I hope you might be able to help me. I have phobias of driving on the freeway, over bridges, and sometimes on city streets. I went to a doctor 10 years ago, but the pills he gave me just put me to sleep. My attacks are quite scary.

Thank you,
Steven

****

I have suffered from anxiety attacks or fear of them for years - sometimes worse at times than others. My problem is being in a place I can't leave if I need to. I am happy to say I can do many things now that I couldn't do at one time but also realize that I just live around the problem. I am very embarrassed for anyone to know about this and have tried to cover it up. Now I'm faced with my daughter getting married and that is a big problem. I can't see myself on the front row of the church and my ex-husband (her dad) and his family behind me. I get upset just thinking about it. I now realize that I need to face this thing and get rid of it. If I could get in a support group it might help.

Thank you,
Ann

****

I need any support or help or information you can possibly give me. Five years ago, at age 21, I had my first of thousands of panic attacks. Not knowing what they were, I ignored them. After several weeks of no sleep, losing 15 pounds, and a million types of phobias starting, I went to my doctor. He told me I was anxious and gave me some sleeping pills and valium. When I stopped taking them everything came back. I fought it off but to no avail. My inner and outer strength were caving in. I felt like I belonged in an institution. A year later I went to a psychiatrist and he gave me an antidepressant and another drug. I've been on and off medication for three and a half years now.

I need other help. Please I beg of you. Help me out in any way. Send me all information regarding Phobics Anonymous. I live in Staten Island, N.Y., and can go to Brooklyn or New Jersey for help.

I'm getting married soon and I want my life to be back to normal again with my new husband.

Thank you so much,
Leah

I have suffered with anxiety and panic attacks for over five and a half years now. In the beginning I was on Imipramine and Xanax. I was off these meds in a year and a half with no meds for a year. The attacks started up again - then I was put on Buspar for about a year. Since then I have been on Valium as needed. Last December 1990 I started with a series of headaches which lasted for three months. Drugs tried were Ibuprofen, Inderal and Anaprox. Finally they died down (I had them every day). Now my anxiety and panic attacks are back again full force. I have been on Prozac now for two weeks. I still need Valium. I guess it takes about four weeks for the Prozac to get into my system.

I will be 46 years old this month. My health is excellent according to my doctors (I have seen more than one). I just feel as if I am going crazy at times. I get head rushes when I feel panic, my swallowing is not easy at times and I am generally scared of each coming day and evening as I never know what it is going to bring.

I am very uncomfortable taking drugs so if you people can suggest an alternative so I can help myself or seek help from others, I would more than appreciate it.

Thank you so very much!
Janet

Can I get help from this group? My problems are twofold.

1. I jump out of bed in a semi-awake panic with a strange sensation (like I'm dying) after falling into a deep sleep. Especially when I feel overtired.

2. In certain unexpected circumstances, like when I soloed an aircraft the second time, I experienced puffing and hyperventilating, feelings of weakness, dizziness, that were uncontrollable. I had to land the airplane, and felt I was lucky to have landed. Yet when I have company in the right seat, these feelings very seldom surface and then only to the extent that only I am aware of something being wrong. Yet they do not interfere with my piloting the aircraft.

Although I have not flown alone since, I look forward to the day I can control my fears. I believe that I have not had enough experience controlling panic, but age and experience may do that for me. Is this possible? Your help is greatly appreciated.

Thank you,
John

****

I was reading the newspaper and I ran across an article on how people suffer from anxiety attacks. I can relate to those people. It's a feeling like you never had before in your life. About four years ago I was driving in early morning traffic on a two lane bridge. This certain morning traffic was heavy, school buses included. I went into one of those attacks right out of the blue. I went out about four times on the bridge before I got across. This scared me so bad I don't drive a vehicle anymore on account of those attacks. It still scares me to even think of hurting someone because I am very - very right with Jesus, I am going to Bible College to become a preacher. So any literature you could supply me with I would appreciate it very much.

Thank you,
Cord

****

I am not anonymous, but just totally phobic. Heights, open spaces, closed spaces, up, down, you name it. I have tried local medical help, also some Rx. I thought perhaps a support group may be what has been missing.

Sincerely,
Jane

****

In a recent column, I first encountered and became aware of your organization. I am now fifty four years of age, and was diagnosed as agoraphobic at age twenty five. With the exception of hospitalization in 1974 for a "nervous breakdown", I have pretty much been functional. I am, and have been employed full time, have raised a family, and for the most part, live an active life. This does not mean however that I have an absence of anxiety.

For the past sixteen years I have been a member of a

twelve step program, and largely, this has kept me out in society.

Recently however, I noticed an increase in anxiety, and a return to some avoidance techniques of the past.

For the above reasons, I am desirous of ascertaining whether or not you have a chapter in my area.

Sincerely,
Paul

****

Would you please send me some information on anxiety attacks? I have been experiencing the panic attacks on and off for some time now. I have finally come to know what they are and would like to get all the information I can about it. My son-in-law is also having the same problem.

Your friend,
Barb

****

After reading an article in the Virginia Pilot newspaper on 29 April 1991, I was very happy that a group was possible. Could you please send me any information you have. I, too, have been living with this disorder and hate my life.

Thank you,
Nancy

I have a sister who has very severe panic attacks. I would like any information you can give me. She seems to be getting worse, she is 62. I've heard of others, and I'd like to be of help. My sister isn't able to get out but we could meet at her place.

Sincerely,
Fern

****

Please send me any information available about support groups and also, if there are any such groups in the greater Boston area.

I suffer from anxiety and am having professional counseling however, I'm aware of the great benefits available with groups.

Sincerely,
Louis

****

I have anxiety and panic attacks quite often. I have seen a Psychologist many times, and it is no longer helping me. I am very interested in getting information on self-help groups in the St. Louis, Missouri metropolitan area.

Thank you for your time,
Cathy

I am in desperate need for something to help me deal with my fear of bugs. Mainly centipedes. I have them in my house and I am a nervous wreck over it.

Thank you,
Kari

****

Please send me information on anything you have. I am very sick in mind and body. I need help. Bad. My panic attacks are really bad and also depression and it all seems hopeless. Please help me.
Thank you and God bless you for this,

Ruth

****

Just finished reading a column about panic and anxiety attacks. Interested in any information you can send me. I suffer from panic and anxiety attacks which makes a prisoner of me. I need help! Is it possible there is a group near my home? I don't go on buses or trains. Would have to take car service. I am a senior citizen living on Social Security only!

Thanking you sincerely,
Glady

Please send me whatever information you have regarding the anxiety problems...

Have been fighting this problem for many years and have many times suspected it caused my "Asthma Attacks" and later led to distinct heart pains. Have just had an angiogram only to find doctors will prescribe Xanax and other medicines to calm me down but am wondering if you have some information that would definitely help my situation...

At any rate, thank you for whatever you can offer in the way of advice.

Sincerely,
Marge

****

Please send some information on "Panic Attacks" before I jump from a tall building.

Sincerely, J.F.

****

Please send me everything you've got on Panic Disorder. My husband has underwent a year of medical tests and with each negative test that came back, his "attacks" have worsened. He fears for his sanity and it has me very worried. Thanks a bunch.

Sincerely
Julie

Please send any information about how to get help with these horrible panic and worry attacks. I read about your organization in a newspaper column. I was not aware of any such help being available except through expensive counseling businesses, which I cannot afford.

Sincerely,
Marian

****

After reading a column in the newspaper, I have decided to ask for your material on panic attacks.
I have suffered the past six months with these attacks and don't know where to turn to for help.

Thank you,
Lucille

****

Please send me information regarding phobias, etc. I need all the help I can get.

Anne

I have had panic attacks for years. I read about your organization in a newspaper article. Please send me information. I really want to put this behind me and get on with my life.

Yours truly,
Caroline

****

My sister and I have been diagnosed as having "agoraphobia". My sister has had it for about seven years, and myself for almost two years. I have not been able to work, and although I am not housebound I cannot go a lot of places without someone I trust.

We have been going to counseling and support groups, ACA, and groups for all kinds of problems.

I think they are helpful and we have made progress, but I think a group that is more focused on phobias such as yours would be wonderful.

Thank you,
Janet

****

I hesitate to write this letter, it's almost like "what's the use" and yet I can't give up. I know there has to be an answer somewhere.

Briefly, in 1983 my family was hit head on by a drunk driver and I sustained a head injury shattering the windshield with my head. I returned to work about six weeks later only to realize I had forgotten my duties. I retrained (I was a secretary) and with much pain and struggle resumed my normal responsibilities at home and work. After a couple of years, I began experiencing panic attacks while driving and I'm sure you know the pattern. I even eventually panicked while shopping and reached the point where I cannot even stay home alone or go anywhere alone. After countless doctors and drugs (which I couldn't take) one doctor discovered an inner ear dysfunction that was caused from the accident.

By this time I had developed so many phobias I don't even have a life anymore.

I miss my productiveness and my independence fiercely!

Is there any hope for me?

Thank you,
Mary

****

I have been suffering since I was a child with what I have only come to know and understand now through therapy as agoraphobia. Now that I understand what is going on, I feel compelled to read anything I can get my hands on, on the subject. As well as talk with other people who have suffered and/or still suffering as I have.

Again, if there is any information you can share with me it would be very much appreciated.

Thank you,
Cori

I developed severe claustrophobia at age forty. I am now fifty-one years old and have recently experienced anxiety attacks. I have tried seeking medical help, but the doctors say I am in excellent physical condition. Any help or information you could send me would be greatly appreciated.

Sincerely
Nancy

****

My daughter is going through a period of panic attacks and I would like to seek her some help.

She is 24 years old and a musician and she teaches voice, graduated with a music degree, but her phobia of being in a closed room and the panic attacks when she is alone in her own home is overwhelming and taking over her talents.

She is on Xanax and is seeing a psychiatrist and reading self-help books. She's still afraid in the house.

Next week I will make her an appointment for a physical check up.

Sincerely yours,
Lorraine

I've been a sufferer of panic attacks for many years and have tried therapy and went through a program called Terrap. You may be familiar with it. It was a wonderful group and it did help a lot, but I feel that there's still a long way to go. My friend (who I met through Terrap) and myself would be very interested in joining one of your groups or possibly even starting one if there's not one in our area.

Thank you,
Marian

****

I have suffered from panic attacks and other anxiety related disorders for the past three years. I have gotten it pretty well under control; however, I do relapse at times. I currently live and work in Washington D.C. metropolitan area, but will be relocating to Glendale, Arizona to attend graduate school in the next couple of months. I am extremely anxious about the move and would be interested in finding out about support groups in that area. I would appreciate any information which you feel would be supportive in this move.

Sincerely,
Jennifer

My husband suffers from panic and anxiety. He has read many books but feels group therapy would be very helpful. We have checked with the local hospital and were told they do not have any kind of group that would be beneficial for him. Do you have a Phobics Anonymous Chapter in our area?

Sincerely,
Pat

****

Thank you for publishing information regarding Phobias. I lecture to small groups on Pre-menstrual Syndrome as well as Chronic Candidacies. So few doctors take the time to care for these sufferers. As a Naturopathic Preventive Health Practitioner, I have developed a specialty in these areas. As you know, phobias can be a part of the PMS Syndrome and your publication will aid me in adding new information to my lecture material. Any additional reading material you suggest will be most appreciated.

Sincerely,
Martha

I would greatly appreciate some information. I am currently being treated for depression and am seeking a support group, but none can be found in my area. I also would like, in the future, to start such a group so that I can help others who may be suffering from this illness.

Very truly yours,
Louise

****

Please send any information you have available for self-help groups which may be in my area or advice how to get one going. I believe such groups can and do help and Lord knows, I am in need. It is of great consolation to know I am not alone!

Sincerely,
Bunny

****

My daughter and I have both been recently diagnosed as having panic attacks. We are currently seeing counselors, but would be interested in any information that you may have regarding self help groups in our area.

Thank you

For a few years my friend and I talked about starting a group such as yours, but didn't know how to go about it. We're so grateful that you can send information that would guide us.

It's sad and ironic that in the same newspaper that held a column with your address, was the obituary of my friend's fifty-one year old husband. She's in a bad way now and could really use a group like this so that she doesn't slip back and become unable to function.

Many thanks,
Bette

****

I would like to receive information on anxiety/phobias. I'm not sure if what I experience has a "name".

Thank you,
Claire

****

Panic attacks have hindered me from traveling and would appreciate some more information on this subject.

I did confront my family doctor with the "inner-ear disfunction theory" and he seemed to not be aware of the problem.

The idea of a self help group sounds encouraging and will appreciate any help you can give me.

Sincerely yours, George

Hello, I am writing to get information for help in starting an anxiety and phobic disorders self-help group. I am a psychotherapist in private practice in my community and several of my patients have requested that I start a group.

Sincerely,
Barbara

****

I have had this disorder for seven years. I am currently involved in the Terrap program here in New Orleans, but not everyone can afford such a program.

I am very interested in starting a support group here in the New Orleans area. We need such a group that gives ongoing support and does not cost a fortune. Please send me any information you have on existing groups and especially on starting a support group.

Sincerely,
Scott

****

I am an attorney and practice law in Baraboo, Wisconsin. From time to time, I am contacted by clients who suffer from anxiety disorders. Please send me information concerning your general background information on anxiety disorders.

Sincerely yours, Dale

I work in an organization with an information and referral service.

We get many requests from those on disability with panic attacks. Private, or even clinic based therapy is not always affordable.

Thank you,
Alice

****

A friend gave me this address to write to in hopes of me finding some help for my agoraphobia and panic disorder that I have suffered with since 1978.

I am very grateful for any help, as I feel very desperate and I want to be my "old self" once more.

Thank you,
Terri

****

I would like to know if Panic Attacks can also be related to Neurotic Compulsive Behavior. I would like to know if Panic Attacks can be started from being harassed and over long periods of time induced stress, and if people who have phobias have cited these conditions as causes of their panic attacks?

Thank you,
Robert

I'm very interested in information on any groups of Phobics Anonymous in my area. I have suffered from panic attacks for eleven years. I am currently in therapy but believe a support group would help me too.

Thank you,
Linda

****

I am looking for a support group for Panic Attacks. I have been under a doctors care for the past four years, but do need a support group to help me get out of this terrible condition.

Thank you,

****

I received your address from an article. I am interested in any literature regarding anxiety and phobias. Although I probably would not start a self help group, I would pass the information to a local group I have attended. I feel this group needs better guidelines to function more effectively. Thank you for anything.

Sincerely,
Gloria

Could you please tell me if there is a Phobics Anonymous meeting anywhere near where I live? I am about 80 miles west of Toronto. Could you please send me information on starting a group. I have been a member of A.A. for ten years, a lot of my drinking was a crutch for my Phobias.

Thank you,
Len

****

I have been suffering for twenty-five years. My self confidence is gone. I need to find a job (I'm a single parent with two kids) and I'm scared to death. I quit drinking, I quit smoking, and I've been supporting us. But I live on the edge all the time. Thank you for any help.

Sincerely,
Connie

****

Please send me information about support groups relating to phobias. I get weird about heights and fears of hurting myself and my three month old baby. I have never acted on any of my weird thoughts, but I want more information and a support group would be great.

Thank you,
Nina

I need help desperately to do something about my panic attacks. I've been in three hospitals, had numerous doctors try everything, but nothing helped.

Could you possibly find any therapy group in the Springfield or West Springfield area?

This has been going on for three years and I really am desperate.

Thank you,
Priscilla

****

I'm seventeen years old and my parents were divorced last year and lately I have had anxiety attacks. I live in a very small town. Please send your information kit to me.

Thank you,
Donna

****

I would appreciate any information regarding your programs for my wife. She is having terrible panic attacks for apparently no reason, and taking too much prescribed medications (in my opinion). Thank you very much.

Sincerely,
Frank

I am not a severe phobic, but know how terrible an attack can be. I believe there are a few like me in this city.

Sincerely,
Lou

****

I am interested in obtaining P.A. literature, to possibly start a group in Toronto, Ontario Canada.

Yours in Recovery
Doug

****

It is nice to know that I'm not the only one who periodically suffers from these malfunctions, but it grieves me to know the extent of such suffering. God bless and keep us all. I wish you health with yours. Thank you .

Sincerely,
Joan

I am currently working with a group of clients that are dealing with varying levels of anxiety and panic disorders and would like for them to have a self-help group to use as an adjunct to or replacement for individual therapy.

Sincerely,
Carol

****

I am falling to pieces with Panic Attacks and have been since High School. No medical doctor has helped me at all, so I am appealing to you.
Your help would be greatly appreciated.

Betty

****

For at least five years now I have suffered from horrible anxiety/panic attacks. I am at the point now where I am afraid I may not be able to work any longer, which would be a disaster financially.

I would so greatly appreciate your letting me know of a support group near where I live. I feel that I could get help from one and am very much in need of that as said above.

Sincerely yours,
Marcia

For about seven years, I have suffered from panic attacks when having to speak in front of groups of people. I would like to do something about it and not let this fear control me anymore.

Sincerely,
Sandra

****

I am a young woman who suffers from panic attacks. I have had them off and on for almost three years. I've been unable to make them go away on my own, so I'm finally trying to get some help for my problem.

Sincerely,
Cynthia

****

I suffer from panic attacks. I think I'm going to die at times. I've even went to the emergency room.

Thank you,
Roy

As a professional social worker I occasionally encounter a patient who suffers with panic and phobia attacks. I would appreciate information on this subject plus a meeting directory for the South Bay area. Thank you for your help as I believe this will be an appropriate referral source.

Sincerely,
Lenore

****

My anxiety disorder has kept me at a job where I'm very unhappy and in general has ruined my life. I've been in therapy for almost twenty years. I'm 42 and I've tried all sorts of medication.

Thank you,
Robert

****

I would like to request information about your organization. I am a psychologist who works with adults and children with phobias, and would like to have information about your services so that I can share it with my clients.

Sincerely,
Vanessa

I recently saw your address in a newspaper column.

As a therapist, I periodically encounter clients dealing with a phobic condition of one sort or another.

Consequently, any information you can send me regarding phobias and your organization will be appreciated.

Thank you in advance for your attention in this matter.

Sincerely,
Bruce

****

Please send me any literature you might have on your 12-Step group. I read about Phobics Anonymous in the Chicago Tribune.

I, myself, am in several 12-Steps groups. I am also employed at a psychiatric hospital and think this program can be of great benefit to many of our patients.

Sincerely,
Barb

****

I have agoraphobia with panic attacks. I am 28 years old, and have had this problem for nine years. I also am hypoglycemic and have Mytro Valve Prolapse.

Thank you,

Per your article in the newspaper, I am requesting information regarding how to start a Phobics Anonymous group. Fellowship House is an alcoholism and substance abuse prevention and treatment center, and I feel that this type of self-help group would be very beneficial to some of our clients.

Thank you,
Mickey

****

I had my first attacks fourteen months ago (I'm 35). I got on a home program, $344.00, but I'm still on a low dose of Imipramine and still get attacks, sometimes. I've come a long way in a year but think a support group would be a big help. The woman I talked to from the course I took said a support group would tend to make me more dependent on someone else. But I think we could help each other with what we've been through and techniques that have helped us. I want to help others to know they're not going crazy, and help them with those scary feelings.

Thanks so much,
Valerie

****

I am suffering from severe agoraphobia. I have been to a psychotherapist on several occasions and have also just completed the Terrap program which both were very helpful. I do believe a support group however, is still needed in my life. I sometimes forget that I am not the only one suffering with this problem.

Thanks!
Kathy

****

I have been suffering with panic and anxiety attacks for six years now. I have been to the hospital and my doctor and both say I am completely healthy. My attacks started when I was and still am under a lot of stress. I've read a lot of books on the subject and they have seemed to help, but not completely. I would like to get into a support group in my area if possible. I don't know of any and neither does my doctor. If you know of any, I would really appreciate it.

Thank you,
Stephen

****

In a recent newspaper article I read about your help for people suffering from different fears or phobias. I have a daughter who has had a nervous breakdown and is now suffering from all sorts of fears, etc. which her psychiatrist doesn't seem to be able to help, except to give her medications. With grateful thanks and any help you might be able to give.

Pat

Do you have any groups in Finland? I have a former exchange student who lived with me for a year. She is 26 years old and has had to drop out of college. She is going to therapy and is taking medication for panic attacks, but both her parents, who are divorced and remarried, don't seem to understand and are giving her a hard time. She wrote me recently, because she felt she had no one else to talk to. She also asked me how this was treated in the United States. Do you have any suggestions for her?

Thanks,
Joann

****

Attacks are paralyzing me, I can not function very well at all and my fear of the next one coming up is unbearable.

Thank you,
Kathleen

****

I am now forty-six years old, I have been getting kind of panicky, (though I have never fainted) when I am in large eating halls with my friends (where I work), because I am worried that I might faint.

Very often, I pretend during these meals, that I need to go to the toilet, and I return after I think I have control of the situation.

I live in Venezuela, but I am using the U.S. address from where the correspondence will be retransmitted to me. I use this method because of the poor postal system in my country.

Yours sincerely,
A.M.

****

As Manager of a Women's Detoxification Center, I find that many women suffer anxiety, and drink to alleviate their symptoms. Please forward to me information which you have available on your Phobics Anonymous organization, and any information you may have on organizations in Canada.

Yours truly,
Norma

****

I too have anxiety attacks. My attacks start with the fear of losing control of my bladder. I am only 21 and have no prior record of this problem (losing urine). I become sweaty and also experience some dizziness like I am going to faint and feel the sensation of having to urinate immediately. I have consulted several doctors (gynecologist and urologist) until I was given a clean bill of health and told to see a psychiatrist.

There is a long waiting period in Montreal before you can see a psychiatrist.

I have passed an evaluation and I am now waiting for some kind of treatment. If you have a group here in Montreal, I feel I could benefit from meeting people with similar problems.

Sincerely,
Kristine

****

Having suffered from panic attacks for many, many years, I would appreciate receiving some information on help groups.

Yours truly,
Violet

****

I was sent this address by my mother because she knows that I do have a Panic Disorder and it's taken me a lot to convince the Doctor here at the Kinross Correctional Facility that I'm not trying to get drugs for getting high off them. But I did get the DOC (Department of Corrections) to give me the drug called Clonazepam (Klonopin) for my attacks. Now it took some time for the Doctor and me to agree on the right dose, but have gotten it to where I don't have my attacks now, and can feel better to function properly . I take 2 mgs. 3 times a day and have for over a years time now. My panic attacks have been in control and I'm so glad that I went over the doctor's head and wrote the head

Psychiatrist in Lansing, Michigan. I also wrote the ADAA (Anxiety Disorder Association of America) and they sent me a folder with a lot of information concerning Panic Attacks & Phobias that's helped me with this problem. I wanted to join their Association so I would receive a news letter with all the latest news concerning Panic Attacks but never did for I didn't have the funds here in prison.

Now I don't have a violent temper or record. In fact I got drunk because I didn't have my medication, and went into a house where I stole some things to buy more booze to control by attacks. And I was sentenced to 7 to 15 years in prison. Now I've been in ever since Aug. 19th of 1988 and I'm now eligible for a program that is called CRP (Community Residential Programming). But I've run into some trouble because of the drug I take. They say that I'm mentally ill and that I can't go. One policy states I can and another says I can't. Now I've written to a Professor of Psychiatry and Director of the Anxiety Disorder Program at the University. of Michigan. Plus he is on the Board of Directors for the ADAA. Now he has written to the DOC here and told them that my medication shouldn't stop me from being in this program. He wrote another doctor and Director of the Mental Health Division for the prison system. And he also wrote to the Director of the CRP programming. But they still have trouble understanding. It seems that I'm not that unwarranted "risk" like they have me classified.

Now I'm trying to get to this program where I'd live and go to work each day and spend my nights there. But these people, or should I say the DOC's Director and others just feel that my being on medication makes me nuts and crazy so I've written to them and sent them a lot of material concerning Panic Attacks. And I also wrote the

Doctor who okayed my medication years ago when the antidepressants made me sick. But they keep saying I'm crazy for having these attacks and just don't understand. And with all the material I've sent them all, I just can't see why they want to keep me from this program. My doctor here and all the nurses on staff say I should be given this chance to go to the center. I'm presently in the process of having a hearing on whether I can go or not. But the way things have been going for me, I don't have much hope that the outcome will be in my favor. And I feel the reason is because the director doesn't understand what panic attacks or phobias really are. Now he has the power to say yes to me going to this program, but I never received a letter in return from him about it. And it seems I've written everyone humanly possible about this issue of panic attacks.

Now I've been misconduct free, or in other words stayed out of trouble while doing my time. Plus I've gotten my SED, & took a Vocational Training in Auto-Mechanics. I am now in the process of taking the state certification tests to be a licensed mechanic in this state. Now if I'm nuts or crazy how could I do all this and have the backing of my doctor and the staff to go to the center? I know you don't know me personally, but neither did the other doctors who wrote letters to all I asked them to. But the one person who could really make a difference just hasn't heard all the true facts on panic attacks and phobias to make any changes in the rules concerning this program. Now I heard that the policies are in for some changes but that at this time I still have to wait.

So I'm asking you out of pure desperation if you'd write the director here in Michigan and explain what a panic attack is and that I'm not crazy for having them.

I'll understand if you don't reply, Marilyn but I pray in God's name that you'll see that I'm not trying to pull the wool over anyone's eyes and that I'm truly sincere about getting out and starting over for my future. A letter from you to the director would help in this matter. I still intend to write some Newspapers about this issue of discrimination for going to a program that'll help me and the state out. I know that I'm asking a lot from you but this issue needs to be addressed!!! And not just for my sake but for others who have the same problems of panic attacks and phobias.

I do hope you'll read this and do what you can for me without causing you any inconveniences that you have in your daily schedule. But I know that I wrote and haven't received any letter in return about this issue. I feel it was just handled by someone else with less authority and that he doesn't even know of the problems concerning me or the issue of this degree.

I do thank you for your time and pray that you will write them about me and this issue. It may not seem like much of an issue to others but this is my life and others we're talking about. I just feel you could make that difference so I thank you again and hope to hear from you soon.

Sincerely & respectfully yours,
Stephen

Please help me. I've got Erythrophobia, which is the fear of blushing. (I've also got obsessive-compulsive disorder, I think.)

Here's my life story: As a child I was incredibly shy. (Some members of one side of my family are very shy also.) Being shy, self-conscious, and very fair-skinned, I would blush easily. It didn't disrupt my life though. But in my early adult years the blushing got worse, much worse. I would blush more often, sometimes getting as red as a tomato. That was years ago and things haven't changed.

I don't know much about masochism, but I've been wondering if the blushing is something like masochism, because it's like I torture myself. It's like I need to be punished or something - the more pain I experience, the better. (I'm not at all a violent person.) This disorder, which I've had since I was a child, has made me have very high standards for myself. I started being this "perfectionist". I started thinking I had to be perfect, and if I didn't get perfect and stay perfect I was no good.

This is what I'm like - If I'm around people and I start to blush, I immediately panic and think "Oh no, I'm starting to blush!" The more important it is that I don't blush, the more I do blush. If there are many people around me I'm going to think "I can't blush, not now! There are all these people here who might see me blush!" Since there are so many people around me I'll probably wind up being as red as a tomato. If there had been only one person around me there would be much less chance I would blush, and if that person had poor eyesight there would've been virtually no chance I would blush.

The Erythrophobia has made me a recluse. The emotional pain I feel when people see me blush is so excruciating, I do the only thing possible - I stay to myself. It's virtually impossible for me to have a job. The psychologist I've been seeing for the last few years keeps trying to get me to apply for Social Security, but I feel if I do get Social Security it might do much more harm than good. I think it could lower my self esteem. (I've also seen a psychiatrist, by the way.)

I'm always trying to think of what I can do to make the Erythrophobia less of a problem. If you know of anything that will help me (medications, books, magazines, things I can do, etc.) would you let me know? I've been reading about alcohol. Based on some things I've read it seems alcohol might help. But based on other things I've read it seems alcohol might not help. Surely you have information on alcohol and similar things. I hope you won't be reluctant to send information on alcohol - I think I'm old enough, wise enough, and cautious enough that there's not much chance I'll become an alcoholic if I do try alcohol. If I do try it, I'll let my doctor know. I welcome any opinions you have, but I really just want the facts.

Please have everyone with knowledge of erythrophobia read this letter. I'll appreciate anything you send me, but also please do everything you can to answer each of the questions I asked in this letter.

Send your response to my doctor

Marilyn,

Please don't interpret my brevity as being insincere, for I have written very few letters in forty years, but never have written a more sincere letter than this one.

Thanks to you, the time you gave personally, especially in those crowded group sessions, my life is nearly back to normal after two very trying and strenuous years. It's hard to believe now, that when I first came to your home in desperation (after seeing a dozen different doctors with no satisfaction), that I couldn't even walk across the street alone. You proved to me that I wasn't going crazy, but was only over stressed and filled with anxiety. You told me to believe in myself and follow the directions in Dr. Weeks' books. Thank you, for you were right, and the combination of your group sessions and Dr. Weeks' books have totally changed my life for the better. I now travel freely and at will, by myself, without any need for any drug. It's impossible to express my gratitude in letter form, so for now I will say, if there is any way I can ever assist you or the troubled men and women you give of your time and effort to help, please do not hesitate to call me.

Forever invested,
Tommy

****

I am writing this letter with great admiration and thanks to Phobics Anonymous, a self-help support group I belong to. P.A. and its founder/director, Marilyn, have helped me find the road to recovery from the horrible panic anxiety disorder (agoraphobia) that I suffer from. Through the group I have discovered that I am not the only person that suffers from this affliction. I felt very alone and that I was possibly going crazy. I could not make anyone (doctors and hospitals included) understand the sheer panic or anxiety I felt just by walking out my front door, or driving, or doing any "normal" activity outside my home (my safe place). I have had this condition since I was 18 years of age (I am 30 years old at present). I have had two remissions in my condition (meaning I could lead a normal life without limitations). I believe I am working on a third remission thanks to all the love and support I get from our group. I am able to do more things with little to no discomfort. Activities or outings that about six months ago I could only think about doing, I am doing now.

I have been hospitalized three times. In all cases, misdiagnosed. Thousands of dollars, tears, and fears later, I was finally referred to Marilyn. Had a Phobics Anonymous group for agoraphobics existed then, I would have saved a lot of pain, incorrect medication, and money. There are many people besides myself afflicted with panic/anxiety related disorders, just think how this support group could help these people. This fellowship is one of a kind. It is run by recovering agoraphobics, which is a plus, because if you have never had a panic attack it is very difficult to understand what is happening to that person at that time. Plus helping people is such good therapy for everyone.

Sincerely,
Joy
Recovering Agoraphobic

I am writing this letter on behalf of Phobics Anonymous and to share with you a little of my story. I started having panic attacks in 1975. At the time I was having them I thought I was going crazy and I was embarrassed about them. I didn't talk to anyone about this, because I thought no one would understand at the time. I was only 20 years old then. My panic attacks kept going on for years, but I tried to block them out like it wasn't happening. I know that these panic attacks stopped me from functioning in our society. I became very isolated and depressed, and afraid of social situations, and my self esteem was shot. I thought I was crazy or mentally ill. I became very depressed in December 1984, and had to be hospitalized. I was misdiagnosed and was given no medication for my condition. I just stumbled along with my life for the next couple of years trying to do the best I could. Then, in October 1985, I was so full of fear that I couldn't come out of my house for the fear that I was going to die or go crazy. When these panic attacks hit, my heart races fast, I feel like I'm losing control of my mind, and I'm going to die. I was hospitalized again and told them of my attacks and the depression I have. They again misdiagnosed me and just dealt with my childhood. They gave me some anti-depressants and sent me on my way.

It wasn't until I went to a doctor in Palm Springs who understood the problem and referred me to Marilyn. In the Phobics Anonymous group I felt I was not alone any more, or crazy, or was going to die from this. At the meetings we discuss our fears, problems and support each other and get the latest education about panic attacks.

Until I started attending the weekly meeting, I couldn't drive my car alone or work or go to supermarkets or social functions. Now I am working and driving alone and am not afraid of social situations anymore. I am still recovering, but I know I can understand my problem and can deal with it and accept it most of the time and function in society.

Sincerely,
Norbert

****

Two and a half years ago I could not leave my home alone or go to the grocery store, restaurants or theaters. I was also not able to leave the desert area away from my safe place (home), because of my illness, Agoraphobia.

With the support and help of Phobics Anonymous, a self help support group, I am now able to do most of these things with little or no problems.

I am just one person who was helped, and there are many more in the desert area that have agoraphobia or panic related problems who recover much more readily because of the self-help support group.

There are people who cannot leave their homes because of the devastating fears they have from these illnesses. Phobics Anonymous helps these people by working with them to desensitize them to the outside world. It is a self-help support group for phobics, run by recovering phobics.

Anxiety and panic related disorders including agoraphobia are the number one mental health problem according to the National Institute for Mental Health. Thanking you for your support and concern.

Sincerely, Renee

Six years ago I moved to the Palm Springs area. We called the Eisenhower Medical Center to see if there was any kind of help for people suffering from this terrible affliction and was told there was no specific help available.

Luckily, I heard a public service announcement on TV for people from Phobics Anonymous. We wrote and were contacted and told about a self help group in the Palm Springs area. It was almost more than I could do to go to the first meeting, but I finally was able to make it to the meetings. It was a great comfort and source of help to learn that I was not alone and other people had the same fears and panic attacks I have been suffering from. We have worked for the past five years with Marilyn, who has headed up this organization, and I am no longer housebound. I am still working at my recovery and have great hope that Phobics Anonymous can continue to offer hope and help to others.

Joni

****

Dear Marilyn,

I'd be interested in a group in the San Mateo, Calif. area. If there is a group please let me know who I can contact. If there is not a group in my area, I'd be interested in starting one and would like to know how to go about it.

I have been suffering with phobias for 10 years (I'm a 40 year old woman). I was leading a normal life for about 8 years. But, it came back last summer. (I had a lot of stress in my life). It came back worse, with more phobias than the first time. I want to get involved with other people with the same problems and help and learn with them.

I'm looking forward to hearing from you. Hopefully, I can help Phobics Anonymous in the future.

Sincerely,
Patti

****

Dear Sir or Madam,

Could you send me information on how I could start a chapter in this area or if there is one here, how I could get in touch with someone about the group? Also, maybe phone number and just name of a person or group leader? How may I obtain a copy of The 12 Steps of Phobics Anonymous? My husband is a recovering alcoholic sober 1 1/2 years, very active in A.A. I've been having my panic attacks for about a month. I can't go out in stores hardly, its rough, the fear is overwhelming. I will appreciate any information you can send me. I am in my fifties.

Thank you, June

P.S. I am very interested in a group about this because I get no emotional support from my husband. He says it's all in my head and he really doesn't care. Its really messed up my normal daily routine. It has limited my driving and comings and goings.

Dear Marilyn,

Thank you for your information of the 12 Steps and contact names.

If my husband and myself stay in this area (we are from the U.K.) I am seriously thinking of trying to get a group started. I know someone who chairs a Co-Dependant's group and I could get feedback from him.

In the meantime, I hope to visit California, then I could stop by and pick up books etc.

Thank you for the support, it reminded me to contact and communicate with higher self (I had forgotten all I "learned" when a crisis hit). I think I needed a sharp reminder, I had been involved in a stressful job, which I am now out of, and learning to meditate once again, so I feel much better. I think you have started a wonderful plan to help people.

Best wishes,
Lynne

****

Dear Marilyn,

The paradox of any Twelve Step Program is that to keep it for ourselves, we must give it away. The more we give, the more we receive. It's a never ending cycle.

The awakening of spirituality does not come in one all-enveloping flash. It's an on-going, never ending process, a journey that is gradual, progressive and healing, a journey that we take one step at a time; one day at a time.

When we carry the message, we don't try to convince, coerce or reform anyone. We cannot change anybody but ourselves. We can only share our story, our experience, faith and hope and the Twelve Steps that brought us to our recovery. If someone has a hole in the soul, we can't repair it for them. Whenever we tried to fix other people, we usually failed. You don't have to be a loser to become a winner.

Dorothy's Additional Interpretation

For each and every one of you, a spiritual awakening takes its own form. One may come into it gradually, feeling the ever growing presence, one day at a time. Each day seems to bring its own awakening. As we let go more and more, we see how our Higher Power works things out for our higher good. Most of the time, we could not have imagined the outcome that was to later develop. Our attitude towards life and people, and ourselves changes ever so gradually but we realize changes are taking place.

When a spiritual awakening comes in a flash, with seeming earth shattering intensity, it's remembered forever. The moment is embedded in the deepest levels of consciousness. I have found that even with such a stupendous awakening into spiritual consciousness, that it still takes time to learn the lessons. The difference between the two awakenings is that the awareness of each step is more pronounced when moving toward what you instinctively now believe in every core of your being.

For me, the awakened spirituality existed long before entering the Twelve Step program. There was a searching, a constant longing for the way to reach it. I knew my goal, finding my own path was the lesson. Each Step, in it's own way, an awakening.

I had two dramatic awakenings. One in December, 1979. In the deepest fit of despair, I cried out for "God's help". Within five minutes, a beautiful light engulfed me. From total despair to instant feelings of overwhelming love had convinced me I'd gone crazy. This experience led me on a quest for getting and keeping that marvelous feeling. Today, in hindsight, I can wonder if I had just let go, and let God, what differences would it have made? Or was it necessary that I learn the hard way and have to wait another 12 years?

In December of 1991, I started working the Twelve Steps in earnest. In January, 1992, there was yet another awe inspiring experience. I really perceived "heaven". It was a short lived 10 days of learning and growing with my Higher Power. Then "hell" seemed to take over. Week after week, day after day, I was having flashbacks of my life. If it hadn't been for the first 10 days of understanding God's goodness in my life, I don't see how I would have survived it. I clung to the Steps, knowing that I had a long climb ahead of me. The big difference was this time, I was learning to let go and let God. Wherever this path was taking me, I was sure I was going to make it.

The days dragged on into weeks, the weeks into months. But, I had a goal, working the Steps, one day at a time. For me, there could be no other way. My past life had to be dealt with, that's where it all started and that's what I needed to work on. The Steps, as I took each one, were and are leading and guiding me.

In hindsight, I see I was working more than one step at a time. I even jumped into Step Twelve because I realized it was an extremely important step. I prayed over it.

I'm not recovered, how can I work Step Twelve? I'm not worthy, how can I carry the message?

The answer became clear, one Step at a time. For me, you see, I'm actually seeing and comprehending how it's working in my life. Each lesson, and everything is a lesson, is bringing me closer and closer. It's truly an amazing journey.

Today, as I sit and write this, I have formally only completed Step Seven, and am preparing to tackle Step Eight. Sure, I dread it in my old way of viewing things, but having seen how Steps Four and Five cleared out so many cobwebs of my mind, I know that Steps Eight and Nine can only do a more thorough cleaning.

Even the writing keeps me on Step Twelve. Sharing my story with others. I've come to realize that the sharing is important. As I learn lessons, it's easier to share one at a time. How could I have possibly shared what I did not experience myself?

"Tried to carry this message to others"

Note the word "tried". It doesn't say that we "do" or we "must", we do the best we can. We simply "try". We do not force, coerce, or attempt to manipulate others into doing what we want. They are only a few of the "shortcomings" we've asked our Higher Power to "remove" in Step Seven.

In the "Twelve Step" book of P.A., even newcomers to the program can work Step Twelve. Twelfth Step work takes many forms. There were times where I've gotten frustrated at other members for not taking more responsibility and doing more to help out, to realize that their mere presence at meetings and sharing what they've learned is the beginnings of Twelfth Step work, the people who help get photocopies done, those who bring in articles to enlighten us, making phone calls to other members, no matter how insignificant it seems, is important, it works. We just have to "try". Doing whatever we are capable of doing at our own particular stages of recovery, and with our own unique talents and abilities.

We are somewhat unique in that we cannot identify ourselves as being addicts, although that could be debatable. We could be addicted to our negative thinking, and actually, even our anxiety. When we're feeling very anxious, or having a panic attack, we certainly know we're alive.

Since we are known as "people pleasers" we do need Twelfth Step work. We need to see a "boundary" on how much we can comfortably do. The essence of the Steps is learning how to take care of ourselves. We'll learn to set appropriate boundaries when working this step. It's part of the process. It helps to view others as if looking at ourselves in a mirror. Looking for myself in others has been very enlightening. We're so good at feeling what we perceive others feel, when we work with each other we instinctively know the fear, anxiety, worry, or whatever other feeling the other member may be experiencing. Thus, it becomes easier and easier to see ourselves.

One defect I've noticed consistently, when a member calls me (and I do the same to others), we seem to worry we're bothering each other. If one is busy, it's appropriate to ask "let's see when would be a mutually convenient time to discuss this issue in more detail"? There would be infinite possibilities. It teaches us, and we learn that in the true spirit of giving and taking, is our own recovery. Taking is also giving. As we humbly take what we need, we have given the other person the gift of giving. There is no way to lose when working Step Twelve.

Practice these principles in all our affairs

It isn't only member to member that this Step Twelve was written for. Practicing the steps in all our affairs is the essence of the Twelve Steps.

We are powerless over everything and it is in our admission of this that we find the first step to liberation.

A power greater than ourselves can restore us to wholeness is the rallying point of Step Two: positive thinking instead of negative; giving up our own defiance in all situations; our right relationship to the Universe, our Higher Power, and to all people.

Step Three is our willingness bringing up into independence because we've learned to depend on our Higher Power and now learning to give up our own "self will" in whatever circumstances we find ourselves.

Our willingness to take our own inventory; defects and assets. This is only the beginning of a lifetime practice. Our inventory shows us our emotional insecurities, our worry, anger, panic, fear, self-pity, anxiety and depression. It reviews our relationships. It gets us on the right track by being able to see our basic problems, the extremes we go through, and how misguided we've been.

The ego deflation of Step Five is only the beginning of true friendship with our Higher Power and all our relationships. This is where we start learning to forgive ourselves and others. We learn how real we really are. How human, and we gain honesty. Here's where we start learning how to trust our Higher Power, and ourselves as well as others.

We became ready to have our Higher Power remove all these defects of character. Here we learn we need to keep trying. We are not perfect, we are simply striving to grow spiritually. We only have to "be ready". Some defects we may not be willing to give up, but we learn to look for our Higher Power's will for us, and the rest takes care of itself. Step Six.

Step Seven is where we move out of ourselves and towards our Higher Power. We learn humility, having experienced where we've come from in each preceding step. Our changing attitude is bringing us closer to our Higher Selves.

Learning to live with others is making a survey of our past, and becoming willing to forgive. This Step brings great insights into harm done to others and ourselves. Learning to give up our extreme judgments. Step Eight.

When we make our amends, we do it in the right time and the right place and in the right way. We are learning quickly now to perceive our Higher Power's will for us and how we can achieve carrying it out. Little by little the ways and means of making amends to ourselves and others are shown to us. We learn the need for discretion and taking responsibility. Step Nine.

Step Ten requires taking a regular personal inventory. It's the first action step. Self-searching is now becoming a habit. We've learned patience and how to examine our motives. We make our amends quickly because we've become very familiar with what has caused our anxieties by working the previous steps. We no longer want to be drawn into past behavior patterns; we want to keep our slate clean.

The prayer and meditation of Step Eleven is individual, as are all the Steps. What works for you is right for you. Here we seek to improve our conscious contact with our Higher Power and only pray for knowledge of our Higher Power's "will" for us and our Higher Selves power to carry it out.

Which brings us to Step Twelve. Our free gift. We've learned that growing spiritually was the answer to our dilemma. Our instincts have become fine tuned and realistic. We no longer have reason to fear or be anxious. Our attitudes towards others, ourselves and life in general has changed. We have learned that true sharing and giving of self caused us to find our true selves, our purpose in life in all our affairs.

A ROUND TUIT

This is a round tuit. Guard it with your life. Tuits are hard to come by, and the round ones are especially rare. It will help you to become much more efficient. For many years you've heard people say, "I'll do this when I get a round tuit." So now you have one, and you can accomplish all those things you put aside until you got a round tuit.

The Seven Major Positive Emotions

The emotion of desire
The emotion of faith
The emotion of love
The emotion of sex
The emotion of enthusiasim
The emotion of romance
The emotion of hope

The Seven Major Negative Emotions
(To be avoided)

The emotion of fear
The emotion of jealousy
The emotion of hatred
The emotion of revenge
The emotion of greed
The emotion of superstition
The emotion of anger

Thy Will Be Done

Make me valiant, make me brave
Let me glisten after pain
as a birch after rain
As storm pressed grasses
rise to the sun
Let me rise from sorrow
"Thy will be done"

DEFINITION
OF
TERMS

DEFINITION OF TERMS

Agoraphobia:

A complex set of fears and avoidance behaviors marked by anxiety, panic attacks, and losing control. Lifestyle can be severely limited. The term agoraphobia is derived from the Greek words "agora", meaning "a place of assembly" and "phobos", meaning "flight-panic". The word agoraphobia was first used by Westphal in 1871. Agoraphobia is sometimes referred to as fear of open spaces or fear of the market place. I choose to more accurately define it from my own personal experience as a fear of the fear reaction. A condition in which a person suffers such incapacitating, debilitating, paralyzing, confusing, intense fear so terrifying, its victim lives in constant fear of repeating the experience which first triggered the reaction of panic attack. Like the ripples of a stone dropped into a placid pool of water, the circles of fear spread out until they encompass the marketplace, the street, the vehicles, and conveyances of ordinary life and indeed everything beyond the agoraphobic's front door.

It is not the fear of a specific place which holds us prisoner under house arrest. It is the fear of having another panic attack and being caught, trapped, or unable to run away, and seek help if that panic attack should occur again.

Agoraphobia, as I shall use the term differs fundamentally and significantly from monosymptomatic phobias such as fear of spiders, death, germs, etc. The person with a specific phobia is afraid of an object outside himself. The agoraphobic fears situations but not quite in the same way. He fears the feelings which arise within himself during a panic attack. The bottom line being, he will lose control, go crazy, or die.

Anticipatory Anxiety (or the "What if...?" Syndrome):
This type of anxiety comes on in anticipation. "What if I get panicky when I go into a situation?" The "What if..." intensity of this anxiety increases gradually. It does not have the extreme, bizarre, and terrifying symptoms spontaneous anxiety attacks do. Many "normal" people have some anticipatory anxiety before going on a stage, making a speech, etc.

Anxiety:
A vague fear, a sense of helpless foreboding which is not directed toward the here and now.

The American Psychiatric Association defines it as "apprehension, tension, or uneasiness that stems from the anticipation of danger, the course of which is largely unknown, or unverbalized". Anxiety is not always unhealthy even when it covers a whole spectrum of distant possibilities. However, one abnormal state is chronic anxiety which is often described as free floating or generalized rather than being specifically anchored to one set of objects or one situation. Anxiety is also abnormal when it is not based on reality, what really could happen, or when it inhibits our daily activities.

Faith Clears The Way

When anxiety and fears arise inviting me to quit.
I meet each one head on sure I can conquer it.
For dauntless I go forth today and every day.
Meeting anxiety and fears
with faith that clears the way.

The Anxiety Scale:

Symptoms are placed in a scale from 1 to 10 for the convenience of discussing the severity of the anxiety without "symptom swapping" which can be contagious.

FUNCTIONAL

1. "Butterflies", a queasy feeling in stomach, trembling, jitteriness, tension, uneasy feeling.
2. Cold or clammy palms, hot flashes and warm all over, profuse sweating, shivering and chills.
3. Very rapid, strong, racing, pounding or irregular heartbeat, tremors, muscle tension and aches, chronic fatigue, exhaustion.

DECREASED FUNCTIONAL ABILITY

4. Jelly legs, wobbly, weak in knees, unsteady feelings, shakiness, need to sit, lean or lie down.
5. Immediate desperate and urgent need to escape, avoid or hide, inability to concentrate, focus or make decisions.
6. Lump in throat, dry mouth, choking, muscle tension, difficulty with swallowing.
7. Hyperventilation, tightness in chest, shortness of breath, smothering sensation, racing thoughts.

LIMITED OR COMPLETELY NON-FUNCTIONAL

8. Feelings of impending doom or death, high pulse rate, difficulty breathing, palpitations, change in eating habits.
9. Dizziness, visual distortion, faintness, headache, nausea, numbness, tingling of hands, feet or other body parts, diarrhea, frequent urination, sleep disturbance.
10. COMPLETE PANIC, non-functional, disoriented, detached, feelings of unreality, paralyzed, fear of dying, going crazy, or losing control, depression.*

*Frequently people experiencing their first spontaneous "panic attack" rush to emergency rooms convinced that they are having a heart attack.

Endogenous Anxiety:

"Endogenous" comes from the Greek word meaning "to be born or produced from within". The latest research shows this condition is a disease whose victims appear to be born with a genetic vulnerability to it. In this anxiety disease, like other diseases, nature has malfunctioned in some way, and like other diseases, it has a life of its own and brings misery and suffering.

Exogenous Anxiety:

"Exogenous" comes from the Greek word meaning "to be born or produced from the outside". It is an ordinary defensive reaction to a justifiable source.

Fear:

A basic emotional response to a specific situation or to an imagined threat. It's a reaction probably both inborn and learned. It is a protective response much like pain and like pain, can be most uncomfortable. Fear is nature's way of alerting us to danger and protecting us from harm. We need a healthy fear of cars for instance so we won't cross the street carelessly. It doesn't mean we should be so frightened of them we won't cross the street at all. Such a persistent fear is an irrational fear.

Irrational Fear:

A persistent, unexplained fear which disrupts our lives and consumes a tremendous amount of emotional energy without providing any benefit.

Panic:

Sudden burst of abrupt and uncontrollable unmanageable terror usually in the face of an immediate threat either real or imagined resulting in the fight or flight syndrome.

Panic Attack:
May be used interchangeably with the term "acute anxiety attacks". Bodily symptoms are the same.

Phobia:
An involuntary fear reaction inappropriate to the situation. It involves a sense of dread so intense the person either does everything possible to avoid it, or experiences extreme discomfort while enduring the source of distress.

Safe Place:
An agoraphobic's "safe place" is their area of security. In the course of events when a phobic returns to their "safe place" the panic subsides. For most agoraphobics, it is usually the home. Once this area is established, any attempts to exceed its boundaries may bring anxiety and if you venture too far. there will be panic.

Setbacks:
Old habits are not easy to break, even when they are bad habits. Therefore, for some unknown reason after doing something successfully you may have a setback and revert back to your old maladaptive habit patterns.

Simple Phobia:
Characterized by dread and avoidance of a specific object or situation, such as highway driving, heights, snakes, and closed in places.

Social Phobia:

An extreme anxiety and panic in social situations, fearing some particular action will be noticed by others, one will be judged by others, and behave in a way leading to extreme embarrassment. Examples are public speaking, eating in public, and dating.

Spontaneous Anxiety Attacks or Panic:

The anxiety surges suddenly, unexpectedly, and for no apparent reason. It seems to overwhelm and panic the body before the mind can fully figure out how to cope with it. It rushes to peak intensity (a "10" - see anxiety scale) very quickly.

When these two companions, the spontaneous attacks and the anticipatory episodes join forces, the victim crosses a threshold into a new realm of progressive disability.

Support Person or Sponsor:

A trusted, recovering, non-judgmental fellow phobic who can be turned to in time of need for assistance, encouragement, and guidance.

We all need a helping hand.
Someone to share with, who will understand.
Special people to see us through,
the glad times and the sad times too.
A sponsor on whom we can always depend.

Symptom Swapping:

This can be a major problem within groups. It happens when a person who is highly verbal and descriptive relates their symptoms and after listening to them, you acquire them. Using only the numbers on the anxiety scale to describe feelings provides an insulation from this phenomena.

Anyway

People are unreasonable, illogical and
self-centered. Love them anyway.
If you do good people will accuse you of
ulterior motives. Do good anyway
If you are successful you win false
friends and true enemies. Succeed anyway.
The good you do today may be forgotten
tomorrow. Do good anyway.
Honesty and frankness make you
vulnerable. Be honest and frank anyway.
People favor underdogs but follow only
top dogs. Fight for some underdogs anyway.
What you spend years building may be
destroyed overnight. Build anyway.
People really need help but may attack
you if you help them. Help people anyway
Give the world the best you have and
you might get kicked in the teeth.
Give the world the best you've got anyway.

So Little Time

I seem to have so little time
for things I'd like to do.
For life is short and I'm the sort
with lots of things in view.
So little time for daydream's
for chats upon the phone.
So little time for making friends
I'd really like to own.
So little time for seeing lands
I'd really like to hike to.
So little time to know myself
as much as I would like to.

ADDITIONAL
RESOURCES
AND
SUGGESTED
BOOKS

Anxiety Addict To Serenity Seeker

SUGGESTED SOURCES OF INFORMATION

1. For any Twelve Step information regarding Anxiety and Panic related disorders, P.A. Chapters, etc.**:
   Phobics Anonymous World Headquarters
   c/o The Institute for Phobic Awareness
   P.O. Box 1180
   Palm Springs, CA 92263

2. The Anxiety Disorder Association of America is a national organization dedicated to alleviating the impact of anxiety disorders on individuals, their families and society. For information, tapes, books, Treatment Directory etc.:
   The Anxiety Disorder Association of America (formerly The Phobia Society of America):
   600 Executive Boulevard, Suite 200
   Rockville, MD 20852-3801

3. For Twelve Step substance abuse issues contact:
   Alcoholics Anonymous World Services, Inc.
   468 Park Avenue South
   New York, NY 10016

4. For Mental Health information contact:
   National Institute of Mental Health Section on Anxiety Disorders
   9000 Rockville Pike
   Bethesda, MD 20892

**(Please enclose a legal size stamped self-addressed envelope with .58 cents postage, and a tax deductible donation to cover printing and handling costs.)

SUGGESTED READING

1. The Twelve Steps of Phobics Anonymous;
   Marilyn Gellis Ph.D., Rosemary Maut M.A.

2. The Anxiety Disease;
   Dr. David Sheehan

3. The Good News About Panic, Anxiety and Phobias;
   Mark S. Gold M.D.

4. Hope and Help For Your Nerves;
   Peace From Nervous Suffering;
   Simple Effective Treatment of Agoraphobia;
   Dr. Claire Weekes M.B., D.Sc., F.R.A.C.P.

5. Breaking The Panic Cycle;
   Don't Panic
   R. Reid Wilson Ph.D.

6. Managing Your Anxiety;
   Outgrowing Agoraphobia;
   Christopher J. McCullough Ph.D.

7. You Have Choices;
   William N. Penzer Ph.D. and Bonnie Goodman, M.S.

8. Anxiety Phobias and Panic;
   Reneau Z. Peurifoy MA. MFCC.

9. Your Phobia;
   Dr. Manny Zane

Excellent newsletters containing the latest up-to-date information and research on anxiety and panic related disorders:

1. National Panic and Anxiety Newsletter
   Cyma J. Siegel, Editor
   1718 Burgundy Place, Suite B
   Santa Rosa, CA 95403

2. Encourage Newsletter
   Pat Merrill, Editor
   13610 N. Scottsdale Road
   Suite 10-126
   Scottsdale, AZ 85254

3. The Mountain Climber
   Franci Warner, Editor
   1209 Ayala Drive
   Sunnyvale, CA 94086

4. Straight Talk
   Joan Orrico, Editor
   P.O. Box 090186
   Staten Island, NY 10309

5. Recovery Road Newsletter
   Candace A. Sharp, Editor
   3316 S. Carpenter Street
   Chicago, IL 60608

6. P.M. News
   Phobia Clinic, White Plains Hospital Center
   Davis Avenue and East Post Road
   White Plains, NY 10601

7. Shirley Green
   ABIL Inc. (Agoraphobics Building Independent Lives)
   1418 Lorraine Avenue
   Richmond, VA 23227

8. Fran Carpenter
   Agoraphobics in Action Inc.
   P.O. Box 140114
   Nashville, TN 37214-0114

9. Sandra Odney
   Panic Awareness & Support Network
   P.O. Box 3603
   Westlake Village, CA 91359

An Excellent 12 Step Recovery Magazine:
   Sober Times - The Recovery Magazine
   P.O. Box 40259
   San Diego, CA 92104

CANADA

10. Free From Fear Foundation
    1400 Bayley Street, Unit 15A
    YMCA/Pace
    Pickering, Ontario, Canada LIW 3R2

11. Agoraphobic Foundation of Canada, Inc.
    P.O. Box 132
    Chomeday Laval, Quebec, Canada H7W 4K2

12. Panic, Phobias and Anxiety Disorders
    Pat Zwartjes, RN
    8307 109 Street
    Edmonton, Alberta, Canada T6G 1E1

12 STEPS OF ALCOHOLICS ANONYMOUS

1. We admitted we were powerless over alcohol - that our lives had become unmanageable.

2. Came to believe that a Power greater than ourselves could restore us to sanity.

3. Made a decision to turn our will and our lives over to the care of God <u>as we understood Him</u>.

4. Made a searching and fearless moral inventory of ourselves.

5. Admitted to God, to ourselves, and to another human being the exact nature of our wrongs.

6. Were entirely ready to have God remove all these defects of character.

7. Humbly asked Him to remove our shortcomings.

8. Made a list of all persons we had harmed, and became willing to make amends to them all.

9. Made direct amends to such people wherever possible, except when to do so would injure them or others.

10. Continued to take personal inventory and when we were wrong, promptly admitted it.

11. Sought through prayer and meditation to improve our conscious contact with God <u>as we understood Him</u>, praying only for knowledge of His will for us and the power to carry that out.

12. Having had a spiritual awakening as the result of these steps we tried to carry this message to alcoholics, and to practice these principles in all our affairs.

THE TWELVE STEPS OF NON-RECOVERY

1. We admitted we were powerless over nothing, that we could manage our lives perfectly and those of anyone else who would allow us to.
2. Came to believe there was no power greater than ourselves and that the rest of the world had problems. The whole world's crazy but thee and me and I'm not too sure about thee.
3. Made a decision to have our loved ones and friends turn their will and their lives over to our care, even though they couldn't understand us.
4. Made a searching moral and immoral inventory of everyone we knew.
5. Admitted to the whole world the exact nature of everyone else's wrongs.
6. Were entirely ready to make others straighten up and do right.
7. Demanded others to either shape up or ship out.
8. Made a list of all persons who had harmed us and became willing to go to any length to get even with them all.
9. Got direct revenge on such people whenever possible, except when to do so would cost us our lives, or at the very least a jail sentence.
10. Continued to take the inventory of others, and when they were wrong promptly and repeatedly told them about it.
11. Sought through complaining and nagging to improve our relations with others as we couldn't understand them, asking only that they knuckle under and do it our way.
12. Having had a complete physical, intellectual, emotional, and spiritual breakdown as a result of these steps, we tried to blame it on others and to get sympathy and pity in all of our affairs.

ORDER FORM
The Institute For Phobic Awareness
Phobics Anonymous World Service Hqtrs.
P.O. Box 1180,
Palm Springs, CA 92263

Please send me the latest edition of:
From Anxiety Addict To Serenity Seeker
Number of books Requested at:

$12.95 each _____ $_____

(Price outside U.S.A. in American currency or
International Money Order)

$15.00 each _____ $_____

The Twelve Steps of Phobics Anonymous
Number of books Requested at:

$ 9.95 each _____ $_____

(Price outside U.S.A. in American currency or
International Money Order)

$12.00 each _____ $_____

California Residents please add:

sales tax _____ $_____

Shipping and Handling (for one book) $ _____ 3.00
Add .50¢ for each additional book $_____
*Total enclosed $_____

Name _____
Phone #(   ) _____
Address _____
City_____State_____Zip_____

*All payments must be in U.S. dollars or International
money orders. Paid to the order of Phobics Anonymous.
Please allow 2-4 for weeks delivery.